The
Reference Shelf ®

Families: Traditional and New Structures

Edited by
Paul McCaffrey

The Reference Shelf
Volume 84 • Number 4
H. W. Wilson
A Division of EBSCO Publishing, Inc.
Ipswich, Massachusetts
2013

The Reference Shelf

The books in this series contain reprints of articles, excerpts from books, addresses on current issues, and studies of social trends in the United States and other countries. There are six separately bound numbers in each volume, all of which are usually published in the same calendar year. Numbers one through five are each devoted to a single subject, providing background information and discussion from various points of view and concluding with an index and comprehensive bibliography that lists books, pamphlets, and articles on the subject. The final number of each volume is a collection of recent speeches, and it contains a cumulative speaker index. Books in the series may be purchased individually or on subscription.

Library of Congress Cataloging-in-Publication Data

Families : traditional and new structures / edited by Paul McCaffrey.
    p. cm. — (The reference shelf ; v. 84, no. 4)
  Includes bibliographical references and index.
  ISBN 978-0-8242-1118-9 (issue 4, pbk.) — ISBN 978-0-8242-1249-0 (v. 84)
  1. Families—United States. 2. Families. I. McCaffrey, Paul, 1977–
HQ536.F3346 2013
306.850973—dc23

2012018997

Cover: Family Portrait © Radius Images/Corbis

Visit: www.salempress.com/hwwilson

Printed in the United States of America

Contents

3

Changing Perspectives on Fatherhood

4

Adoption and the Changing Face of Families

5

Families Across Cultures

6

Family, Finances, and the Economy

Preface: Contemporary Perspectives on Family Life

The family is the singular social unit for human beings. Families bridge the inner, private world of the individual with the global, public world for every level of social strata in which they live. Families provide the environment in which individuals' potential can be fully or less than fully realized. How individuals develop determines how and with what degree of success they will be able to function in society. Ultimately, how individuals function determines how societies succeed or do not succeed. Appreciating the varied architecture of families is the only way to understand the smaller unit of the individual and the larger unit of society.

Families are far more than collections of individuals who are biologically related. They are dynamic, highly reactive systems in which each member affects and is affected by all other members. Families are minisocieties with their own mores, rites, rules, traditions, cuisines, climates, and identities. Family environments determine the relative importance of relationships and emotions, work and leisure, culture and altruism, food and faith, creativity and routine, and liberty and sacrifice. The emotional sense of belonging to a family is what allows individuals to feel existential security and confidence when facing nonfamily individuals—that is, the rest of the world. But families are also more than minisocieties. They are the breeding places of individual development, including family members' capacities for psychological and physical intimacy and personal valuation and meaning, and allow individuals to come to stand out, a part of and apart from all others.

As human beings have evolved, families have taken almost every conceivable shape, form, and size, even to the degree that some families are only recognizable as such because they share the basic functionality of other families: the protection and growth of healthy individual members for the protection and survivability of the societies that support them. Though the small social unit of two opposite-sex parents with any number of children has been the prevailing definition of family in Western (especially American) eyes, the anthropological, sociological, and historical record suggests that family structures have always adapted to time and place, circumstances and weather, poverty and plenty, war and peace, and closeness to or distance from other families. The changes to today's models of family are actually just a continuation of the nature, shape, and structure of families of the past, the most recent step in a social and personal history that is marked by successful development, growth, and adaptation to human progress and survivability. The multiplicity of family structures evident today is simply the latest branch to grow on the human sociobiological tree.

The current state of affairs and the need to get a clear fix on the direction of familial structural change can be accounted for in the rapid rate of change. Social institutions more easily maintain identity, functionality, relevance, and continuity by evolving slowly. Many descriptions of family exist, but since the 1960s the description "slowly changing social institution" is not among them. The changing and multifaceted family form is deeply tied to developments in contraception methods and practice. This revolution, which has been taking place for over fifty years, has seen a sharp decline in marriage's centrality and popularity and the rise of new and widely, if not universally, accepted familial structures. American behaviors, attitudes, and values about family reflect a nervous, exasperated, proselytizing, uneasy panic and a calm, nonjudgmental, democratic, promotional acceptance of a fluid family architecture.

How one views family correlates strongly with issues of economic class, educational level, age, race, religion, ethnicity, marital status, gender, and the diversity of one's social circle. Though individual differences abound, and though what is true for one group does not necessarily represent what all individuals in that group believe, younger, more liberal, secular, female, and African American subgroups are, in general, more likely to endorse the emergence of multiple structures than older, conservative, religious, male, and Caucasian subgroups.

As the attitudes about and accepted forms of family undergo significant change, the social institution of marriage is changing just as quickly. In 1960, 72 percent of all US adults were married; fifty years later, slightly more than half of all US adults are married. This coincides with a decreasing belief in the importance and necessity of being married. While marriage is declining in all major societal subgroups, the lower one's economic station and level of education, the less likely one is to be married. The decline is even more significant as two models of marriage—same-sex and interracial marriage—are on the rise, as is the cohabitation of unmarried adults.

Several reasons explain the decline in marriage, at least in part. The first is age. Today there is a tendency to marry later; on average, people are marrying five years later than was the case fifty years ago. Second is the capacity to end marriage. There are currently more divorced and separated men and women in the general population than ever before. In 1960, 5 percent of the US adult population was divorced or separated. Today that figure is almost 15 percent. Third is economics. Women, as they achieve greater financial parity with men, face less pressure to marry for reasons of financial security—though marrying as a means of enhancing financial security remains an important motivator. This economic trend is likely to continue because of an educational trend: women now exceed men in educational achievement, with women obtaining more terminal and advanced degrees. But being in love, having a partner with whom to go through life, and simple companionship remain stronger motivators than the improvement of income. Fourth is the prevalence of couples living together either before or without marriage. More adults cohabitate than ever before in US history; as many as 44 percent of Americans have cohabitated at some point in their adult life, two-thirds of whom consider "moving in together" a step toward eventual marriage. While marriage is undergoing significant challenges as a universal social institution, even among those who do not believe in the principle of state-licensed marriage, it is not expected to become an extinct social institution.

While marriage has declined, family has never been held in such high regard, at least in most of its current and varied forms. The essence of family is conceptual, defined in part by the observer and by having or planning to have children.

One easily recognizable familial model is the household that consists of two opposite-sex parents, one income, and children. This traditional structure is often called the "nuclear family"; however, the nuclear family is in decline relative to the rise of other, also recognizable, forms that family has not traditionally taken. The most common structural variant is the two-income household with one or more children that now represents over 60 percent of all US households. While few observers would consider two cohabiting adults living on their own as forming a family, most observers would view two cohabiting, nonmarried adults with one or more children as forming a family. Indeed, observers view the single parent with one child as just as much a family as two parents with children. Also interesting is the prevailing view that while two married adults without children do not form a family, two married adults who want but do not have children do constitute an accepted family structure. It seems that the nature of family requires more than two people unless the two-person unit wishes it were at least a three-person unit. The essence of the family relational structure is not that of a couple (or what the social sciences calls "dyadic") relational structure. Couples are about the "two as one"; families are about the "two as many."

The family structure for which there is no significant historical evidence but that is growing in prevalence and acceptance is that of the gay or lesbian couple who live together (independently of being legally married) and who have or wish to have children. To the extent that family is what the observer says, this model structure has gone from being nearly unrecognizable and unacceptable as a "true family" to a structure that one of two US adults today readily label a real family. Researchers predict that this trend will continue. Within the general adult population, there is a bipolar distribution of those who accept gay and lesbian-headed families and those who reject them. As an aggregate, those who reject gay and lesbian families typically also reject the legality of gay and lesbian marriage. The group that falls under this distribution curve tends to be made up of older, politically conservative, and religiously traditional or fundamental individuals with modest contact with people who are gay or lesbian. The group under the curve that accepts gay or lesbian-headed households that have children or plan to have children tends to be made up of individuals who are younger, have a higher mean educational level, are politically liberal or moderate, hold self-described flexible religious tenets, and can name one or more family members or friends who are gay or lesbian. Social science researchers interpret the variance of this bipolar distribution as best explained by the degree of familiarity with a first-order gay or lesbian relative or close friend. Those with such exposure recognize gay and lesbian families as families; those without do not see this structure as representing what is intrinsic to being a family.

This age is a robust one for families. There have never been greater numbers or percentages of people living in families. Most people live in families or in social structures that a majority of the adult population would describe as families. Even among homeless individuals, the majority live within a kind of family structure, even as that family is itself homeless.

There has never been a better time in US history to live in families. The clear majority of adults describe being in their families as gratifying or highly gratifying. Most adults consider their family to be the most important element in their life, ahead of having a spouse or partner, wealth, success, popular or peer recognition, or a secure retirement plan. Among those who do not, the majority still see family as the single most important structure for society and for the individual. Even many of those who report their own family experience as horrible, toxic, or abusive still consider the idea of family to be fundamental to human happiness, identity, and meaning.

Social institutions exist because they promote the survival and well-being of the individual, who in turn serves the needs of the institution. Social institutions adapt in order to continue to execute these functions. The traditional nuclear family structure was perhaps the best model to support and promote individual and societal well-being at the time of its greatest prevalence. Other structures are now evolving to serve various segments of the general population because adaptive mechanisms can better fulfill "why" there are families in the first place. The many faces of family are alive and well, and they seem to be here to stay.

Paul Moglia, PhD
June 2012

1

Who Is Family Today?

(The Washington Post/Getty Images)

James Abbott (left) with children Caleb, 14 (second from left), and Alfred Gri-Abbott, 11 (far right), and husband, David Gri, as they pose for a portrait at their home in Oakton, Virginia, on Sunday, February 5, 2012. Virginia state law forbids gay couples from adopting a child together, and the General Assembly is moving to pass a bill allowing private agencies to turn away prospective gay parents for religious or moral reasons.

Family Redefined

By Paul McCaffrey

In 2010, *Time* magazine and the Pew Research Center conducted a poll analyzing American attitudes toward marriage. The results were striking. Around 40 percent of respondents agreed with the statement that marriage is becoming obsolete. Such attitudes are reflected in shifting family structure in the twenty-first century and the growing prevalence since the 1950s of more diverse and unorthodox family units. Though the conventional nuclear family—composed of a married mother and father and their biological children—is still the dominant structure, it has been waning for the past sixty years as single-parent families, stepfamilies, cohabitating families—those with unmarried domestic partners—and other arrangements have taken on greater prominence.

While marriage rates have declined and new family structures have become more common, the biological underpinnings of family have stayed central, as has the role of parents, whether biological or adoptive, single or step. A 2009 census report noted that approximately 93.8 percent of all children reside with at least one biological parent. Of the remaining 6.2 percent, 1.9 percent lived with one or more adopted parents. This left around 4.2 percent living without a biological or adoptive parent; of these, around 60 percent resided with grandparents. Biology notwithstanding, according to some estimates, up to 54 percent of children will live apart from one of their parents by the time they are fifteen years old.

Though single-parent families are by no means a new phenomenon, thanks to soaring divorce and out-of-wedlock birth rates, their numbers have tripled during the last several generations and are expected to continue growing. In 1960, fully 87 percent of children under eighteen were being brought up by two married parents, compared to only 9 percent being raised by single parents. According to census data, in 2009, that 87 percent had fallen to 64.7 percent while the 9 percent had risen to 27.3 percent. Currently, over 40 percent of births are to unwed mothers, and about one in four children live with a single parent. Of those children who live with one parent, about 86 percent reside with their mothers.

Single parenthood is not an easy proposition. While most married and cohabitating families can rely on two incomes, a single-parent household generally only has access to one. In addition to being the sole provider, the single parent is frequently the only caregiver. These responsibilities are hard for one person to fulfill and research bears this out. Single-parent families, especially those headed by mothers, are more likely to fall into poverty. Children in these families are twice as likely to develop psychiatric problems and suffer from drug and alcohol abuse; they are also dropping out of school and committing crimes at higher rates. Even so, researchers maintain that attributing these statistics to the single-parent family alone is ill advised. "You need to be careful in interpreting the data because you don't have the inner family details," Dr. Per-Anders Rydelius, a professor at Sweden's Karolinska Institute, observed. "This is really a complex situation and you cannot put it just on the single-parent family. There are many other complex factors that we have a hint of but no detailed information on."

The plight of single parents—and single mothers in particular—is not helped by popular attitudes. According to a Pew Research Center study, the majority of the American public, 69 percent, though accepting on the whole of working mothers, cohabitating households, gay families, and other nontraditional arrangements, were more skeptical of single motherhood and perceived it as a potential threat to society. "Working mothers are acceptable to almost everybody," Andrew Cherlin, a sociologist at Johns Hopkins University, commented. "Two parents who are unmarried are tolerated or acceptable. But many people, including single parents themselves, question single-parent families. There's still a strong belief that children need two parents."

Single parenthood is not the only family structure to grow more prevalent with the increase in divorce rates and out-of-wedlock births. Nor is it the only one to suffer from varying degrees of social disapproval. Stepfamilies have become especially common over recent generations. The US Bureau of the Census reports that 7.5 percent of children under eighteen have at least one stepparent, and according to the Pew Research Center, more than four in ten Americans now have a stepchild, stepparent, stepsibling, or a half sibling. These rates seem particularly linked to the age of the respondent's demographic; the younger the respondents, the more likely it is that they have stepfamilies. Thirty percent of the Pew respondents reported having a step or half sibling, 13 percent claim one or more stepchildren, and 18 percent have a stepparent who is still living. For those between the ages of eighteen and twenty-nine, fully 52 percent have a step or half relative. What is meant by the term "stepfamily" has also evolved. "It used to be that stepfamilies mainly referred to divorced parents who remarried," Andrew Cherlin observed. "Now, unmarried people who have children from a previous relationship may start a stepfamily without either partner having been married."

Like single-parent households, stepfamilies face their own set of challenges. Age-old tales about wicked stepparents and stepsiblings have painted stepfamilies into an unenviable corner; many reject the label in favor of the more innocuous "blended family" or some other construction. Still, the stigma attached to stepfamilies is not altogether unwarranted. Various studies have pointed to a so-called Cinderella effect, wherein stepchildren suffer greater rates of abuse and neglect at the hands of their stepparents compared to their biological parents. There is also data to suggest that stepchildren tend to leave home earlier, citing family conflict as the cause.

On a larger level, building bonds of kinship within stepfamilies can take years and success is never assured. According to Pew, these connections are rarely as strong as those enjoyed by biological families. But that does not mean that people lower their expectations, with some holding on to the ideal of a perfectly blended family as depicted in the television series *The Brady Bunch*. Consequently, many researchers feel that just as the stigma associated with a stepfamily is not entirely helpful, neither are the elevated hopes implied by calling it a blended family. As Brenda Ockun, the publisher of the online magazine *StepMom*, commented, "People come together with their own traditions and history, and in trying to define the new stepfamily, they struggle to determine what it's supposed to look like. Calling them a blended family can create pressure to instantly bond and look like the first family."

In 1990, barely 3 percent of families were headed by unmarried couples. That figure had doubled to 6 percent eighteen years later, the Pew Research Center reported. The accuracy of this data is open to some dispute. Unlike marriages and divorces, there are no official statistics on cohabiting families, so estimates may over- or underreport them. Moreover, the dynamics of cohabiting families tend to be a bit more fluid and less stable than conventional marriages. Still, while precise figures are unavailable, the consensus is that cohabiting families are expanding rapidly. As W. Bradford Wilcox, the director of the National Marriage Project at the University of Virginia, commented, "today more than 2.5 million kids are living in cohabiting homes—up more than 12-fold from the 1970s. And more than 40% of kids will spend some time in a cohabiting household, either with their own biological parents or with one parent and an unrelated adult."

Cohabiting families are surprisingly diverse, so it is difficult to make generalizations about them. They can contain two biological parents, composing a typical nuclear family minus the parents' marriage. Or they can be structured more along the lines of stepfamilies. Either way, cohabitation enjoys some economic advantages over single parenthood, providing families with two potential incomes and allowing them to cut down on their living expenses by consolidating. Cohabitation also eases the caregiving burdens.

Nevertheless, cohabiting families have disadvantages, especially if one of the adults is not a biological parent of the children. In this regard, cohabiting families share some of the same downsides as stepfamilies. Even when the cohabiting family is headed by both biological parents, there is still more instability than in families where the parents are married. On the whole, cohabiting families tend to have fewer financial resources than married families, and couples are more likely to split up. Some researchers take an especially bleak view of such families. Even controlling for income levels and other factors, studies still find, according to Wilcox, "that children in cohabiting families are significantly more likely to suffer from depression, delinquency, drug use, and the like." Indeed, according to some research, children raised in cohabiting families have poorer outcomes than those raised in single-parent households. Still, cohabiting families are viewed more positively. According to a Pew poll, 43 percent of respondents disapproved of cohabiting couples raising children compared to 69 percent for single mothers.

In 2010, the US Bureau of the Census estimated that there were nearly 600,000 same-sex couples in the United States. Of these, about one in four was raising children. Most of these children, about 84 percent, were the biological offspring of one of the parents and many were the product of a previous heterosexual marriage. Though same-sex marriage and civil unions have been legalized in a number of states over the past decade or so, many states still do not sanction them. As a consequence, of these 600,000 or so couples, most do not have their unions officially recognized by the government. This makes adoption more difficult since many states give preference to married couples in adoption proceedings. Nevertheless, same-sex families are growing. Between 2000 and 2009, for example, gay adoption rates more than doubled, with 18 percent of same-sex households reporting an adoptive child in the house, up from 8 percent just nine years earlier. Government officials estimate that gay families account for about 4 percent of all adoptions in the United States.

Though gay and lesbian couples continue to face discrimination, with most states not recognizing same-sex unions and two states—Utah and Mississippi—outlawing same-sex adoption, the majority of the public accepts same-sex families. In fact, only about 43 percent disapprove, a rate equal to that for cohabiting families, and given the trends of the past generation, that figure is expected to fall in the years ahead. Though same-sex families may be the targets of prejudice, studies tend to support the view that children raised in such structures fare just as well as those raised with a married mother and father. Bryan Samuels, the commissioner of the US Department of Health and Human Services's Administration on Children, Youth, and Families, declared, "The child welfare system has come to understand that placing a child in a gay or lesbian family is no greater risk than placing them in a heterosexual family."

Amid the growth of new types of family units, there has also been a return to larger, multigenerational households, those in which adult children continue to reside with their parents, for example, or families move in with relatives, where three generations—children, parents, and grandparents—may share a home. In 1940, according to the Pew Research Center, nearly one in four households were multigenerational; in 1980, however, a mere 12.1 percent were categorized as such. The prevalence of multigenerational households tends to depend on economic factors. During times of high unemployment, it makes more sense for families to pool their limited resources. In the midst of the global financial crisis of 2008 and 2009, 16.7 percent of the population, nearly five million more people than in 2007, lived in multigenerational households. Though these arrangements are often the result of unfortunate circumstances, they illustrate that during difficult times, people fall back on their families.

Though rates of marriage may be falling and many may question the institution's continued relevance in the face of the new family structures that are emerging, the family unit itself, even amidst all these changes, still retains its preeminent place in American society. More than three in four people polled by Pew named their families as the most important thing in their lives, and 85 percent say their family today is as close or closer than the one in which they were raised. How a family is built and defined may have shifted, but its value has not. Whether headed by traditional, single, step, cohabiting, or same-sex parents, the family is in no danger of becoming obsolete.

Address to the Iowa House of Representatives

By Zach Wahls
January 31, 2011

Good evening, Mr. Chairman, my name is Zach Wahls.

I'm a sixth-generation Iowan and an engineering student at the University of Iowa, and I was raised by two women. My biological mom, Terri, told her grandparents that she was pregnant, that the artificial insemination had worked, and they wouldn't even acknowledge it. It actually wasn't until I was born and they succumbed to my infantile cuteness that they broke down and told her that they were thrilled to have another grandson. Unfortunately, neither of them lived to see her marry her partner Jacki of fifteen years when they wed in 2009.

My younger sister and only sibling was born in 1994. We actually have the same anonymous donor, so we're full siblings, which is really cool for me. I guess the point is that my family really isn't so different from any other Iowa family.

When I'm home, we go to church together. We eat dinner, we go on vacations. But, we have our hard times, too; we get in fights. Actually, my mom, Terri, was diagnosed with multiple sclerosis in 2000. It is a devastating disease that put her in a wheelchair, so we've had our struggles.

But we're Iowans. We don't expect anyone to solve our problems for us. We'll fight our own battles. We just hope for equal and fair treatment from our government.

Being a student at the University of Iowa, the topic of same-sex marriage comes up quite frequently in classroom discussions. The question always comes down to, "Well, can gays even raise kids?" And the conversation gets quiet for a moment, because most people don't really have an answer. And then I raise my hand and say, "Actually, I was raised by a gay couple, and I'm doing pretty well."

I scored in the 99th percentile on the ACT. I'm actually an Eagle Scout. I own and operate my own small business. If I was your son, Mr. Chairman, I believe I'd make you very proud. I'm not really so different from any of your children. My family really isn't so different from yours. After all, your family doesn't derive its sense of worth from being told by the state, "You're married, congratulations!"

No, the sense of family comes from the commitment we make to each other to work through the hard times so we can enjoy the good ones. It comes from the love that binds us. That's what makes a family.

So what you're voting for here isn't to change us. It's not to change our families. It's to change how the law views us, how the law treats us. You are voting for the first time in the history of our state to codify discrimination into our constitution, a constitution that but for the proposed amendment is the least amended constitution in the United States of America.

You are telling Iowans that some among you are second-class citizens who do not have the right to marry the person you love. So will this vote affect my family? Would it

> *The sense of family comes from the commitment we make to each other to work through the hard times so we can enjoy the good ones. It comes from the love that binds us. That's what makes a family.*

affect yours? In the next two hours, I'm sure we're going to hear a lot of testimony about how damaging having gay parents is on kids. But in my nineteen years, not once have I ever been confronted by an individual who realized independently that I was raised by a gay couple. And you know why? Because the sexual orientation of my parents has had zero effect on the content of my character.

Thank you very much.

How America Changed

By Haya El Nasser and Paul Overberg
USA Today, August 10, 2011

What changes two decades have wrought.

The USA is bigger, older, more Hispanic and Asian and less wedded to marriage and traditional families than it was in 1990. It also is less enamored of kids, more embracing of several generations living under one roof, more inclusive of same-sex couples, more cognizant of multiracial identities, more suburban, less rural and leaning more to the South and West.

Results of the 2010 Census have been pouring out all year, an avalanche of statistics detailing the population characteristics of states, counties and cities. But the Census represents more than just a current snapshot.

The end of the first decade of the 21st century marks a turning point in the nation's social, cultural, geographic, racial and ethnic fabric. It's a shift so profound that it reveals an America that seemed unlikely a mere 20 years ago—one that will influence the nation for years to come in everything from who is elected to run the country, states and cities to what type of houses will be built and where.

The metamorphosis over just two decades stuns even demographers and social observers.

"It was always predicted that we would be diverse, but it's happened faster than anyone predicted," says Cheryl Russell, former editor in chief of *American Demographics* magazine, now editorial director of New Strategist Publications, publisher of reference tools. "Diversity and the rapid growth in diversity is one of the reasons we have a black president today. That's one thing that would never have been predicted."

The black-white racial dynamics that have dominated much of the nation's history have been scrambled by the explosive growth of Hispanics. In most southern states where the black-white legacy has deep roots, Hispanics have accounted for most of the population gains during the past decade.

"An entire Venezuela's worth of Hispanics was added in just those two decades," says Robert Lang, an urban sociologist at the University of Nevada–Las Vegas. That's about 30 million, or half of the nation's growth since 1990.

"Everything about America now has to do with diversity that we could hardly recognize in 1990," says William Frey, demographer at the Brookings Institution. The change will be felt for years to come as whites and blacks age and young Hispanics dominate in more places.

"By 2050, Americans will look back at the controversies around immigration, controversies about diversity and wonder what the big deal was," Lang says.

The starkest evidence of the cultural revolution the nation has undergone in two decades lies in the first government reporting of same-sex households.

"That is huge," Russell says. "Usually, attitudinal change occurs as one generation replaces another" but this happened faster.

"In 1990, people were still thinking of family as what you saw on TV sitcoms," Frey says—mainly mom and dad and two kids. "It still stuck in people's minds as the norm."

The Facts Behind the New Norm

Who's Home

The traditional nuclear family—one or two adults and their young children—continues to ebb. In its place, a grab bag of alternatives has appeared or begun growing after decades of decline:

Among families. Various forms of three generations under one roof; adult children returning to their parents' home, sometimes with a spouse and their own children or both; blended families that include stepparents or stepchildren; and extended families that include a parent, a child, cousins and others, related or not.

Among unrelated people. A wide variety of living arrangements have flourished among all ages: unmarried partner couples, both same-sex or opposite sex, sometimes with their own or related children or adult roommates.

Living solo. The share of one-person households continues to grow, up from 25% in 1990 to 27%. The recession has slowed the trend by forcing some young adults to live with parents or roommates. But as Baby Boomers flood into their empty-nesting years and beyond, the trend could accelerate. In many Western European countries, more than one-third of households consist of just one person.

Multigenerational households. At the other end of the spectrum, a growing share of homes includes more than one generation of a family. The average household size has stopped shrinking and begun to grow for the first time in a half-century, partly buoyed by the influx of immigrant families.

Immigrants are more likely to have young children and live with siblings, parents or other relatives. By one broad definition, 16% of U.S. households are multigenerational (two or more), up from 14% in 1990, according to the Pew Research Center. The Census defines multigenerational as three or more generations of the same family. In 2010, they made up 4% of households.

Fewer kids. Only one-third of households now have children, and the share of households that have kids under age 18 dropped in 95% of counties, changing the flavor of neighborhoods in cities and suburbs.

The opposite is happening in areas populated predominantly by immigrants. The 1.9 million-person gain in the under-18 population since 2000 was fueled completely by racial and ethnic minorities. Hispanic fertility is at 2.9 births per woman, much higher than the national average of 2.1.

At 24%, the proportion of residents who are 18 and under is at an all-time low, according to the Population Reference Bureau. It was 25.6% in 1990. Twenty-three states and Washington, D.C., lost 10% or more of their child populations just in the last decade.

Having children increasingly has become detached from marriage. The share of births by unmarried women has risen from 26% to 41% since 1990 and could be headed higher. Among Hispanics, it's 53%; among blacks, it's 73%. In several European countries, half to two-thirds of all children are born to unmarried women.

Remix

One of the most significant demographic trends of the past 20 years is the explosive growth of Hispanics. Now at 50 million—almost one in six Americans—Hispanics have more than doubled their numbers in 1990.

The Hispanic boom has spread far beyond traditional immigrant gateways such as California and Florida, altering the American landscape in states such as Kansas and North Carolina.

Just more than 1% of North Carolina's 6.6 million residents were Hispanic in 1990. In 2010: Almost 7% of 9.5 million people were.

Asians grew at a similarly rapid rate but they still account for a small share of the population (4.7%). Since 2000, more Asians were added (4.3 million) to the population than blacks (3.7 million).

Hispanics surpassed blacks in 2003. African Americans' presence in some traditional strongholds is shrinking. They are leaving cities and heading for the suburbs or returning to the South.

Fifty-seven percent of the USA's blacks live in the South, the highest since 1960. Some are retirees settling in Florida and North Carolina; others are professionals lured by thriving metropolitan areas in Texas and Georgia.

Most of Chicago's population declines since 2000 were due to a loss of more than 181,000 black residents. There were declines in Cleveland, Philadelphia, Dallas and Atlanta. The black population in Washington, D.C., is slipping below 50%.

The USA's racial and ethnic balance has been further upset by the growing number of Americans who claim more than one race.

The change happened in 2000, when the government first allowed people to pick two or more races on Census forms. The 9 million who did so make up almost 2% of the population, up from 1.6% in 2000.

One in seven new marriages include spouses of different racial or ethnic backgrounds, according to the Population Reference Bureau. In 2010, 5.6% of children under age 18 reported two or more races compared with 2.1% of adults.

The Census projects that less than half of the U.S. population will be white and not Hispanic by 2042—a moving target that will be influenced by future immigration and fertility patterns.

Gender Evolution

Gender roles have been redefined.

One of the biggest changes is the delay and eclipse of marriage. Half of women who marry wait until 26 to do so, up from 24 in 1990. For men, half don't marry until they are older than 28, up from 26.

Part of the delay may stem from higher education levels. Women have made such giant leaps that they now dominate men at every level of higher education in earning degrees. The most recent Department of Education statistics show that 51% of doctoral degrees went to women in 2007–08, up from 42% in just 10 years.

"For a lot of women, marriage is a disadvantage," Russell says. "Women would end up supporting the men."

The educational gender gap is widening, but men's life expectancy, still lagging women's, is rising at a faster rate.

Since 1990, life expectancy for men who make it to retirement has grown at almost three times the rate that it has for women, according to preliminary 2009 data from the National Center on Health Statistics.

A 65-year-old man today is expected to live another 17.3 years, women 20 years—up 15% for men and just 6% for women.

In 1990, a 65-year-old man was expected to live 15.1 more years and women 18.9.

The same is happening for those who reach age 75: Men's life expectancy has gained 14%, women's 4%.

Much of the gain for men is the result of lower lung cancer rates (men smoked more before the anti-smoking crusade began a generation ago) and better heart disease treatment and prevention.

Men have shown steady annual gains of 0.2 years in life expectancy in recent years while the rate for women gained less or stayed flat.

Where We Live

The pull of suburbia did not let up despite an urban renaissance fueled by empty nesters and the young and childless. More than half of Americans—about 158 million—are suburbanites. In 1990, just over 48% were. In just 20 years, almost 40 million more people lived in suburbs.

Rural areas continued their decline, their population remaining stagnant over 20 years at 50 million. Rural residents now make up only 16% of the total population, down from 20% in 1990.

"Remote rural counties grew the least and the outer suburbs of large metro areas grew the most during the 20-year period," says Kenneth Johnson, demographer at the University of New Hampshire's Carsey Institute. "In rural areas, farm counties grew the least and retirement counties grew the most."

The nation is tipping south and west. The allure of Sun Belt states such as California and Florida was in full bloom 20 years ago, but no one saw the population explosion that hit states throughout the region, from North Carolina to Nevada.

> *"We didn't appreciate how old the white population would get in 20 years," Frey says, and how diverse the younger population would get. "The future is people of all races and ethnicities."*

"We knew people were moving to the Sun Belt, but we didn't know people were moving to the interior part of the Sun Belt," Frey says. "This time, California didn't even gain a seat in Congress, but Nevada, Arizona and Utah all gained seats. These are the new pioneering areas of the U.S."

At the same time, growth slowed in the Northeast and Midwest, where less than 40% of the U.S. population lives now compared with more than 44% in 1990. More than 37% now live in the South and 23% in the West. For the first time, more people live in the West than the Midwest. Twenty years ago, the West first surpassed the Northeast.

"It's not something we would have foreseen, this emptying out of the industrial Midwest," Frey says. "This decade has made that much more permanent, much more dramatic."

Because of suburbanization, cities that were mere specks on the map 20 years ago are major urban centers today. Frisco, Texas, for example, a northern suburb of Dallas, was a hamlet of 6,142 in 1990. In 2010: 116,989.

"It's the newest city in America with more than 100,000 people," says Lang, who coined the term "boomburbs."

Life Stages for Americans

Tweens? twentysomethings? Young professionals? Oldest old?

Partly because of longevity, largely because of economic and cultural influences, life stages are stretching far beyond the five traditional categories—kids, teens, young adults, middle-aged and old. That gives marketers more sales pitches to customize for age niches.

Children go from being children to the in-between stage of tweenhood that precedes teenage years. Young adults, staying in college longer and many moving back home after they graduate, are in a new stage of delayed adulthood.

"It's partly the extension of childhood to about age 30 at this point," Russell says. "Because of education, the time it takes to establish a career and marry, people are about 30. That's when, interestingly, voting rates rise."

In 2010, 24 million adult children lived at home, she says, many of them because they can't find jobs or can't afford housing.

"That's one of the surprises," Russell says. "Who knew in 1990, when Boomers were young adults, that they would be so family-oriented? First, they were family-oriented by choice and now it's by necessity."

People are living longer and older people are working longer, creating new degrees of aging.

The 85-plus population climbed from about 3 million in 1990 (1.2% of the population) to 5.5 million—1.8%—in 2010.

"We didn't appreciate how old the white population would get in 20 years," Frey says, and how diverse the younger population would get. "The future is people of all races and ethnicities."

What Is Family?

By Heather Somaini
The Next Family, July 8, 2011

I was with my family this past weekend for the 4th of July—hopefully you were with yours. On the way home as I watched our babies sleep on the plane, I started to think about how much I miss my family, how much I need them and how much I want them around more.

We're an odd bunch, our clan. My grandparents were products of the Depression and had an unbelievable work ethic matched with a strong sense of humor. They believed that you could be anything you wanted but hard work was the only way to get there. They passed down a strong sense of self, with tongue firmly planted in cheek. They all picked themselves up by their bootstraps and when they made mistakes, they picked themselves up again. They suffered. They fought back. They came from hearty stock.

Growing up in this family had its fair share of knocks. I always knew I was loved, deeply, and that every single one of my relatives would kill for me. We can pick on one of our own but if an outsider even looked sideways, let alone had something critical to say about one of us, the wagons would circle. My family is an impenetrable force that no one can pierce. I know that when we're together, we are a force—probably a force to be reckoned with (as I say with a grin).

Families are sort of amazing when you think about it. In my family, we're all stuck with each other no matter what because blood means a tremendous amount to us. My mom and I were talking about a family that disowned one of their own for being gay. She was in shock because to her, blood is blood. You don't get the option of rejecting your own. You're stuck with them for good or bad, and you'd better start figuring it out because they're not going away. I mean if you could reject a relative for being gay, why not reject the one that drinks too much or makes bad financial decisions or the one that got pregnant way too early?

Oh wait; if we did that, then we'd all be rejected! The beauty of my family is that they accept me. It has not always been easy and that's probably more my fault than anyone else's, but as I've come to accept who I am, it's been easier to see that they've always been there for me. They've always wanted the best for me. They've always accepted my choices, even if they were looking at me sideways the whole time.

As I watched my baby boy and baby girl sleep next to me on that plane, I thought about what I would do for them as they grow older. How I am already so fiercely protective of their future selves, how I want them to experience life in all its complexity and make decisions that in the end they will be proud of. I want to be there

> *My mom and I were talking about a family that disowned one of their own for being gay. She was in shock because to her, blood is blood.*

to watch them fail and then pick themselves up again. I will whisper in their ear all the encouragement they need to stand up again and when that doesn't work, I'll bark at them until they get up just to make me stop. I can only hope they are the best parts of me.

My wife Tere was out of sorts as we prepared to leave my parents' house in Tennessee for the trek back to Los Angeles. She seemed mad or upset at me. Eventually she broke down and told me she was sad about going home, how my parents feel like family to her and that gives her hope. Hope that she has a place in the world, a place that is bigger than she. Hope that her children will have those same people around them to make sure they are loved with big, all-squeezing arms. Hope that in this odd clan of ours, she will be as fiercely protected as I was. Hope that she will one day be whole. I think that's all we can ever hope for—being whole . . . or maybe just a little less broken than we are today.

I wish I could convince Tere that she needn't worry. No one gets rejected in our family—even the ones that marry in. We have a number of in-laws that are still with us long after the marriage ended. Her place is secure. My family has actually confided that they'd probably keep her over me in a divorce. See, that's how they keep me on my toes, right when I was getting comfortable. We're an odd bunch.

Freer, Messier, Happier

By Jeremy Adam Smith
Yes! Magazine, December 2, 2010

These days, moms, dads, kids, grandmas—even neighbors—are sharing the work of family.

In 1946, when my grandfather mustered out of the army and married my grandmother, he set up what looked like the ideal family at the time. His wife quit her job and he started work driving a crane in a Massachusetts quarry—a job he would do for the next forty years, working up to six days a week, sometimes 12 hours a day. When I asked him if he faced any challenges raising his three children, he replied, "I never did. My wife took care of all that. She brought the kids up." This arrangement came with a rigid hierarchy: "She worked for me," said my grandfather of his wife. "I always said, 'You work for me.'"

By the time my mother and father met in Dracut High School in 1963, the same year that Betty Friedan published *The Feminine Mystique*, more and more people were starting to question this division of labor between men and women. The following year, Congress formally abolished sex discrimination at work. I was born in 1970. "I wanted to be closer to you than my father was to me," my dad told me when I interviewed him for my book, *The Daddy Shift*. "I wanted to participate more in my kids' lives." Even so, my parents never questioned for a moment that he would make most of the money and she would change most of the diapers.

By 1988—the year I graduated from high school—only 29 percent of children lived in two-parent families with a full-time homemaking mother. And like many Baby Boomer couples, my parents split in 1991—the same year I met the woman who is today my wife. By the time we became parents in 2004, my wife and I were stepping into a family landscape that was totally different from the one my grandparents faced in 1946.

For one thing, we never assumed that one of us was the natural breadwinner and the other a natural caregiver—instead, we saw those as roles that we would share and negotiate over time. For a year, I took care of my son while my wife went to work, and as we visited San Francisco's playgrounds, I met other stay-at-home dads, gay and lesbian parents, single mothers and fathers, and multiracial and immigrant families. I watched these disparate kinds of families manage to knit themselves into a community.

The right-wing "family values" movement has painted these trends as a crisis, but no one I know experiences them that way. Instead, we seem to share a positive (if often unarticulated) vision of the family as diverse, egalitarian, voluntary, interdependent, flexible, and improvisational. Many people hold these ideals without necessarily being conscious of their political and economic implications—and they're not making politically motivated choices. In researching *The Daddy Shift*, for example, I didn't interview any breadwinning moms and caregiving dads who adopted their reverse-traditional arrangement for feminist reasons. They almost always framed their work and care decisions as a practical matter, a response to brutally competitive labor and childcare markets.

> *Today's parents are pioneering new relationships among moms, dads, neighbors, relatives, and community, largely in response to challenging economic conditions—and they're doing it with little or no support from marriage, divorce, and medical leave policies designed to support married, heterosexual, nuclear families.*

These day-to-day challenges can prevent us from seeing the bigger picture. We tend to see decades of battles over divorce, single moms, interracial marriage, same-sex marriage, and even immigration as isolated "issues." In fact, each of these issues is a frontline in a wider conflict over family ideals.

Each is part of a larger debate about what kind of society we want to be: one rooted in solidarity, cooperation, nurturance, and inclusiveness, the other in ideals now being most forcefully articulated by the Tea Party movement.

Today's parents are pioneering new relationships among moms, dads, neighbors, relatives, and community, largely in response to challenging economic conditions—and they're doing it with little or no support from marriage, divorce, and medical leave policies designed to support married, heterosexual, nuclear families. Those policies need to change, and we're the ones who are going to have to change them.

Women at Work, Men at Home

Economics have always shaped family. For most of human history, extended families were consolidated business units, growing and making what they needed to live and then selling the surplus to other families. The sole-male-breadwinner, nuclear family came with the rise of industrial capitalism, when fathers marched off to factories and mothers tended homes that became more mechanistic and consumerist as time went on. Today, we are in the throes of another economic and technological evolution that is transforming our most intimate family relationships. As money and people move across borders, barriers against intercultural marriage are dissolving. Today, one in seven new marriages is interracial.

Meanwhile, jobs are becoming more portable, less stable, and more technically demanding—and the recession has hit hardest in male-dominated sectors of the economy.

For almost every decade for the past 100 years, more and more women have gone to college and work. Over the past three years, men have been much more likely to lose their jobs than women, who are concentrated in fast-growing, high-skill industries like health care and education. Between 2009 and 2010, men with college degrees saw their median weekly earnings drop 3 percent while the income of women with degrees grew by 4.3 percent. Today, young women's pay exceeds that of their male peers in most metropolitan areas.

These trends have changed the way moms and dads relate to each other and to their children. As men lost the ability to reliably support families on one income, families responded by diversifying. Men have developed emotional and interpersonal skills by taking care of children—since the mid-1990s, the number of hours dads spend with kids has nearly doubled—and women have gone to school and to work. In the eyes of many couples, equity between parents has moved from a nice ideal to an urgent matter of survival.

And it's a strange but true fact that these changes to the structure of heterosexual families are what's driving acceptance of gay and lesbian marriage and parenthood. In August of 2010, Judge Vaughn Walker explicitly recognized this connection when he overturned Proposition 8, an amendment to California's constitution that defined marriage as being between "one man and one woman." In his decision, Walker wrote:

> The evidence shows that the movement of marriage away from a gendered institution and toward an institution free from state-mandated gender roles reflects an evolution in the understanding of gender rather than a change in marriage. . . . The exclusion [of same-sex couples] exists as an artifact of a time when the genders were seen as having distinct roles in society and in marriage. That time has passed.

Jeremy Adam Smith wrote this article for What Happy Families Know, *the Winter 2011 issue of* YES! Magazine. *Jeremy is a John S. Knight fellow at Stanford University and the author of* The Daddy Shift *(Beacon Press, 2009), from which parts of this essay were adapted.*

Gay Couples: A Close Look at This Modern Family

By Sharon Jayson
USA Today, November 5, 2009

So many gay couples today have kids that it has become a cultural phenomenon—there's even a new TV show about a modern family that includes a gay couple with an adopted baby.

One in five male couples and one in three lesbian couples were raising children as of the 2000 Census. That's way up from 1990, when one in 20 male couples and one in five lesbian couples had kids.

But Census numbers are just part of a new comprehensive analysis of research on gay parenting since the 1970s in new book *Lesbian and Gay Parents and Their Children: Research on the Family Life Cycle*, by Abbie Goldberg, an assistant professor of psychology at Clark University in Worcester, Mass.

Gay households have more in common than not with their heterosexual counterparts who are also raising kids, the research shows. "The sexual orientation of a parent has really little to do with their parenting," Goldberg says.

That idea comes through loud and clear in pop culture, in TV shows such as *Modern Family*, in which two gay men adopt a Vietnamese infant, and among celebrities as gay stars are increasingly having or adopting children.

Demographer Gary Gates of the Williams Institute at the University of California–Los Angeles also has studied same-sex families. His new analysis of the 2008 American Community Survey showed that 31% of same-sex couples who identify themselves as spouses are raising kids compared with 43% of heterosexual couples. That survey marked the first available Census data about same-sex spouses and gay U.S. families. Gates says same-sex couples who identify as married are similar to heterosexual couples in many ways, including the fact that almost one-third are raising children.

Among findings outlined in Goldberg's book:

- The transition to parenthood is similar for both homosexual couples and heterosexual couples.
- Children of gay couples don't differ from their peers raised by heterosexual couples in terms of their mental health, self-esteem, life satisfaction, social skills or number of friends.
- Children in gay families are teased more about their families and their sexuality but are not teased more overall.

> *Gates says same-sex couples who identify as married are similar to heterosexual couples in many ways, including the fact that almost one-third are raising children.*

Stephanie Woolley-Larrea, 36, of Miami says she and her partner, Mary Larrea, 49, have tried to prepare their 7-year-old triplets (two girls and a boy) to face such ridicule, but "it's been a non-issue."

Her kids know "their family is not like everybody else's" but "think it is much more unusual that they are triplets than that they have gay moms."

Goldberg's analysis also included phone interviews that began in 2005 with adoptive parents in 30 states, including 30 to 35 male couples, 40 lesbian couples and 50 to 60 heterosexual couples. They were interviewed before adoption and three months after, with two annual follow-ups so far.

"Gay men are just as likely to want to parent as straight men, but are less likely to parent because of all the barriers in their way," Goldberg says.

Her analysis also suggests that children of gay parents are no more likely to identify as gay themselves.

Sociologist Tim Biblarz of the University of Southern California–Los Angeles says too little long-term, large-scale research exists to conclude that being raised by same-sex couples doesn't affect sexual identity.

"That's an area that the next decade of research might really be able to pioneer."

More Gay Men Embrace Marriage, Fatherhood

Changing laws, surrogacy programs create options for same-sex couples

The Associated Press, August 10, 2008

The cost remains high, and a good lawyer is essential. Yet despite complications, the idea of becoming a biological dad with help from a surrogate mother is gaining allure among gay men as the status of "married with children" grows ever more possible.

With same-sex marriage now legal in California even to nonresidents, and Massachusetts extending its 4-year-old gay-marriage policy to out-of-staters, in-wedlock parenting is suddenly a realistic option for gays and lesbians nationwide, even if their home state won't recognize the union.

Fertility clinics and surrogacy programs report increased interest from gay men, while couples who already have children are getting married—or considering it—to provide more security for those kids.

"We wanted our daughter to know her parents were married—that was the big thing for us," said Tommy Starling of Pawley's Island, S.C., who wed his partner of 12 years, Jeff Littlefield, on July 11 in Hollywood.

Daddy and Dad

Among those at the ceremony was their daughter, Carrigan, who was born in California two years ago.

Starling said he and Littlefield had tried previously to adopt a child in South Carolina, but encountered anti-gay hostility and instead opted to become parents through a surrogacy program run by Los Angeles–based Growing Generations. Since 1996, it has matched hundreds of gay men with surrogate mothers who are paid to carry an implanted embryo produced from a donor egg fertilized with the client's sperm.

"Our journey to parenthood was not easy, cheap or fun," Starling and Littlefield wrote in an account of their family. "The result, however, has been the most amazing experience in the world; being called Daddy and Dad by our loving daughter."

'Something to Prove'

Starling, 36, and Littlefield, 52, face the likelihood that their marriage will not be recognized anytime soon in South Carolina, one of 26 states with constitutional amendments banning same-sex marriages.

In contrast, Joe and Brent Taravella, who are raising three children in South Orange, N.J., already have a civil union and are optimistic that New Jersey will soon join California and Massachusetts in legalizing same-sex marriages.

"As a couple with kids, you really see the importance of it, trying to get as many protections as you can," Joe Taravella said.

They have a 2-year-old daughter through a surrogacy handled by Growing Generations, and twins born in May 2007 through a surrogacy arranged by a New Jersey lawyer, Melissa Brisman.

"My relatives were screaming with excitement when they found out we were going to be parents," Joe Taravella said. "I think we still have something to prove, to show America we can do a great job with these kids."

Becoming a Biological Dad

Brisman, who specializes in reproductive legal issues, said laws dealing with surrogacy vary widely from state to state, as do the options for same-sex couples who become parents.

"Legally, being able to get married will help in some states but not others," she said. "I would never tell clients to get married. . . . But I tell them straight out, 'If you do get married, it's going to be easier.'"

The Taravellas (Brent has taken Joe's last name) both donated sperm—a fairly common practice among gay male couples who say they don't care which partner is the biological dad. Some other couples decide to have two biological babies simultaneously, each providing sperm and using two surrogates.

Among the enterprises offering such services for prospective gay fathers is the Fertility Institutes, which has offices in Los Angeles, Las Vegas and Mexico, and plans to open a

> *"Our journey to parenthood was not easy, cheap or fun,"* Starling and Littlefield wrote *in an account of their family. "The result, however, has been the most amazing experience in the world; being called Daddy and Dad by our loving daughter."*

branch soon in New York City even though New York is among a half-dozen states banning paid surrogacy.

"It's not going to happen in New York as the law stands now," said the Fertility Institutes' director, Dr. Jeffrey Steinberg. "You can't bring the surrogate into the state, but we can make the arrangements, fly the client elsewhere."

Overall, Steinberg says inquiries from gay men to his offices have increased 30 percent in the past six months.

"There are more couples that had been holding off because of the marriage situation who are now starting to show up," he said. "We've definitely seen an upswing."

'Surrogacy Is Getting Easier'

For now, adoptions, rather than surrogacy, remain the most common way for gay men to become fathers, but Steinberg believes a shift is under way.

"Adoption is not getting any easier—surrogacy is getting easier," he said. "You rarely hear horror stories about surrogacy."

In fact, there are occasional surrogacy cases which become anguishing—including lawsuits by surrogate mothers seeking custody of the child, and wrenching cases in which triplets or quadruplets are conceived, and a debate ensues over whether any of the fetuses should be aborted.

Lawyers say airtight contracts can head off such problems, but legal costs run high. Beyond that, there usually are medical costs in the tens of thousands of dollars, and fees to the egg donor and surrogate that together can exceed $25,000.

Dr. G. David Adamson, director of Fertility Associates of Northern California and president of the American Society for Reproductive Medicine, says gay couples considering the option of surrogacy should receive thorough medical and psychological counseling, as well as candid legal advice.

"What we've tried to do is have consent forms that make it very clear what the intentions of the people are," he said. "Who's going to be the mom, who's going to be the dad, what might happen if relationship ends, if someone dies."

"If you don't have an exit strategy, the usual result is that you have potentially several years of litigation, which is extremely damaging to the child," Adamson added. "It's incumbent on everyone to be very thoughtful about entering these arrangements."

A Social Support System

The challenges of gay fatherhood can seem relatively less daunting in gay-friendly communities such as New York, where Jeffrey Parsons and Chris Hietikko are raising a 2-year-old son, Henry. They've also remained in touch with the surrogate mother, a lesbian who lives with her own family in Oregon.

"As gay men, so much depends on where you live, what your social support system is like," said Parsons, a 41-year-old psychology professor at Hunter College.

"Our child will go to school with other kids with gay parents," he said. "I had a job option upstate, but I knew he'd be the only kid like that there."

Parsons, who has been conferring with Hietikko about getting married, says he's a rarity among gay men his age—even as a youth, realizing he was gay, he was convinced he'd become a father.

More typical are men like Jeff Littlefield, who said that in his 20s, "I'd completely given up on the idea of ever having a child."

Littlefield was raised in Utah as a Mormon. In that family-focused culture, he regretted the prospect of not providing his mother with a grandchild.

When he and Starling did have their daughter, they rushed out to introduce the infant to her ailing grandmother—who died just a few days later. The girl's name, Carrigan, is her grandmother's maiden name.

"My mom was able to hold her," Littlefield said. "It was magical."

SPLC Lawsuit Challenges Defense of Marriage Act, VA for Refusing to Recognize Legally Married Same-Sex Couples

SPLC.org, February 1, 2012

Tracey Cooper-Harris served for 12 years in the U.S. Army and received multiple commendations. But because she's in a marriage with a person of the same sex, the government refuses to grant her the same disability benefits as heterosexual veterans.

In a federal lawsuit filed today, the SPLC challenged the constitutionality of the Defense of Marriage Act (DOMA) as well as the law that governs the Department of Veterans Affairs policy.

"The government's refusal to grant these benefits is a slap in the face to the gay and lesbian service members who put their lives on the line to protect our nation and our freedoms," said Christine P. Sun, deputy legal director for the SPLC. "Especially given the recent repeal of Don't Ask Don't Tell, it's shocking that the federal government continues to demean Tracey's years of service and the service of many others in this way."

While in the Army, Tracey reached the rank of sergeant and served in Kyrgyzstan and Kuwait in support of Operation Enduring Freedom and Operation Iraqi Freedom. She received more than two dozen medals and commendations and was honorably discharged in 2003.

Five years later, she married her partner, Maggie, in Van Nuys, Calif. In 2010, she was diagnosed with multiple sclerosis (MS), which the VA has determined is connected to her military service. There is no known cure for MS, a disabling disease that attacks the brain and central nervous system.

Tracey received disability benefits, but the VA denied her application for additional compensation to which married veterans are entitled—benefits meant to help ensure financial stability for spouses—even though her marriage is legally recognized in California. The denial also means the couple will not be permitted to be buried together in a national veteran's cemetery.

The VA's decision was based on its definition of a spouse, spelled out in federal law, as "a person of the opposite sex who is a wife or a husband." Even if the department were to change its definition of spouse, DOMA would prevent the VA from approving the benefits because it defines marriage for all federal purposes as "a legal union between one man and one woman as husband and wife."

"I dedicated 12 years of my life to serving the country I love," Tracey said. "I'm asking only for the same benefits the brave men and women who served beside me enjoy. By refusing to recognize our marriage, the federal government has deprived Maggie and me of the peace of mind that such benefits are meant to provide to veterans and their families."

The lawsuit, filed in the U.S. District Court for the Central District of California, charges that DOMA is unconstitutional because it discriminates on the basis of gender and sexual orientation. It also challenges the VA's definition of "spouse" as discriminatory.

> "I dedicated 12 years of my life to serving the country I love," Tracey said. "I'm asking only for the same benefits the brave men and women who served beside me enjoy."

"This discriminatory policy devalues the military service of countless Americans, solely on the basis of their sexual orientation," said Randall R. Lee, co-counsel in the case and partner-in-charge of WilmerHale's Los Angeles office, which is working with the SPLC on a *pro bono* basis. "It sends a disturbing message to gay and lesbian service members that the courage, commitment, and sacrifice they make on behalf of their country are not valued as much as the service of heterosexual military veterans."

The lawsuit is not the first time the SPLC has fought for equal benefits for military personnel. In the early 1970s, the SPLC challenged the military's refusal to grant equal benefits to married servicewomen. Joseph Levin, SPLC's co-founder, argued the case, *Frontiero v. Richardson*, before the U.S. Supreme Court in 1973. The Court held that the military must provide married women in the armed forces with the same benefits as married men. It was the first successful sex discrimination lawsuit against the federal government.

"More than four decades ago, we fought on behalf of female service members when the military refused to provide them the same benefits as male service members," Levin said. "Sadly, we are once again forced to fight for the equal treatment of service members and their families. All service members and their families make the same commitment and sacrifices for their country. They all should receive the same benefits."

Other attorneys on the case include Caren Short of the SPLC and Matthew Benedetto, Daniel Noble and Eugene Marder of WilmerHale.

Fighting for Family

Michigan law leaves behind gay and lesbian parents— and their children too

By Tara Cavanaugh
Between the Lines, July 21, 2011

With practiced patience, James McDonald manages snack time for a two-year-old who is surprisingly chatty for her age.

"She's everything for her age," he laughs. "She's incredibly smart. We joke she's two going on 20."

The precocious toddler is lucky to have a stay-at-home dad who will no doubt nurture her natural intelligence. She's also lucky to have fathers who temporarily relocated to California just to be able to adopt her and her half brother. The family now lives in Ypsilanti.

Michigan doesn't allow same-sex couples to adopt together, which means that gay and lesbian couples that want to become parents have to carefully survey their options. But no matter how much they plan, Michigan law doesn't even consider children from same-sex parents, and these families can be fractured in an instant.

Everyone knows that parenting can be an uphill battle. But gay and lesbian couples who dare to parent in Michigan are climbing a mountain.

A First and Last Day of School

The first day of school is about more than clean backpacks and fresh pencils—it's a marker that the child has grown a year older. It's a reminder that kids grow up fast.

On a first day of school in September 2009, Renee Harmon showed up at the home of her three children and former partner Tammy Davis. For ten years, the two raised the family they planned together, but then they broke up. After Harmon moved out, she had an informal custody agreement with Davis and saw the kids regularly.

That morning, Harmon rang the doorbell. She had never missed a first day of school. Her arms were full with coffee and bagels, new kids' clothes and a camera.

But Davis' new partner opened the door and told Harmon to go away—that she couldn't see the kids anymore.

Harmon snapped. She had worried about this. No one was going to prevent her from seeing her kids. She broke a window and crawled inside. Davis and her girlfriend tackled Harmon and dragged her out.

Harmon stood in the driveway and waited.

Davis brought out the children when the bus pulled up. They broke away from Davis and ran up to Harmon, crying. "We love you, Nay—Nay!" they yelled.

Harmon hasn't seen her children since.

Harmon's lawyer, Dana Nessel, hears a story like this once a week.

What Michigan Law Doesn't Say

Harmon is suing for custody of her children. It's a difficult case to make, Nessel says, because Harmon and Davis "never tried to adopt. They didn't think they could."

Truth is, the two of them couldn't adopt together. In Michigan, a single adult can adopt a child, and so can a married couple. But unmarried couples cannot adopt, and same-sex couples can't marry. Michigan won't even recognize same-sex marriages performed in other states.

And even though Michigan adoption law doesn't explicitly say that an unmarried couple can't adopt, the judges who grant adoptions have come to that conclusion.

These judges are likely influenced by the powerful figures who have attacked same-sex parent adoption. In 2004 Attorney General Mike Cox issued an opinion against same-sex parent adoption. Also, in 2002, a state Supreme Court justice issued an opinion that judges in Washtenaw County shouldn't perform same-sex parent adoptions. The chief judge responded by telling clerks to stop accepting adoption applications from same-sex parents.

What does this mean for Harmon and the children she hasn't seen in two years? It means that she and her two lawyers, Nessel and Nicole Childers, have to try and prove to the courts that Harmon intended to parent the children with Davis, which she did, and that they functioned as a family, which they did.

But before they can do that, they have to fight for the right to bring evidence before the court. That's because Harmon was never a legal parent. Her ability to present her evidence is a question waiting for consideration by the Michigan Supreme Court right now.

If it refuses her case, then Harmon is set on suing in federal court. This, of course, would mean starting the long legal process all over again.

Harmon isn't afraid of climbing the mountain. Her kids are at the top.

Everyday Dangers

Gay and lesbian parents have to worry about much more than a potential breakup, Nessel says. All sorts of problems await them in everyday life.

For example: the problem of health insurance. Nessel knows of one family whose kids lost their health insurance because their legal mother lost hers. The kids now use Medicaid services.

"So now they have terrible insurance," Nessel says, "and the state has to pay for that. And here they have another parent who wants to put them on her insurance, but of course the employer won't allow that because they're not legally her kids."

Some kids with same-sex parents have even ended up in foster care when they lose their only legal parent.

Stories like these can prevent couples from becoming parents, Nessel says. She remembers two women who wanted to adopt a baby from a pregnant teenager. They asked Nessel how they could protect themselves as parents.

"They fought and fought about who would get to adopt the baby," Nessel says. Finally, they decided whoever had the best health insurance should be the legal parent.

"But the other one broke down crying and said 'I know too much, I've heard too much, I've read too many stories, I can't raise a child knowing that at any time my child will be taken away from me. It would break my heart. I'm not a strong enough person. I can't go through this. There's no guarantees.'"

The women broke up, and one adopted the child. "So who won in that scenario?" Nessel asks angrily.

Few state lawmakers have tried to do anything about this problem. A bill to make same-sex parent adoption legal has been introduced at least three times, explains Emily Dievendorf, director of policy for Equality Michigan. But each time, the bill hasn't even made it past committee to the state House or Senate floor for debate.

In Michigan, a single adult can adopt a child, and so can a married couple. But unmarried couples cannot adopt, and same-sex couples can't marry. Michigan won't even recognize same-sex marriages performed in other states.

"Any time there is a committee hearing almost everybody offers testimony—and we're talking about psychologists, social workers—as to why this needs to happen and that having two parents is in the best interest of the child," Dievendorf says. "It's overwhelming testimony that delaying this is a terrible idea. And it will look like it should move with logic and scientific evidence in support behind it, and then it doesn't go anywhere."

At home in Ypsilanti, McDonald shakes his head at the legislature. "These kids need homes," he says. "That should be what the legislators should be looking at. There are people, whether they're same-sex couples or not, who are able, willing and wanting to provide those homes. Shame on them for standing in the way of that."

Knowing Where to Look

Hands Across the Water is an adoption agency in Ann Arbor. In June it won an award from the Human Rights Campaign for helping gay and lesbian parents adopt. The HRC gives out awards like this because many adoption agencies don't welcome gay or lesbian parents.

The agency's founder and director, Kathi Nelson, has noticed something interesting about these aspiring parents: At the monthly information meetings, they're quiet, and they don't ask their questions until everyone else leaves.

In response, Nelson is planning the agency's first information meeting specifically for gay and lesbian parents. She's looking for someone from the LGBT community to be on the agency's board of directors, and she asked a gay parent—McDonald—to lead a support group. He held the first meeting last month.

"I would like that people just to know that it can happen," McDonald says. "That it's a possibility. And it is a struggle, but that's what the group is there for, to help you through the phases of your process."

A Mother's Warning

What would Harmon say to any gay or lesbian couple that is considering adoption? "I would warn them," she says. "I never thought this would happen to me.

"We were together nineteen years. When you're in love and you're planning a family and you've been together so long, it never enters your mind that something like this could happen. Be careful."

Mostly, though, Harmon is angry that her children aren't protected: "They didn't ask to be born in this situation and to have no rights."

Harmon has become a sort of poster child for the cause of same-sex parent adoption, and she's been contacted by other parents in the same situation, looking for help. "My advice to them was just do what you can to be able to see your children," she says.

She'll keep sending her kids birthday cards and letters, even though they are sent back. She'll keep working with her lawyers, even though she has to throw fundraisers to pay the bills.

She's doing everything she can.

2

Contemporary Motherhood

(Brand New Images)

The evolving portrait of contemporary motherhood includes women having children later in life, single motherhood by choice, and Web 2.0 mommy bloggers.

American Mothers: Finding a Balance

By Paul McCaffrey

During the late twentieth and early twenty-first century, popular conceptions of motherhood have undergone a metamorphosis. In the United States, the traditional view of motherhood was that mothers stayed in the home. In general, they did not pursue careers but dedicated their lives to running households and raising children. The idea that motherhood was the central calling of women's lives became a widely idealized principle in American culture.

A number of women found the expectation of motherhood that was placed on them to be restrictive. During the "second-wave" feminist movement that started to take shape in the early 1960s, many women began rebelling against this prevailing model. The "first-wave" feminism of the mid-to-late nineteenth and early twentieth century was concerned primarily with legal issues related to gender equality. It helped to secure the Nineteenth Amendment to the Constitution, giving women the right to vote. Second-wave feminism, also known as the Women's Liberation Movement, was more concerned with social and cultural matters. It focused on issues such as equality in the workplace and freeing women from the restrictions of traditional gender roles, and societal expectations that confined them to the home.

In her seminal book *The Feminine Mystique* (1963), Betty Friedan wrote of "the problem that has no name—which is simply the fact that American women are kept from growing to their full human capacities." In Friedan's view, the roles and expectations mapped out for women by society prevented them from realizing their full potential and deprived the larger American community of the benefits of that potential. Friedan argued that there were few ways for women to define themselves outside of the traditional family model.

The Feminine Mystique discusses the plight of mothers Friedan researched during the late 1950s, mothers who, despite fulfilling the role that society expected of them, felt that something was missing. "Each suburban wife struggled with it alone," Friedan writes. "As she made the beds, shopped for groceries, matched slip-cover material, ate peanut butter sandwiches with her children, chauffered Cub Scouts and Brownies, lay beside her husband at night—she was afraid to ask even of herself the silent question—'Is this all?'"

"The only way for a woman, as for a man, to find herself, to know herself as a person," writes Friedan, "is by creative work of her own. There is no other way." Yet employment was not always the solution. "If a job is to be the way out of the trap for a woman, " she wrote, "it must be a job that she can take seriously as part of a life plan, work in which she can grow as part of society."

Though the discontent and yearning she evoked was not universal and was even antithetical to some, Friedan's sentiment spoke to many women, and these concerns became central to second-wave feminism. "The problem that has no name" continues to be reflected in research data. In a 2012 Gallup poll, 28 percent of stay-at-home mothers reported suffering from depression, as compared to 17 percent of both working mothers and working women. "In fact," writes Sharon Lerner for *Slate*, "stay-at-home moms fare worse than these two groups by every emotional measure, reporting more anger, sadness, stress, and worry. They were more likely to describe themselves as struggling and suffering, and less likely to see themselves as 'thriving.'"

The Women's Liberation Movement modeled itself after the Civil Rights and anti-war movements of the 1960s. The movement achieved a number of victories, particularly in the realm of reproductive, employment, and housing rights. Yet its major goal—the ratification of the Equal Rights Amendment (ERA) prohibiting discrimination based on gender—was never accomplished.

As the Women's Liberation Movement pushed its agenda, other currents were at work in society that eroded the economic and social foundations supporting the traditional ideal of motherhood. Birth control became widely accessible, allowing women to put off having children and giving them more freedom to pursue careers. Educational opportunities expanded as well. Fewer women became married, women elected to have fewer children, and divorce rates increased. Single women and single mothers became a growing presence in the labor force. Economic factors also made it more difficult for families to support themselves on only one income. Increasingly, mothers were compelled by financial necessity to enter the workforce. While the Women's Liberation Movement advocated for career building as an act of autonomy, there was an element of necessity as well. To provide for themselves and their families, many women had no choice but to find work.

Of all the social trends of the latter half of the twentieth century, few are more significant than the migration of women into the labor force. For mothers, the pattern is especially pronounced. In 1950, fewer than one in five women with children under the age of eighteen worked outside the home. By the late 1990s, more than seven in ten had jobs. As of 2010, of the roughly 25,300,000 married couples with children under the age of eighteen, over 64 percent earned two incomes, and less than 30 percent were supported by the father alone. In nearly 3 percent of these families, the traditional model was turned on its head, with the father staying at home and the mother serving as the sole breadwinner. The earnings of wives and mothers have increased as well. In 1970, a working wife earned about 26.6 percent of her family's income. By 2010, that had grown to 37.6 percent, and currently around 40 percent of working wives earn more than their husbands, a figure that would have been unimaginable during the era in which Betty Friedan wrote *The Feminine Mystique*.

The pace and diversity of these social and economic changes has redefined motherhood. Fifty years ago, the typical mother was married with several children and did not participate in the labor force. Today, most mothers have careers, and a growing number of them are unmarried. In addition, woman are having fewer children and having them later, sometimes postponing motherhood until well after they turn thirty-five.

The increasing prevalence of single mothers can be attributed to a host of factors, including the decrease in marriage rates and the growing economic independence of women. Nevertheless, the increase of births among unmarried women is striking. In 2010, single mothers accounted for approximately 41 percent of all newborns. Fifty years earlier, in 1960, single mothers accounted for 5.3 percent of all newborns. Still, single mothers are a distinct, if growing, minority. In 2010, 66 percent of children under the age of eighteen lived with two married parents. Only 23 percent lived with just their mothers. In addition, the term "single mother" is not especially precise. Many single mothers, in fact, have a partner with whom they live but to whom they are not married.

Statistically speaking, children raised by single mothers—or single fathers—are at a disadvantage when compared to those brought up in traditional two-parent households. They are more likely to grow up poor, and, according to a Swedish study reported on by Emma Ross for the Associated Press, "twice as likely as those in two-parent families to develop serious psychiatric problems and [drug] addictions later in life." Though the data is clear, the causes of greater rates of mental illness are not. Researchers have varying theories, with some blaming this rate on the comparative lack of financial resources among single parents. Others posit a more complex assortment of factors. Ross cites "the level of hostility between the parents who separate, the quality of the parenting, the timing of divorce, and the extent and quality of the social network, which includes school, friends and adult role models." Whatever the underlying causes, the fact remains that the risk is not so elevated as to be determinative. Most children raised by single parents, like most raised by two parents, end up leading normal lives.

The 1950s model of motherhood that Betty Friedan and the Women's Liberation Movement rebelled against was constructed in the midst of the post–World War II Baby Boom, a period of elevated birth rates in the United States. In the late 1950s, for example, though contraception was more accessible, if not readily available, the total fertility rate stood at 3.7 children per woman. The typical mother rarely had just one child, and the average had between three and four. In the decades since, that number has fallen drastically. By the late 1970s, it was more than cut in half, declining to 1.8. In 2012, the rate stood at around 2.06.

As women concentrate more on their careers, they are often choosing to have children later in life. In 1990, for example, 9 percent of births were attributed to women over thirty-five, whereas 13 percent were to teenagers. As of 2008, those statistics were reversed, as births among women over thirty-five outpaced those among teenagers 14 percent to 10 percent. In 1970, the average age at which a mother first gave birth was around twenty-one. By 2008, that age had increased to 25.1. Though it is more difficult for women to become pregnant later in life, and though later pregnancies carry more risk, as a group older mothers frequently have some advantages over their younger counterparts. In general, they tend to be more financially stable, with advanced educations, and are more likely to be married. Describing the overall pattern, Susan Bianchi, a sociologist at the University of California at Los Angeles (UCLA) comments, "It's clear that young adult transitions are being postponed . . . Children born to highly educated mothers increasingly are born later in life. The mothers are usually married, and they have a much higher chance of raising children in a stable marriage that lasts through a child's childhood."

The developments described above reflect a comprehensive transformation of motherhood in America. In many respects, the changes demonstrate a triumph for second-wave feminism. Over the past fifty years, women and mothers have gained a degree of autonomy that would have been unthinkable when Friedan first described "the problem that has no name." Mothers today are out in the workforce, and asserting themselves economically. They are choosing motherhood on their own terms, postponing it to build careers, and deciding whether or not it will take place as part of a marriage or some other relationship.

The emerging twenty-first-century vision of motherhood also brings with it new challenges. Mothers today have more financial obligations than in the past, serving as earners and providers, and sometimes as their family's only earner and provider. The stay-at-home mom, the model of the "Feminine Mystique," on the other hand—though growing scarcer in the face of economic and social change—has not disappeared entirely, and continues to influence what society expects of mothers and what mothers expect of themselves. Finding the right balance between these expectations, between the old role of nurturer and the new role of provider, represents a new challenge for twenty-first-century mothers.

Midlife Mamas: It's Worth the Wait

By Karen West
Seattle Woman Magazine, 2009

We've all seen the headlines: Women's biological clocks start ticking in their late 20s. Fertility declines with age. Women who want it all find it's too late.

Tell that to the burgeoning number of "midlife mamas"—women all over the country having babies later in life, and for some, on their own terms.

Many are resetting their biological clocks to establish careers, build financial nest eggs and travel the world. Others become older moms unexpectedly after years of unsuccessful attempts. And some prolong having children until they find the right partner or "retire" into parenthood. They are rewriting the book on motherhood—and aging—in America.

Midlife mamas—whether they are gay or straight, divorced or married, use donor sperm, in vitro fertilization, conceive naturally or adopt—agree that age and a sense of readiness have personally given them the wisdom and patience to be better, more content mothers. In interviews with more than 30 older moms in the Seattle area, almost all said they were happier having children later in life. And research shows that women who wait are even living longer.

"I was a pretty squirrelly twenty-something, a relentlessly striving thirty-something and by comparison a sensible forty-something," says Bonnie Albin Fraik, who discovered she was pregnant at age 41 while living on her sailboat in Puerto Vallarta. She had financial resources, a stable marriage, plenty of options "and perhaps a little accumulated wisdom."

The wave of new, older mothers is spreading across the country.

- In 2006 more than 600,000 babies (one in seven) were born to moms 35 and older in the United States, according to Centers for Disease Control statistics.

- The birthrate for women 45 and older tripled between 1990 and 2006, according to the CDC, and the actual number of births to moms 45 and older has quadrupled (up from 1,638 in 1990 to 6,956 in 2006).

- Later celebrity moms, such as Julia Roberts, Madonna, Nicole Kidman and Salma Hayek, grace the covers of magazines on supermarket news racks.

- Support groups for older moms, including Seattle's Fabulous Mamas Over 40 and 80's Ladies With Babies, are being formed in just about every city in the country. There's even a new magazine, *Plum*, that targets pregnant women over 35.

"Women now have the option to define for themselves when they're ready for family, rather than sticking to a schedule set by social convention," writes Elizabeth Gregory in her book, *Ready: Why Women are Embracing the New Later Motherhood* (Basic Books, 2007). "As a society, however, we have yet to come to terms with the phenomenon of later motherhood, and women who decide it makes sense to delay pregnancy often find themselves confronted with alarmist warnings about the dangers of waiting too long."

New Later Moms

Having children at a later age is not new, but U.S. Census data shows a dramatic increase in the number of women choosing to start their families at age 35 or older. Gregory, director of the women's studies program and professor of English at the University of Houston, calls them "new later moms."

In a telephone interview from her home in Houston, Gregory, 51, points out that her grandmother had the old-fashioned kind of later motherhood by having her eighth child when she was 39. That's the same age Gregory was when she gave birth to her first. She notes that in 2005, one of every 12 first births in the U.S. was to a woman 35 or older, compared with 1970, when one in every 100 first children had an older mom. After the first child, many new later moms, including Gregory, go on to have more kids.

"This is a generation of women with more clout," says Gregory, who adopted a second child at age 48. "The difference from the later moms of years past is that the new later moms have more cultural capital: more education and higher wages. . . . They are established in their jobs and secure in their senses of self so they can focus on their kids' development rather than their own."

Debbie Kobelansky, 50, is one of those new later moms. She made a conscious decision to start her family later in life, mainly because she also married later. Starting a family later allowed her to establish her career as a health care risk management consultant in Seattle and develop the financial means to help support her family. "I did so much traveling in my 20s and 30s, so I don't feel like I am missing out on anything," says Kobelansky. "I don't have the conflict younger women feel who may just be establishing their careers."

She and her husband first decided to become foster parents and later adopted those children, who are now 5 and 7. The couple fostered both children as infants, but the adoption process took 18 months for one and nearly three years for the other.

Leslie MacGregor, 42, didn't even think about having kids until she was in her 30s. She was busy traveling and working long hours as a vice president of advertising for a global technology company. "I feel much more content and comfortable with a baby after 40 than I did with my first one," she says. "The experience feels more natural, less worrisome and more enjoyable."

The mother of three boys, now ages 7, 5, and 2, MacGregor was fortunate to conceive immediately with each child. Shortly after having her first baby in California, the family moved overseas and she had two more children, one in London and the other in Amsterdam.

The Waiting Game

Not all older mothers make a conscious decision to wait. Sometimes Mother Nature decides for them.

Julie Clark, for example, always wanted children, even as a teenager. She had had an early abortion at age 17, which, she says, "I didn't want but felt pressured into," and then in her 20s lost two babies through miscarriage in her first marriage. "Although I developed a career and a full life without children, having children was my dream from age 17 until 41, when I finally got them. It was worth the wait."

"This is a generation of women with more clout," says Gregory, who adopted a second child at age 48. "The difference from the later moms of years past is that the new later moms have more cultural capital: more education and higher wages. . . . They are established in their jobs and secure in their senses of self so they can focus on their kids' development rather than their own."

Clark, of Bellingham, was 41 and 43 when she had her daughters, now 4 and 6. She met her husband at age 39 and they began trying to have children shortly after they married. "I was lucky at my age to get pregnant within a few months," she says.

She wanted to have another baby but assumed she wouldn't get pregnant while exclusively breast-feeding. But when her daughter was five months old, she did get pregnant. Sadly the baby died five months into her pregnancy. It was a heartbreaking time, but several months later she got pregnant again and gave birth to another daughter.

For Alex Sanso, 46, the concept of motherhood evolved over the years as she settled into a long-term relationship with her female partner. She never thought of herself as the mommy type. She liked children and loved spoiling her niece and nephew, but admits it was nice to give them back to mom at the end of a fun-filled day. "I always thought I was too selfish and interested in too many other things to actually want to raise a child."

But after a few years, she and her partner started exploring adoption. "A child started to feel like a missing piece for us and my feelings shifted," she says. "Then, almost like the proverbial ticking clock, at age 39, I suddenly had to do it." Her realization happened while riding the subway to work one day in Tokyo, where she was a designer for Disneyland. "I was surrounded by all these cute kids and their families on their way to Disneyland, and it hit me."

Instead of adopting, they researched sperm banks in California and had four vials shipped to Japan. Using her own egg, Sanso's doctor performed an intrauterine insemination in his office while she held hands with her partner and her mother. The first insemination was successful and she gave birth to a healthy boy, now 6.

Sanso says she never felt like an "older" mother. "We were living in Tokyo at the time, so it was more unusual that we were two women trying to start a family than the fact that I was older."

Menopausal Mamas?

Despite acquiring wisdom and patience with age, many older moms still have their share of worries: sleep deprivation, mortality and menopause, to name a few. "I became perimenopausal as I became a new mother," Debbie Kobelansky says. "Talk about conflicting hormones!"

Others ask themselves: Will I be able to physically keep up with my active kids? Will I be around to see my children graduate from high school, marry and have children of their own? Will my own parents be around long enough to develop relationships with their grandchildren?

Jeanne Flohr, an administrator at O'Dea High School in Seattle, had a bittersweet experience with the birth of her third child at age 44. Her mother died unexpectedly just 12 days after her son was born last May—three days before Mother's Day.

"She only held him a few times and he will never know her as his sister, brother and cousins did," Flohr says. "Mom was a wonderful teacher, an avid reader, and enjoyed exploring the city and parks with her 13 other grandchildren, and it makes me very sad to know Charlie will not experience her joie de vivre."

Flohr already had two children, then ages 12 and 13, when she unexpectedly became pregnant. Although it was a shock, she and her husband welcomed the news. Her teenage children had a slightly different view at first. "Once I was showing, they were embarrassed to be seen with me 'cause it means, you know, Mom and Dad. . . . Then, after Charlie arrived, they didn't like me walking them to and from school with the stroller; otherwise they were good with it."

Katie Perry, 45, worries that she won't be able to have a relationship with her grandchildren. If she could do things over again, she says she would have had children earlier, "just so that I physically had more energy and could be around for a longer period of their lives."

Perry had her first baby when she was 38 and the second at 40. She didn't make a conscious decision to have her baby later in life but waited until she found the right partner. "Life was full of adventure and travel and work. I was in and out of long-term relationships. Although I always knew I wanted to have a family, I really started thinking about family and future at age 35. At age 37, I found a person to do that with."

The stress of caring for elderly parents while nurturing a toddler also is a factor for many older moms, including Bonnie Albin Fraik, 47. Her ailing father died of

Alzheimer's disease in 2007, shortly after she had her baby. She remembers "being wiped out with an infant/toddler while my father was falling into dementia. I would have liked to have spent more time with him."

A Sense of Community

Menopausal moments and being part of the sandwich generation don't usually come up in conversation at new parent support groups. That's why Suji Quay started her own last year, exclusively for new mothers over 40. "I was at different stages in life than most of the other moms and I wanted to talk with women my own age," she says.

The group started out with just a few older moms meeting in neighborhood coffeehouses in Seattle. It has since changed its name to "Fabulous Mamas Over 40" and has grown to more than 40 members from Marysville to South Seattle. The group, now being led by Elise Gordon of Lynnwood, sponsors semi-monthly "meet-ups," including mom's nights out, trips to the zoo, museums and parks.

For Gordon, 45, "Fabulous Mamas" has given her an outlet to share parenting strategies, discuss aging issues and swap "older mom" stories with women of her generation. "Between taking care of ailing parents, running a household, taking care of kids and working, older mothers need support," Gordon says. "They need to know there are a lot of other moms out there dealing with the same issues."

Society and the medical community seem to be warming up to older mothers. The fact that she was 41 when she became pregnant didn't faze Albin Fraik's perinatologist. "On my first visit, he told me he didn't blink unless you were over 50, so being 41 was nothing."

Dr. David Luthy, medical director of obstetrics and gynecology at Swedish Medical Center, says women over 40 having children is commonplace nowadays, especially in King County where the birthrate among older mothers leads the country. "It certainly doesn't raise any eyebrows in our office."

He cautioned, however, that complications can arise, such as preeclampsia or diabetes, with mature maternity.

Leslie MacGregor, who had two of her three children overseas, found the medical approaches in the U.S. to be vastly different from those in Europe. She was 35 when she had her first baby in California and "everything was very clinical and all about testing and monitoring the baby."

She had a completely different experience three years later with her second child born in London. "The European model is all about pleasing the mother," she says. She had an even better experience with her last child born in Amsterdam.

The Dutch, who believe birth should be natural, not medical, take a non-interventionist approach to pregnancy. So when MacGregor instructed her doctor in Amsterdam to give her an epidural for her last delivery, he just smiled and said he would see what he could do. "I was moaning like I was in a tribal community and screaming for an epidural," she recalls. "All these Dutch women were looking at me like I was a crazy American who wanted painkillers." She never did get the epidural because her baby was born within the hour.

As they left the hospital, she was pleasantly surprised to learn that a nanny had been assigned to them for the first two weeks. "That's just the way they do things. It's such a different mentality."

She hopes that mentality will eventually find its way to the U.S. Gregory, who spent several years studying older mothers, says American society is slowly adjusting to older motherhood. "There's been this great anxiety about women over 35 having children, but the story so often is very different. Doctors and society have discovered that older moms are doing just fine."

Karen West, 50, is a Bainbridge Island–based writer and mother of a 6-year-old girl and a 10-year-old boy.

Why I Left My Children

By Rahna Reiko Rizzuto
Salon.com, February 28, 2011

My husband is the one who wanted kids. But I learned I didn't have to live with them to be a good mother.

In 2001, 16 days after my youngest son's third birthday, I walked out the door of my Brooklyn, N.Y., brownstone with one piece of luggage. I was leaving my family. Two sons, age 5 and 3, and my childhood-sweetheart husband, my partner for 20 years.

I had been awarded a grant to live in Japan for six months to interview the survivors of the atomic bomb. It was an honor that my husband had encouraged me to apply for, and we were in complete agreement, in fact he insisted, that I should go. The question was not how he and the kids would manage—he had plenty of help from a loving caretaker who had become part of our family, and from actual blood relations living down the block and flying in from halfway around the world. The wild card was me: How would I do, living in a foreign country where I did not even speak the language, living on my own for the first time ever in my 37-year-old life?

My marriage did not survive.

The question I am always asked is, "How could you leave your children?" How could you be the mother who walks away? As if my children were embedded inside me, even years after birth, and had to be surgically removed? As if I abandoned them on a desert island, amid flaming airplane debris and got into the lifeboat alone?

Hyperbolic. Inflammatory. But that's part of the point. Because my relationship with my children survives. In fact, it has improved.

It was a matter of months—perhaps two—when my husband and I began fighting long distance. Our marriage ran aground on expectations, promises and old habits. Shoulds. What we should be doing, what we should want, what we should do or say. We had been together since I was 17. We had spent more of our lives together as a couple than we had apart. And we destroyed our marriage in less time than it takes a credit card company to report you for nonpayment.

I will not tell you the children never noticed I was gone. Though there were plenty of times I could not get them to stop watching *Barney* to talk to me on the telephone, I also received some very sad phone calls and transcribed e-mails, including one that said, "When I called you last night I felt like I really missed you very much." But when they arrived in Japan to live with me four months after I left, I was the one who was in trouble. They were happy—in love with their father and with me—thrilled with the temples and the trains and the samurai castles and the bean cakes shaped like fish. I was in "mommy shock." Without a strong marriage to support me, after four months alone and in a new country I had grown to love but was only just beginning to understand how to navigate, I had no idea what to do with these bouncing balls of energy. Even feeding them, finding them a bathroom, was a challenge.

It raised a little issue for me that I have neglected to mention: I never wanted to be a mother.

> *I was afraid of being swallowed up, of being exhausted, of opening my eyes one day, 20 (or 30!) years after they were born, and realizing I had lost myself and my life was over.*

I was afraid of being swallowed up, of being exhausted, of opening my eyes one day, 20 (or 30!) years after they were born, and realizing I had lost myself and my life was over.

Yet their father wanted a family. He begged. He promised to take care of everything; he removed every possible obstacle I could think of. He would be the primary caretaker if I would just have them.

It all makes sense now, doesn't it? I am a cold bitch. I was never a mother in anything but name. I am probably one of those women who will be arrested for going to a nearby bar and leaving my children asleep in a house with a faulty pilot light: a house in flames.

I am a bad mother.

But that's not true either.

My problem was not with my children, but with how we think about motherhood. About how a male full-time caretaker is a "saint," and how a female full-time caretaker is a "mother." It is an equation we do not question; in fact we insist on it. And we punish the very idea that there are other ways to be a mother.

My trip to Japan changed me. I went from being uncertain, ambivalent, loving but overwhelmed, to being a damned good mother. My marriage failed, and I gave primary physical custody to my husband. But I kept joint custody, and I did not take the house in Hawaii and jump a plane into the sunset. I moved down the block and began the long, hard work of proving to my children, and myself, that I am here.

These days, my sons live and sleep at their father's house. They can walk to their "other house"—mine—which they do several times a week. They come over after school and get picked up at bedtime, and in between I help them with their homework, we cook dinner together, eat and clean up together, and we talk about the day. Normally, we get in a few rounds of Quiddler or Yahtzee, or we Hulu episodes of old TV shows, like "Jamie Oliver's Food Revolution," that we missed because we were on the plane coming home from a two-week vacation in Hawaii with their grandparents. And we cry together when Jamie cries, and when a 16-year-old girl talks about how she might only have seven years to live. We do a lot of hugging, even in public, even though they are now boys entering their teens.

I had to leave my children to find them. In my part-time motherhood, I get concentrated blocks of time when I can be that 1950s mother we idealize who was waiting in an apron with fresh cookies when we got off the school bus and wasn't too busy for anything we needed until we went to bed. I go to every parent-teacher conference; I am there for performances and baseball games. My former husband is there too. Though it was not easy for him, he has made it possible for me to define my own motherhood, and for our sons to have a life of additions, rather than subtraction, of a relative peace, rather than constant accusation.

Yesterday, on a blog, I read a plea from a young woman who was planning to go to a residency and leave her 2- and 4-year-old children. "Am I crazy?" she wrote. "Someone tell me." I thought about answering, but I didn't know what to say. Would I do it again? Yes. Should she do it? Only she can answer that question. Then I looked at the date and realized: She was already gone.

Mother Huckster

How the mommy blog became a brand

By Sarah McAbee
Bitch Magazine, Spring 2011

"Mommy blog": The label is simultaneously approachable and derisive, potentially political, and way too cute. Unlike tech bloggers, food bloggers, celebrity bloggers, or design bloggers, mommy bloggers are a huge and diverse group that has been nominally defined not by their content, which ranges from parenting to design to education to activism, but by the one-size-fits-all mantle of motherhood. And as mainstream media outlets introduce mommy bloggers to audiences beyond the blogosphere, the emphasis is on the "mommy" rather than the "blog." Writers who have developed their websites into major online brands are treated as novel and authentic new pundits on mothering and womanhood, but not much else.

When Heather Armstrong of the blog Dooce appeared, via Skype, on *Oprah* in 2009, the success of her blog—the $40,000 a month in ad revenue, Dooce's transition from personal blog to media empire—was mentioned only in passing. The story Oprah really wanted was how blogging, in Armstrong's words, saved her life during a period of severe postpartum depression. She spoke of the many readers and commenters who wrote in to assure her that her feelings were normal, as well as to offer support when she decided to be hospitalized for treatment. "Isn't this new for us?" Oprah responded, noting that in earlier days, PPD was a condition left unmentioned, even between women. The casual use of "us"—as in "just us girls"—tethers Armstrong's contributions as a blogger to her femaleness and mother status, not to her broader role as an author (she's written two books since starting Dooce) or wildly divisive Web 2.0 figure. It's even more telling that Oprah's emphasis on Dooce's story wasn't that the Internet facilitated a dialogue on PPD, but that a woman was bringing the subject up at all. Despite Armstrong's attempt to discuss the blog itself, the story was reduced to one mom talking to others.

Even more dispiriting is the offline media treatment of the biggest mommy blogger of them all, Ree Drummond. Drummond, who started her blog, The Pioneer Woman, in 2006, now receives 22 million hits a month. Her 2009 cookbook, *The Pioneer Woman Cooks*, became a *New York Times* bestseller based on her blog fame; the just-released book about how she met her husband, *Black Heels to Tractor Wheels*, has been optioned by Columbia Pictures (with Reese Witherspoon rumored to be in early talks to play the lead). In addition, she hosts multiple weekly

---

sweepstakes and quiz posts that draw tens of thousands of comments. Like Dooce, The Pioneer Woman has become its own media brand and counts its hits and advertising dollars by the million, including partnerships with HP, Macy's, and other major companies. But when Drummond appears on *The Bonnie Hunt Show*, *Good Morning America*, or the *Today* show, the producers have her make a sheet cake or a pot roast. Even when hosts take conversation with Drummond beyond the book-tour boilerplate, they stick to the Pioneer Woman's romantic narrative of Girl Meets Cowboy, while her incredible success as a media brand is left undiscussed.

Despite the complexity of these blogging powerhouses, the mainstream media seems content to categorize them as just, well, moms. Not professional bloggers, not businesspeople, not brands in and of themselves. Despite all the potential and power in these women's blogs and the hundreds authored by other women for whom "mother" is just one in a list of identifiers, mommy bloggers—especially those who haven't hit the big time yet—are often confined to an easily caricatured realm. In a March 2010 article for the *New York Times* titled "Honey, Don't Bother Mommy. I'm Too Busy Building My Brand" (and located in, naturally, the style section), Jennifer Mendelsohn, who was herself once included on a list of top 50 "lesser-known mom bloggers," opens her article by invoking a tableau of thirty something women gathering to talk shop about the business end of mommy blogging at something called Bloggy Boot Camp. "Teaching your baby to read?" Mendelsohn posits. "Please. How to hide vegetables in your children's food? Oh, that's so 2008." Though her writing loses much of its snark by the end of the piece, Mendelsohn's feigned shock at mothers coming together to talk page views and PR rules comes off as condescending (or sour grapes). When she quotes the organizer of the conference acknowledging that the attendees "want to be seen as professional," she follows up by noting that the organizer herself "went barefoot for much of the day and said 'You guys!' a lot." Get it? These women could never really be professionals, because they're just moms!

Parenting columnist Liz Gumbinner, on her personal blog, Mom-101, was among the bloggers to call Mendelsohn out on her antimom subtext, though she also acknowledged the better parts of the article, in which the conference attendees discussed the community building aspects of their medium as well as the current conversational flash point—how bloggers with community roles as peers and mentors navigate relationships with advertisers and corporate sponsors. Still, she wrote, "I wish [the article] had opened with the yearning of bloggers for the community to return to good writing, and the evidence that in the end, that's mostly what pays off, and not this [search engine optimization] bullshit or obsession with stats." Instead, Gumbinner noted, by opening her article with shallow depictions of mommy bloggers as greedy, inane wannabe writers, Mendelsohn threw open a door for commenters like one on the *Times'* Motherlode blog who sneered that "nature abhors a vacuum, so these people fill up their lives with each other. . . . There is something pathetic about the clingy, needy plea for attention and affirmation." Much of the response elsewhere was similarly gendered. And really, why shouldn't it be, when the coverage of mommy bloggers attracts readers by trading on the idea of them as flighty former career women with time on their hands?

When smear pieces like Mendelsohn's and TV morning shows characterize mommy blogs as "kaffeeklatsches" or one mom just sharing her recipes, they ignore the charged internal culture that is the true subtext of the mommy blogosphere. While nonblogging *Times* commenters may find mommy blogs too touchy-feely and histrionic (you know, like women are), insiders know that the big personalities and topics can be just as polarizing as, say, Lady Gaga is to the Internet at large. For example, the phrase "I hate Dooce" gets more than 61,000 hits when Googled. In a nod to that prodigious group of critics, Armstrong created a section of Dooce called "Monetizing the Hate," where cut-and-pastes from particularly nasty e-mails and comments are surrounded by lucrative advertisements from the likes of Amazon, ensuring that anyone who wants to drink some of the haterade will also drop some change into the Dooce retirement fund. The Pioneer Woman doesn't seem to evoke quite so many negative reactions, but the criticisms all fall along the same lines—why are we supposed to believe P-Widdy is just like us when, by some estimates, her blog is pulling in cash by the millions?

> *When [Mendelsohn] quotes the organizer of [Bloggy Boot camp] acknowledging that the attendees "want to be seen as professional," she follows up by noting that the organizer herself "went barefoot for much of the day and said 'You guys!' a lot."*

It's now evident that mommy bloggers' criticism of each other has actually become a hallmark of their genre. The active, extensive networks that rocket a blogger to virtual stardom can work just as quickly to disseminate gossip, court controversy, and shit-talk a personality and her readers/groupies. Some of the complaints are generic and long-standing: Way back in 2006, blogger Ilyka Damen noted the "objectification" of mommy bloggers' offspring through obsessive attention to detail, seemingly denying their children or families crucial privacy. Some are about disproportionate representation: Countless writers have argued that mommy blogging seems overwhelmingly white and middle class. And those at the top of the heap—the professional mommy bloggers with their sponsored giveaways and book deals—are criticized for seldom (or never) acknowledging the privilege of their circumstances.

Take the now-notorious story of Dooce and the Maytag. In 2009, Armstrong, whose blog is a full-time job for her, her husband, and a guy she's nicknamed Tyrant, purchased a $1,300 Maytag washing machine, which broke down. She embarked on a series of dead-end attempts at resolution with the company, and reaching the end of her patience, asked a customer service representative, "Do you know what Twitter is? Because I have [more than] a million followers on Twitter." The rep was unmoved by the proclamation, but Armstrong's tweets later that day ("DO NOT EVER BUY A MAYTAG") sucked Maytag into a PR nightmare that escalated one minor problem into a disaster witnessed by millions. While brand managers quickly began using the event as a case study for customer service in the age of social media, Armstrong's fellow mommy bloggers attacked her for what they argued was a wanton misuse of her influence. Anna Viele of ABDPBT.com accused Armstrong of "brand bullying" and joked that "Dooce getting her washer fixed in like 8 seconds after complaining on the Internet" was not quite the "*Sí! Se puede!*" anticorporate moment Armstrong and her husband made it out to be.

At the root of all these criticisms is an ideal of authentic connection and self-presentation, whether in blogging's capacity for community building or its real-life, warts-and-all tone. When a blog becomes a branded powerhouse, the blogger-reader dynamic shifts from a peer-to-peer interaction to a relationship much more aspirational (or jealous) on the part of the reader-commenter. Maybe it's because we don't all have the time or pageviews to attend networking summits and corporate promotional events, or the resources to renovate a guest house during an economic recession. More likely, it's a pattern familiar to any subculture—those who are the first to go mainstream get tagged "sellout" and are perceived to be abandoning their core audience. That the mommy bloggers who do are the ones likely to be featured in the *New York Times* or welcomed onto daytime television only complicates this relationship further. The mainstream media's selective representation of bloggers like Dooce and The Pioneer Woman as unpolished, normal women with stories to tell rings about as true for some readers and fellow bloggers as the "Stars Are Just Like Us!" features in supermarket rags.

The way in which the mainstream media indirectly (or even directly) characterizes mommy bloggers has alienated so many bloggers that the term itself has for years been contentious. Julie Marsh, of the popular blog The Mom Slant, argues that the term has been "distorted" by a "new wave of mommy bloggers [who] just want to make money or at the very least, gather up as many goodies from the swag piñata as they possibly can." Arwyn, of the feminist blog Raising My Boychick, uses Jennifer Mendelsohn's *Times* article to illustrate how the term is "kyriarchy in action," writing that "the 'mommy blogger' as described in the *NYT* is solidly middle class . . . she is understood to be straight, by way of being married. She is assumed to be white, by being both middle class and married."

The term can come off as deliberately dismissive, particularly for women who write professionally in other spheres. Blogger and freelance writer Meagan Francis tells the story of taking a travel-writing assignment, only to be handed a press pass stamped "MOMMY BLOGGER." Joanne Bamberger, AKA blogger PunditMom, has argued that coverage of women's conferences like BlogHer relies on the "mommy blogger" tag to discredit or reduce them, while mixed gender or majority-male blog events like the YearlyKos convention are treated as newsworthy political events. The "mommy blog" label is also indiscriminately applied to almost any female blogger who has a family and blogs independently, no matter her site's subject matter—Babble's current list of top 50 mom blogs includes Kristen Chase's Mominatrix sex-advice column; Stefanie Wilder-Taylor's Baby on Bored, which is well known for its focus on supporting those in recovery from alcohol and drug abuse; and Jessica Gottlieb's blog, which addresses, among other things, her work with the United

Nations High Commissioner for Refugees. The inclusiveness of the "mommy blogger" label can be a positive reflection of women's online community networks, but it's clearly limiting for the blogs and bloggers to which it's assigned.

The one-size-fits-all category of "mommy blogger" will persist as long as deliberately limited portrayals of personalities like Dooce and The Pioneer Woman define the term. By emphasizing the domestic and ignoring the professional aspects of these figures, the media ensures that even the blogosphere's mommy moguls fit neatly into the dominant pop culture narrative in which women have to choose between the competing worlds of family and career/creative work. Instead, bloggers like Armstrong and Drummond have actually made a business of their home life, blurring the boundaries between the domestic and the public spheres. Although not every blogger may ever be able to monetize motherhood in the same way, the simple act of blogging—about anything—while female will eventually challenge the current stereotype of the mommy blogger so much that even the media will someday have to get over it. I'll blog to that.

Sarah McAbee lives in Austin and recommends The Pioneer Woman's recipe for chicken piccata.

The Mommy Option:
1 in 4 Moms Stay-at-Home

By Elizabeth Gettelman
Mother Jones, October 1, 2009

Yesterday, the Census Bureau released its new report on stay-at-home moms, one that's now being hailed as proving the myth of the "opt-out revolution." The opt-out theory goes like this: high wage earning, highly educated women land promising and high paying jobs, only to leave them once they have babies. The trend has been debated, and now, if you believe *The Washington Post*, has been debunked.

This is seen as either a good thing, read: women are able to balance work and motherhood and carry on doing both without having to make tough choices to leave or give up parenting. Work/life balance problem solved, strong feminists can have their job, and baby too. Or the report's results are actually much more complicated than that and mean that women who want to choose to stay home can't now for a host of reasons, that those who do have little choice in the matter (many of whom are also feminists, and all of whom are feminine), that more women are actually just losing their jobs, and that the data doesn't capture the true state of stay-at-home motherhood.

I Open Door #2

The report's take-home message, that stay-at-home moms are actually younger and of lower income and education (and less white) than the opt-out theory would suggest, does less to say that other mothers aren't making hard work/life choices and says more about the nearly 1 in 4 moms who *do* stay at home, that they simply don't have options to begin with (jobs to go back to, for example), the choices that older, more established workers and women have when deciding how to support their family and career.

And keep in mind that the Census definition of stay-at-home mom is rigid and doesn't account for all sorts of work/life sacrifice decisions women make:

> For this report stay-at-home mothers are those who have a husband who was in the labor force all 52 weeks last year, while she was out of the labor force during the same 52 weeks to care for the home and family.

So if a woman freelances and/or works part-time and cares for kids during the rest of it, those moms aren't counted. Mothers who are in the labor force even for a

> *Mothers who are in the labor force even for a total of 1 week, or have husbands who are out of the labor force for 1 week, or who don't report the primary reason they were out of the labor force as "to care for home and family" are considered office-working moms.*

total of 1 week, or have husbands who are out of the labor force for 1 week, or who don't report the primary reason they were out of the labor force as "to care for home and family" are considered office-working moms. Also, this eliminates single moms (other than the independently wealthy ones) from the equation, even ones who might find ways to stay at home. And whither lesbian couples? Is it surprising then, that under this strict definition the majority of stay-at-home moms are ones who may have likely never entered the workplace in the first place?

There are other tidbits in this report that are worth noting. For example, guess which household size has been steadily increasing its share over the past several decades? Families of uno. Since 1970, while family sizes of 5 or more, 4, or 3 people have been steadily declining, the percentage of families with 2 or 1 member have been rising. One member households have seen the biggest gains, from 17.1% in 1970, more than doubling to 28.6% in 2007. Not so good for downsizing our cities and staving off global warming through efficiencies.

Also, this report focused on mothers almost exclusively, though there's a chart on page 12 that shows the stark contrast between stay-at-home mom- and fatherhood. Of all mothers, 17.1% stay at home full time; of all fathers, only 3.4% stay at home. Five times more moms than dads, whatever their backgrounds. Meaning the income inequality elephant-in-the-room is one not to be ignored in this race to define all the choices women do and don't have.

As The Economix' David Leonhardt points out, over time the report actually found *an uptick* in stay-at-home motherhood, from 19.8% of married-couple families with children younger than 15 with a stay-at-home mother in 1994 to 23.7% in 2007. (The Economix says last year but the Census report, though released now, covers data from 2007.) Which means that we should look, without the focus on opting out or not, at the forces that are contributing to the fact that moms are now in greater proportion out of the workplace than in it. If that's by choice, would that make everyone feel better? Sure, because we value choice, but sometimes choices are lousy.

Elizabeth Gettelman is the managing editor at Mother Jones.

The Jewish Mother I Never Thought I'd Be

By Kim Brooks
Salon.com, September 28, 2011

I believed that smothering, overprotective moms like mine just had boundary issues. Then I had kids of my own.

I always knew my mother was different, different from the other mothers in the way she dressed, the way she spoke, but most obviously, the way she mothered. I remember a slumber party where instead of a sleeping bag, she urged me to bring a small, inflatable mattress because the dust on the floor was liable to aggravate my allergies. I remember a little boy in a play group whom she threatened with physical harm after he pulled a chair out from under me. And I remember the nagging—the questioning of whether or not I'd finished my homework, my college applications, my thank you notes, my chores—the questions asked not once, not twice, not three times, but on so many separate occasions that the words began to feel as though they arose not from my mother's mouth but from some dark and tormented place inside my soul.

If I'd lived in the Jersey suburbs or Chicago's north shore, I might have recognized these qualities as the psychological price to be paid for all the benefits of having a loving, smothering, highly invested, over-involved Jewish mother. But because I lived in rural-suburban central Virginia where Jews were about as common as AFL-CIO leaflets, I didn't know what to make of her. I only knew that I loved her, and that she loved me, and that on a daily basis, she drove me absolutely, positively crazy. I am 33 years old, and sometimes she still drives me crazy. The difference now is that since the birth of my son and daughter, I have steadily, inexorably been creeping toward the realization that I, too, am a Jewish mother, that the uniquely Yiddish bouquet of neurosis and psychopathology is likely woven into the double helix of my DNA. Is there a support group for this? Are there interventions?

It seems to me the term "Jewish mother" has little do with Judaism or Jewishness itself, but rather describes a style of mothering that can be broken down into four distinct but inter-connected components: anxiety in all its guises (arising from the mother and transferred to the child with the efficacy of an intravenous transfusion); overprotectiveness; high, at times unreachable, expectations; and finally, the ability and willingness to inflict shame, guilt and self-martyrdom to shape a child's (and in this case "child" could mean 40-year-old man's) character and moral worth.

Now my children aren't yet preschool age, so I've really only had experience with the first two components, anxiety and overprotectiveness. But, boy, have these

This article first appeared in Salon.com, at *http://www.Salon.com*. An online version remains in the Salon archives. Reprinted with permission.

53

experiences been illuminating. Let's begin with anxiety, which is really the beginning and the end, the alpha and omega of the Jewish mother paradigm.

My first moment as a Jewish mother came not when my son was born, but a few months later when he had his first upper-respiratory infection. I was sleeping heavily after several nights of mucus-suctioning and nebulizing treatments, sleeping the sleep of the dead, and all at once, though he was not crying or coughing, though he had not uttered a peep, my eyes flicked open, and I shot up in bed. How was he? Was everything going to be OK? Was he wheezing? Was he going to get pneumonia? Was the pediatrician we'd chosen really the best one in town? How was the humidity in his room? Why hadn't I bought one of those grocery-store cart germ cover thingies? The questions went on and on. The anxiety was a real, physical thing inside me. It had a weight, a color, a texture. It wouldn't let up; it demanded to be answered or fed or reassured back to sleep. Only there was no real reassurance it would accept, no permanent soothing. For the first time I understood what a relative had once told me: "A Jewish mother is only as happy as her unhappiest child." At the time, I had scoffed and thought, "Please. It's called boundaries. It's called having your own identity and sense of self. It's called getting a grip." Now I feel as though the adage has come back to haunt (or nag) me.

> *In short, I'm the worst Jewish mother in the world. I make Alexander Portnoy's mother look like a laid-back Earth mama.*

If the non-Jewish mother thinks, "What's the worst that could happen?" the Jewish mother thinks, "What's the worst that can happen: Let's consider."

For four years now, I've considered.

I've harassed pediatricians and nurses, demanded extra conferences with preschool teachers, contacted speech therapists and occupational therapists over delays other mothers probably wouldn't have noticed, stressed over magnet school applications three years before they're due. I've found it difficult to restrain myself from grabbing a playground bully by the arms and giving him a good shaking. I've written out itineraries for baby sitters with years of experience. I've gotten up in the middle of the night and stood over my children's sleeping bodies just to make sure they're breathing, and breathing well. In short, I'm the worst Jewish mother in the world. I make Alexander Portnoy's mother look like a laid-back Earth mama.

When I reveal these peculiar behaviors and fixations to other "Jewish mothers," especially those to whom I am related, they nod and press their lips together and give me a look that seems to say, "Is there anything you've forgotten? Is there anything else you should perhaps be worrying about?" There's nothing Jewish mothers love more than out-Jewish-mothering other Jewish mothers. I remember emailing my mother a picture of my 1-year-old daughter standing happily on the beach. The reply came back almost instantly via text message: "No shoes? Aren't her little feet going to burn?"

I remember other conversations with my mother-in-law that went something like this:

Mother-in-law: How are you? What are you up to today?

Me: Oh, just finishing up some work. Not gonna pick the baby up at daycare until 4 today.

M-I-L: Four o'clock? PM?

Me: Yup.

M-I-L: What'll he do there for so long?

Me: I don't know? Baby stuff?

M-I-L: I hope he doesn't get bored.

Me: I'm sure he'll be fine.

M-I-L: I guess if he's bored he'll just go to sleep.

Me: I guess.

Silence.

Me: Maybe I'll just go get him now.

When I tell this to my own mother over the phone, I can almost hear her smile. "Ah," she says. "Now you see. Little Miss You-did-this-wrong-you-did-that-wrong understands."

Kind of, I do. But that doesn't mean I have to accept it. I start thinking that surely if I better understood the origins of this Jewish mother mentality I could somehow tame it. And about a year ago, I came close.

My son had just recovered from a tonsillectomy. It was an awful surgery, and in my despair I began googling "tonsillectomy recovery" and stumbled across an article in *Tablet* about Lower East Side moms in 1906 who rioted after a principal at P.S. 100 arranged for doctors from Mount Sinai to come to the school and perform tonsillectomies on kids with chronic tonsillitis. Apparently, having heard rumors that uptown doctors were being dispatched to the school to "cut the throats of Jewish children," a throng of mothers descended on the school. The article describes how, "greeted by locked doors, the screaming throngs surrounded the schools and began smashing windows and pounding on doors. On Essex Street, some white-hot mothers clambered up ladders in an attempt to break into P.S. 138 through the second-floor windows."

At last, I thought, some Jewish mothers who make me look calm and reasonable. But of course, this happened in 1906 and many of these Jewish mothers, poor immigrants from Eastern Europe, had come from places where horrible, unfathomable acts were committed on Jewish children, not to mention Jewish parents, Jewish men and women, Jewish anybody—see Kishinev pogroms of 1903—a massacre where the *New York Times* described "babies . . . literally torn to pieces by the frenzied and blood-thirsty mob."

What's the worst that could happen? The terrible truth is that it probably already has.

I know what you're thinking. I can see the hate letters coming in already: *Generalized Anxiety Disorder, anyone? She clearly needs to relax, have a drink, go on a vacation.* I couldn't argue with any of this. And I'm sure others will point out how there are plenty of "Jewish mothers" who aren't even Jewish, just as Amy Chua pointed out in her controversial essay how not all Asian mothers are "tiger mothers," and not all "tiger mothers" are Asian. People will argue that culture or ethnicity is beside the point. Maybe, but I for one couldn't help wondering when I read Chua's essay if the people who were so offended by the exaltation of the tiger mother (or the ones who will surely be offended by the notion of a stereotypical "Jewish mother") are in reality put off more by style than substance.

I mean, don't all mothers basically want their children to succeed, to excel, to be healthy and safe, to be valued and appreciated or admired by a worthwhile community, to prosper greatly and to suffer little? I believe nearly all mothers would like these things; what differs is the resources at their disposal to achieve them and the cultural tools (pride, shame, guilt, tradition) they employ toward their end.

What an awful burden we mothers and fathers, Jewish and not, have to bear—to hatch a thing we love more than ourselves into a world so fundamentally unworthy. I'm reminded of Grace Paley's exquisitely beautiful story about an old Jewish lady watching two young fathers out her window—aptly titled, "Anxiety."

And I'm reminded of an interview in which Philip Roth recounted how after the publication of *Portnoy's Complaint*, a reporter asked his mother if she considered herself a "Jewish mother." He told how she gave an answer "worthy of Pascal," replying simply, "All mothers are Jewish mothers."

It has to be true. How could it be otherwise?

Kim Brooks is a graduate of the Iowa Writers' Workshop. Her fiction has appeared in Glimmer Train, One Story, Epoch, *and other journals. She lives in Chicago and has just finished a novel. You can follow her on Twitter @KA_Brooks.*

Obama's Young Mother Abroad

By Janny Scott

The New York Times, April 20, 2011

The photograph showed the son, but my eye gravitated toward the mother. That first glimpse was surprising—the stout, pale-skinned woman in sturdy sandals, standing squarely a half-step ahead of the lithe, darker-skinned figure to her left. His elastic-band body bespoke discipline, even asceticism. Her form was well padded, territory ceded long ago to the pleasures of appetite and the forces of anatomical destiny. He had the studied casualness of a catalog model, in khakis, at home in the viewfinder. She met the camera head-on, dressed in hand-loomed textile dyed indigo, a silver earring half-hidden in the cascading curtain of her dark hair. She carried her chin a few degrees higher than most. His right hand rested on her shoulder, lightly. The photograph, taken on a Manhattan rooftop in August 1987 and e-mailed to me 20 years later, was a revelation and a puzzle. The man was Barack Obama at 26, the community organizer from Chicago on a visit to New York. The woman was Stanley Ann Dunham, his mother. It was impossible not to be struck by the similarities, and the dissimilarities, between them. It was impossible not to question the stereotype to which she had been expediently reduced: the white woman from Kansas.

The president's mother has served as any of a number of useful oversimplifications. In the capsule version of Obama's life story, she is the white mother from Kansas coupled alliteratively to the black father from Kenya. She is corn-fed, white-bread, whatever Kenya is not. In "Dreams From My Father," the memoir that helped power Obama's political ascent, she is the shy, small-town girl who falls head over heels for the brilliant, charismatic African who steals the show. In the next chapter, she is the naïve idealist, the innocent abroad. In Obama's presidential campaign, she was the struggling single mother, the food-stamp recipient, the victim of a health care system gone awry, pleading with her insurance company for coverage as her life slipped away. And in the fevered imaginings of supermarket tabloids and the Internet, she is the atheist, the Marxist, the flower child, the mother who abandoned her son or duped the newspapers of Hawaii into printing a birth announcement for her Kenyan-born baby, on the off chance that he might want to be president someday.

The earthy figure in the photograph did not fit any of those, as I learned over the course of two and a half years of research, travel and nearly 200 interviews. To describe Dunham as a white woman from Kansas turns out to be about as illuminating as describing her son as a politician who likes golf. Intentionally or not, the label obscures an extraordinary story—of a girl with a boy's name who grew up in the years before the women's movement, the pill and the antiwar movement; who married an African at a time when nearly two dozen states still had laws against interracial marriage; who, at 24, moved to Jakarta with her son in the waning days of an anticommunist bloodbath in which hundreds of thousands of Indonesians were slaughtered; who lived more than half her adult life in a place barely known to most Americans, in the country with the largest Muslim population in the world; who spent years working in villages where a lone Western woman was a rarity; who immersed herself in the study of blacksmithing, a craft long practiced exclusively by men; who, as a working and mostly single mother, brought up two biracial children; who believed her son in particular had the potential to be great; who raised him to be, as he has put it jokingly, a combination of Albert Einstein, Mahatma Gandhi and Harry Belafonte; and then died at 52, never knowing who or what he would become.

Obama placed the ghost of his absent father at the center of his lyrical account of his life. At times, he has seemed to say more about the grandparents who helped raise him than about his mother. Yet she shaped him, to a degree Obama has seemed increasingly to acknowledge. In the preface to the 2004 edition of "Dreams From My Father," issued nine years after the first edition and nine years after Dunham's death, Obama folded in a revealing admission: had he known his mother would not survive her illness, he might have written a different book—"less a meditation on the absent parent, more a celebration of the one who was the single constant in my life."

Dunham, for whom a letter in Jakarta from her son in the United States could raise her spirits for a full day, surely wondered about her place in his life. On rare occasions, she indicated as much—painfully, wistfully—to close friends. But she would not have been inclined to overstate her case. As she told him, with a dry humor that seems downright Kansan, "If nothing else, I gave you an interesting life."

Ann Dunham, who jettisoned the name Stanley upon emerging from childhood, was just 17 years old in the fall of 1960 when she became pregnant with the child of a charismatic Kenyan named Barack Hussein Obama, a fellow student at the University of Hawaii who was more than six years her senior. She dropped out of school, married him and gave birth shortly before their union ended. In the aftermath, she met Lolo Soetoro, an amiable, easygoing, tennis-playing graduate student from the Indonesian island of Java. They married in 1964, after Ann's divorce came through, but their early life together was upended by forces beyond their control. On Sept. 30, 1965, six Indonesian army generals and one lieutenant were kidnapped and killed in Jakarta, in what the army characterized as an attempted coup planned by the Communist Party. Students studying abroad, including Lolo, whose studies were sponsored by the government, were soon summoned home. A year later, in 1967, Ann graduated with a degree in anthropology, gathered up her 6-year-old child and moved to Indonesia to join her husband.

The four years that followed were formative for mother and son—and are a subject of curiosity and an object of speculation for many Americans today. These were

The four years that followed were formative for mother and son—and are a subject of curiosity and an object of speculation for many Americans today. These were years in which Ann lived closely with the young Obama, who at the time was called Barry; she impressed upon him her values and, consciously and unconsciously, shaped his emerging understanding of the world.

years in which Ann lived closely with the young Obama, who at the time was called Barry; she impressed upon him her values and, consciously and unconsciously, shaped his emerging understanding of the world. She made choices about her own life too, setting an example that in some ways Obama would eventually embrace, while in other ways intentionally leaving it behind.

The white woman and her half-African son made quite a pair traveling in Indonesia together. Elizabeth Bryant, an American who lived in the city of Yogyakarta at the time, remembers a lunch held at another expatriate's house that Ann and Barry attended. Ann arrived in a long skirt made of Indonesian fabric—not, Bryant noticed, a look that other American women in Indonesia seemed to favor. Ann instructed Barry to shake hands, then to sit on the sofa and turn his attention to an English-language workbook she brought along. Ann, who had been in Indonesia for nearly four years, talked about whether to go back to Hawaii. "She said, 'What would *you* do?'" Bryant recalled when I spoke to her nearly 40 years later. "I said, 'I could live here as long as two years, then would go back to Hawaii.' She said, 'Why?' I said it was hard living, it took a toll on your body, there were no doctors, it was not healthy. She didn't agree with me."

Over lunch, Barry, who was 9 at the time, sat at the dining table and listened intently but did not speak. When he asked to be excused, Ann directed him to ask the hostess for permission. Permission granted, he got down on the floor and played with Bryant's son, who was 13 months old. After lunch, the group took a walk, with Barry running ahead. A flock of Indonesian children began lobbing rocks in his direction. They ducked behind a wall and shouted racial epithets. He seemed unfazed, dancing around as though playing dodge ball "with unseen players," Bryant said. Ann did not react. Assuming she must not have understood the words, Bryant offered to intervene. "No, he's O.K.," Ann said. "He's used to it."

"We were floored that she'd bring a half-black child to Indonesia, knowing the disrespect they have for blacks," Bryant said. At the same time, she admired Ann for teaching her boy to be fearless. A child in Indonesia needed to be raised that way— for self-preservation, Bryant decided. Ann also seemed to be teaching Barry respect. He had all the politeness that Indonesian children displayed toward their parents. He seemed to be learning Indonesian ways.

"I think this is one reason he's so *halus*," Bryant said of the president, using the Indonesian adjective that means "polite, refined, or courteous," referring to qualities some see as distinctively Javanese. "He has the manners of Asians and the ways of Americans—being *halus,* being patient, calm, a good listener. If you're not a good listener in Indonesia, you'd better leave."

Indonesia was still in a state of shock when Ann arrived in 1967 for the first of three extended periods of residence that would eventually add up to the majority of her adult life. The details of the attempted coup and countercoup remain in dispute even today, as do the particulars of the carnage that followed. But it is known that neighbors turned on neighbors. According to Adrian Vickers, the author of "A History of Modern Indonesia," militias went door to door in villages, abducting suspects, raping women, even targeting children. "The best way to prove you were not a Communist was to join in the killings," Vickers writes. Bill Collier, a friend of Ann's who arrived in Indonesia in 1968 and spent 15 years doing social and economic surveys in villages, told me that researchers were told by people living near brackish waterways that they had been unable to eat the fish because of decaying corpses in the water. Many Indonesians chose never to speak about what had happened.

The Jakarta that greeted Ann Soetoro and her son was a tapestry of villages— low-rise and sprawling—interwoven with wooded areas, paddy fields and marshland. Narrow alleys disappeared into warrens of tile-roofed houses in the rambling urban hamlets called *kampungs.* Squatter colonies lined the canals, which served as public baths, laundry facilities and sewers, all in one. During the long rainy season from November through March, canals overflowed, saturating cardboard shanties and flooding much of the city. Residents traveled mostly on foot or by bicycle or bicycle-propelled rickshaws called *becaks.* Power outages were common. There were so few working phones that it was said that half the cars on the streets were ferrying messages from one office to the next. "Secretaries would spend hours just dialing and redialing phone numbers trying to get through," Halimah Brugger, an American who moved there in 1968, told me. Westerners were rare, black people even rarer. Western women got a lot of attention. "I remember creating quite a sensation just being pedaled down the street in a *becak,* wearing a short skirt," Brugger said. Letters from the United States took weeks to reach their destination. Foreigners endured all manner of gastrointestinal upsets. Deworming was de rigueur.

Yet the city had a magical charm. People who were children in Jakarta in that period, including Barack Obama, reminisce about the sound of the Muslim call to prayer in the days before public-address systems, and the signature sounds called out by street vendors wheeling their carts through the *kampungs.* Tea was still served on the veranda of the old Hotel des Indes. Ceiling fans turned languidly in the mid afternoon heat, and kerosene lamps flickered in the houses lining the narrow alleys at night. For anyone of no interest to government security forces, life was simple. For a foreigner, it was possible to arrive in Indonesia in 1967 largely ignorant of the horror of just two years before. "I was quite naïve about the whole thing," Brugger said. "It was all over then. I never felt the slightest bit endangered." Years later, many people would look back on the late 1960s and early 1970s as a honeymoon period, Vickers writes. Restrictions on the press eased, a youth culture flowered, literary and cultural life thrived. It was, some later commented, Indonesia's Prague Spring.

When Ann arrived, Lolo was in the army. His salary was low. On her first night in Indonesia, Ann complained later to a colleague, Lolo served her white rice and *dendeng celeng* —dried, jerked wild boar, which Indonesians hunted in the forests when food was scarce. But when Lolo completed his military service, his brother-in-law Trisulo used his contacts as a vice president at the Indonesian oil company Pertamina to help Lolo get a job in the Jakarta office of the Union Oil Company of California. By the early 1970s, Lolo and Ann had moved into a rented house in Matraman, a middle-class area of Jakarta. The house was a *pavilyun,* an annex on the grounds of a bigger main house. It had three bedrooms, a kitchen, a bathroom, a library and a terrace. Like the households of other Indonesians who could afford it, it had a sizable domestic staff. Two female servants shared a bedroom; two men—a cook and a houseboy—slept mostly on the floor of the house or in the garden. The staff freed Ann from domestic obligations to a degree that would have been almost impossible in the United States. There were people to clean the house, prepare meals, buy groceries and look after her children—enabling her to work, pursue her interests and come and go as she wanted. The domestic staff made it possible, too, for Ann and Lolo to cultivate their own professional and social circles, which did not necessarily overlap.

By January 1968, Ann had gone to work as the assistant to the American director of Lembaga Indonesia-Amerika, a binational organization financed by the United States Information Service and housed at the U.S. Agency for International Development. She supervised a small group of Indonesians who taught English classes for Indonesian government employees and businessmen being sent by U.S.A.I.D. to the United States for graduate studies. It would be an understatement to say she disliked the job. "I worked at the U.S. Embassy in Djakarta for 2 horrible years," she wrote to a friend. As Obama describes the job in his memoir, "The Indonesian businessmen weren't much interested in the niceties of the English language, and several made passes at her." Occasionally, she took Barry to work. Joseph Sigit, an Indonesian who worked as the office manager at the time, told me, "Our staff here sometimes made a joke of him because he looked different—the color of his skin."

Joked with him—or about him? I asked.

"With and about him," Sigit said, with no evident embarrassment.

Two years later, at 27, Ann was hired to start an English-language business-communications department in one of the few private nonprofit management-training schools in the country. The school, called the Institute for Management Education and Development, was started several years earlier by a Dutch Jesuit priest with the intention of helping to build an Indonesian elite. Ann trained the teachers, developed the curriculum and taught top executives. In return, she received not just a paycheck but also a share of the revenue from the program. She also became a popular teacher. Ann's classes "could be a riot of laughter from beginning to end. She had a great sense of humor," said Leonard Kibble, who taught part time at the institute in the early 1970s. Some of the laughter involved Ann's still-incomplete mastery of the Indonesian language. In one slip that Kibble said Ann delighted in recounting, she tried to tell a student that he would "get a promotion" if he learned

English. Instead of using the phrase *naik pangkat*, she said *naik pantat*. The word *naik* means to "go up, rise, or mount"; *pangkat* means "rank" or "position." *Pantat* means "buttocks."

That same year, on Aug. 15, 1970, shortly after Barry's ninth birthday and during what would turn out to be the only visit by her mother, Madelyn Dunham, to Indonesia, Ann gave birth to Maya Kassandra Soetoro at Saint Carolus Hospital, a Catholic hospital thought by Westerners at that time to be the best in Jakarta. When Halimah Brugger gave birth in the same hospital two years later, she told me, the doctor delivered her baby without the luxury of a stethoscope, gloves or gown. "When the baby was born, the doctor asked my husband for his handkerchief," Brugger said. "Then she stuffed it in my mouth and gave me 11 stitches without any anesthesia." Ann tried out three different names for her new daughter, all of them Sanskrit, before settling on Maya Kassandra. The name was important to Ann, Maya told me; she wanted "beautiful names." Stanley, the name Ann felt burdened with as a child, was not on the list.

In Indonesia, Ann was a striking figure who did not go unnoticed. "Maybe just her presence—the way she carried herself," said Halimah Bellows, whom Ann hired in the spring of 1971. She dressed simply, with little or no makeup, and wore her hair long, held back by a headband. By Javanese standards, she was, as Felina Pramono, an Indonesian colleague, put it, "a bit sturdy for a woman." She had strong opinions—and rarely softened them to please others.

"She used to tear me apart," says Kay Ikranagara, one of Ann's closest friends, in a tone that sounded almost fond. Ann told her she needed to be bolder and stronger. She made fun of her inadequacy in the kitchen. She told her she should give her housekeeper explicit instructions, not simply let her do whatever she wanted. "With everybody she was like that: she would tell them what was wrong with them," Ikranagara said. Family members were not spared. "She was very scathing about the traditional Indonesian wife role," Ikranagara recalled. "She would tell Maya not to be such a wimp. She didn't like this passive Indonesian female caricature. She would tell me not to fall into that."

Ikranagara was the daughter of a development economist from the University of California who taught at the University of Indonesia in the late 1950s. She lived in Jakarta as a teenager, studied anthropology and linguistics in the 1960s at Berkeley and then returned to Jakarta, where she met her husband. She met Ann while teaching part time at the management school and writing her dissertation in linguistics. They had a lot in common: Indonesian husbands, degrees in anthropology, babies born in the same month, opinions shaped by the 1960s. They were less conscious than others of the boundaries between cultures, Ikranagara told me, and they rejected what they saw as the previous generation's hypocrisy on the subject of race. "We had all the same attitudes," she said. "When we met people who worked for the oil companies or the embassy, they belonged to a different culture than Ann and I. We felt they didn't mix with Indonesians, they were part of an insular American culture." Servants seemed to be the only Indonesians those Americans knew.

But by the early 1970s, Lolo's new job had plunged him deeply into the oil-company culture. Foreign businesses in Indonesia were required to hire and train Indonesian partners. The exercise struck some people as a sham: companies would hire an Indonesian director, pay him well and give him little or nothing to do. Trisulo, Lolo's brother-in-law, told me he did not recall the exact nature of Lolo's job with Union Oil. His son, Sonny Trisulo, said it may have been "government relations." Whatever it was, Lolo's job included socializing with oil-company executives and their wives. He joined the Indonesian Petroleum Club, a private watering hole in Central Jakarta for oil-company people and their families, which offered swimming, tennis and dining. Ann was expected to socialize, too. Any failure to do so reflected badly on Lolo. "It's the society that asks it," Ikranagara said. "Your husband is supposed to show up at social functions with you at his side, dressed in a *kain* and *kebaya*," a costume consisting of a traditional, tightly fitted, long-sleeved blouse and a length of unstitched cloth wound around the lower part of the body. "You're supposed to sit with the women and talk about your children and your servants."

Ann begged off. "She didn't understand these folks—the idea of living an expatriate life that was so completely divorced from the world around you, that involves hiding yourself away in these protective cells of existence," Maya said. "That was peculiar to her, and she was bored by it." Ann complained to her friend Bill Collier that all those middle-aged white Americans talked about inane things. Lolo, she told Collier, "was becoming more American all the time." Occasionally, the young Obama would overhear Lolo and Ann arguing in their bedroom about Ann's refusal to attend his oil-company dinners, at which, he writes in "Dreams From My Father," "American businessmen from Texas and Louisiana would slap Lolo's back and boast about the palms they had greased to obtain the new offshore-drilling rights, while their wives complained to my mother about the quality of Indonesian help. He would ask her how it would look for him to go alone and remind her that these were her own people, and my mother's voice would rise to almost a shout.

"'They are *not* my people.'"

The relationship between Ann and Lolo appears to have begun deteriorating even before Lolo took the oil-company job. As Obama describes it, something happened between them when Lolo was called back to Jakarta during the time of unrest in Indonesia and they spent a year apart. In Hawaii, Lolo was full of life, regaling Ann with stories from his childhood, confiding his plans to return to his country and teach at the university. Now he barely spoke to her. Some nights, he would sleep with a pistol under his pillow; other nights, she would hear him "wandering through the house with a bottle of imported whiskey, nursing his secrets." Ann's loneliness was a constant, Obama writes, "like a shortness of breath."

Ann had pieced together some of what happened in Indonesia in 1965 and afterward from fragmentary information that people let slip. Her new Indonesian friends talked to her about corruption in government agencies, police and military shakedowns, the power of the president's entourage. Lolo would not talk about any of it. According to Obama, a cousin of Lolo's finally explained to Ann what happened when her husband returned from Hawaii. Upon arriving in Jakarta, he was taken away for questioning and told he had been conscripted and would be sent to the jungles of New Guinea for a year. It could have been worse: students returning from Soviet-bloc countries were jailed or even vanished. Obama writes that Ann concluded that "power had taken Lolo and yanked him back into line just when he thought he'd escaped, making him feel its weight, letting him know that his life wasn't his own." In response, Lolo made his peace with power, "learned the wisdom of forgetting; just as his brother-in-law had done, making millions as a high official in the national oil company."

Lolo had disappointed Ann, but her refusal to conform to his culture's expectations apparently angered him as well. "She didn't know, as little I knew, how Indonesian men change when suddenly their family is around," Renske Heringa, a Dutch anthropologist and close friend of Ann's in the 1980s who herself married a man who was half Indonesian, told me. "And how Indonesian men like women to be easy and open abroad, but when you get to Indonesia, the parents are there, the family is there, you have to behave. You have to be the little wife. As a wife, you were not supposed to make yourself visible besides being beautiful. By the time I knew Ann, she was a hefty woman. She didn't care about getting dressed, wearing jewelry, the way Indonesian women do. That was not her style. He expected her to do it. That is one reason she didn't stick it out. She absolutely refused to. I understand why he couldn't accept it."

One morning in January 2009, at the offices of the management school for which Ann had worked, I met a man in his late 50s named Saman. Like some Javanese, he went by a single name. Speaking in Bahasa Indonesia, with Ann's former assistant Felina Pramono translating, he told me that he worked as a houseboy for Lolo and Ann in the early 1970s. One of seven children from a family of farmers, Saman moved to Jakarta as a teenager to find work. When he worked for Ann and Lolo, his duties included gardening; taking care of a pet turtle, dog, rabbit and bird; and taking Barry to school by bicycle or *becak*. Ann and Lolo paid Saman well and treated all four members of the household staff equally, he said. He remembered Lolo as stern and Ann as kindhearted.

Ann would finish teaching at 9 in the evening and sometimes not return home until midnight, Saman said. She seemed barely to sleep. She would stay up, typing and correcting Barry's homework, then get up again before dawn. On one occasion, Saman said: "She got home late with a student, but the student didn't see her home properly. So he dropped her near the house, and Soetoro got very mad because of that." An argument ensued, which Saman overheard. "He said: 'I've warned you many times. Why are you still doing this?'" Saman recalled. Whether Lolo's worry was infidelity or simply what others might think is unclear from Saman's story. After the argument, he said, Ann appeared in the house with a towel pressed to her face and blood running from her nose. It is difficult to know what to make of the nearly 40-year-old recollection. No one else I interviewed suggested there was ever violence between Ann and Lolo, a man many people described as patient and sweet-tempered.

When one fellow teacher, an Indonesian man whom Ann befriended, asked about her husband in 1968 or 1969, she told him grimly: "I'm never asked. I'm told."

Reflecting on her marriage some years later, Ann told another Indonesian friend, Yang Suwan, resignedly: "Don't you know that you don't argue and you don't discuss with a Javanese person? Because problems don't exist with Javanese people. Time will solve problems."

With her children, Ann made a point of being more physically affectionate than her mother had been with her, she told one friend. She was cuddly and would say, "I love you," according to Maya, a hundred times a day. She was playful—making pottery, weaving decorations, doing art projects that stretched across the room. "I think that we benefited a great deal from her focus when we were with her, when she was beside us," Maya told me. "So that made the absences hurt a little less." Where her children were involved, Ann was easily moved to tears, even occasionally when speaking about them to friends. She preferred humor to harping, but she was exacting about the things she believed mattered most. Richard Hook, who worked with Ann in Jakarta in the late 1980s and early 1990s, said she told him that she worked to instill ideas about public service in her son. She wanted Barry to have a sense of obligation, to give something back. She wanted him to start off, Hook said, with the attitudes and values she had taken years to learn.

"If you want to grow into a human being," Obama remembers her saying, "you're going to need some values." When necessary, Ann was, according to two accounts, not unwilling to reinforce her message. "She talked about disciplining Barry, including spanking him for things where he richly deserved a spanking," said Don Johnston, who worked with Ann in the early 1990s, sometimes traveling with her in Indonesia and living in the same house. Saman said that when Barry failed to finish homework sent from Hawaii by his grandmother, Ann "would call him into his room and would spank him with his father's military belt." President Obama, through a spokeswoman, said his mother never resorted to physical discipline.

One evening in the house in Matraman, Saman said, he and Barry were preparing to go to sleep. They often slept in the same place—sometimes in the bunk bed in Barry's room, sometimes on the dining-room floor or in the garden. On this occasion, Barry, who was 8 or 9 at the time, asked Saman to turn out the light. When Saman did not do it, he said, Barry hit him in the chest. When he did not react, Barry hit him harder, and Saman struck him back. Barry began to cry loudly, attracting Ann's attention. According to Saman, Ann did not respond. She seemed to realize that Barry had been in the wrong. Otherwise, Saman would not have struck him.

"We were not permitted to be rude, we were not permitted to be mean, we were not permitted to be arrogant," Maya told me. "We had to have a certain humility and broad-mindedness. We had to study. . . . If we said something unkind about someone, she would try to talk about their point of view. Or, 'How would you feel?' Sort of compelling us ever toward empathy and those kinds of things and not allowing us to be selfish. That was constant, steady, daily."

It was clear to many that Ann believed Barry, in particular, was unusually gifted. She would boast about his brains, his achievements, how brave he was. Benji Bennington, a friend of Ann's from Hawaii, told me, "Sometimes when she talked about

Barack, she'd say, 'Well, my son is so bright, he can do anything he ever wants in the world, even be president of the United States.' I remember her saying that." Samardal Manan, who taught with Ann in Jakarta, remembered Ann saying something similar—that Barry could be, or perhaps wanted to be, the first black president.

"What do you want to be when you grow up?" Lolo asked Barry one evening, according to Saman.

"Oh, prime minister," Barry answered.

What mattered as much as anything to Ann, as a parent, was her children's education. But that was not simple. Indonesian schools in the late 1960s and early 1970s were inadequate; there were not enough of them, the government controlled the curriculum, teachers were poorly trained. Westerners sent their children to the Jakarta International School, but it was expensive and difficult to get into. Obama attended two Indonesian schools, one Catholic and one Muslim. The experience cannot have failed to have left a mark. The Javanese, especially the Central Javanese, place an enormous emphasis on self-control. Even to sneeze was to exhibit an untoward lack of self-control, said Michael Dove, who got to know Ann when they were both anthropologists working in Java in the 1980s. "You demonstrate an inner strength by not betraying emotion, not speaking loudly, not moving jerkily," he said. Self-control is inculcated through a culture of teasing, Kay Ikranagara told me. Her husband, known only as Ikranagara, said, "People tease about skin color all the time." If a child allows the teasing to bother him, he is teased more. If he ignores it, it stops. "Our ambassador said this was where Barack learned to be cool," Kay told me. "If you get mad and react, you lose. If you learn to laugh and take it without any reaction, you win."

With time, Ann's thinking about Barack's future changed. "She had always encouraged my rapid acculturation in Indonesia," he wrote in his memoir. "It had made me relatively self-sufficient, undemanding on a tight budget, and extremely well mannered when compared with other American children. She had taught me to disdain the blend of ignorance and arrogance that too often characterized Americans abroad. But she now had learned, just as Lolo had learned, the chasm that separated the life chances of an American from those of an Indonesian. She knew which side of the divide she wanted her child to be on. I was an American, she decided, and my true life lay elsewhere."

In early 1971, Ann told Barry that he would be returning to Hawaii. He would live with his grandparents in Honolulu and attend Punahou School, a respected prep school within walking distance of the Dunhams' apartment. "She said that she and Maya would be joining me in Hawaii very soon—a year, tops—and that she'd try to make it there for Christmas," he wrote in "Dreams From My Father." Ann's uncle Charles Payne told me he suspected that her mother, Madelyn, played a part in the decision. "Madelyn always had a great concern about Barack getting a good education," he said. "I think that was her defense against his racial mixture—that education was the solution to whatever problems that would bring."

As Obama later described his send-off, an Indonesian co-pilot who was a friend of Ann's escorted him to the plane "as she and Lolo and my new sister, Maya, stood by at the gate."

Ann uprooted Barry, at age 6, and transplanted him to Jakarta. Now she was uprooting him again, at barely 10, and sending him back, alone. She would follow him to Hawaii only to leave him again, less than three years later.

When we spoke last July, Obama recalled those serial displacements. "I think that was harder on a 10-year-old boy than he'd care to admit at the time," Obama said, sitting in a chair in the Oval Office and speaking about his mother with a mix of affection and critical distance. "When we were separated again during high school, at that point I was old enough to say, 'This is my choice, my decision.' But being a parent now and looking back at that, I could see—you know what?—that would be hard on a kid."

He spoke about his mother with fondness, humor and a degree of candor that I had not expected. There was also in his tone at times a hint of gentle forbearance. Perhaps it was the tone of someone whose patience had been tested, by a person he loved, to the point where he had stepped back to a safer distance. Or perhaps it was the knowingness of a grown child seeing his parent as irredeemably human.

"She was a very strong person in her own way," Obama said, when I asked about Ann's limitations as a mother. "Resilient, able to bounce back from setbacks, persistent—the fact that she ended up finishing her dissertation. But despite all those strengths, she was not a well-organized person. And that disorganization, you know, spilled over. Had it not been for my grandparents, I think, providing some sort of safety net financially, being able to take me and my sister on at certain spots, I think my mother would have had to make some different decisions. And I think that sometimes she took for granted that, 'Well, it'll all work out, and it'll be fine.' But the fact is, it might not always have been fine, had it not been for my grandmother. Had she not been there to provide that floor, I think our young lives could have been much more chaotic than they were."

But he did not, he said, hold his mother's choices against her. Part of being an adult is seeing your parents "as people who have their own strengths, weaknesses, quirks, longings." He did not believe, he said, that parents served their children well by being unhappy. If his mother had cramped her spirit, it would not have given him a happier childhood. As it was, she gave him the single most important gift a parent can give—"a sense of unconditional love that was big enough that, with all the surface disturbances of our lives, it sustained me, entirely."

Janny Scott (jannyscott@gmail.com), a reporter for The New York Times, *went on leave in 2008 to write* A Singular Woman: The Untold Story of Barack Obama's Mother, *from which this article is adapted. Editor: Lauren Kern (l.kern-MagGroup@ nytimes.com).*

3

Changing Perspectives on Fatherhood

(Marcy Maloy)

Parenting for men today may often mean adopting life choices once reserved only for women, as more men opt to experience stay-at-home fatherhood.

Fatherhood Across the Spectrum

By Paul McCaffrey

The concept of fatherhood in the United States has evolved more during the late twentieth and early twenty-first centuries than perhaps any other time in history. Economic and social developments have altered gender roles and societal mores such that the responsibilities of the approximately seventy million American fathers have shifted dramatically.

Traditionally, fatherhood has occurred within the confines of marriage in the United States. But American marriage rates have fallen off considerably. In 1960, 72 percent of adults over the age of eighteen were married. By 2011, that number had declined to slightly over 50 percent. In 1960, men married for the first time at the age of 22.8 on average. By 2010, that had increased to 28.2. Today's Americans are marrying later in life, or not at all. In 1960, 85 percent of American adults had been married at least once. Today, that figure is closer to 70 percent. "Marriage is less likely to anchor the adult life course," according to W. Bradford Wilcox, the director of the National Marriage Project at the University of Virginia. "It's less likely to ground children's experience with family life [and] plays a less central role as an institution in American life."

As marriage rates have declined and divorce rates spiked, more and more children in the United States are born out of wedlock or are raised in a household that is not headed by married biological parents. Instead, children are often brought up by unwed parents or in single-parent homes. In 1960, roughly 5 percent of births were to unmarried mothers. By 2008, that number had increased to 40 percent. "In the minds of Americans, getting married and becoming parents are two different things," Wilcox states. "Their top priority is being a parent, second to having a successful marriage. People have separated the two things. Years ago, they were closely linked to one another."

Because of these societal changes, many children in the United States grow up without their biological fathers in the home. According to the Pew Research Center, 11 percent of American children lived apart from their fathers in 1960. Fifty years later, that figure had risen to 27 percent. (Within that same timeframe, children living apart from their mothers increased from 4 percent to 8 percent.) Though fathers may live in separate households, they are rarely completely removed from their children's lives. According to Pew, 27 percent of fathers who live apart from the children report no contact with them, 21 percent see their children several times a year, 29 percent several times a month, and 22 percent visit with them more than once a week.

The impact of absent fathers on society is significant. Statistics show that children who grow up without a father in the home are more likely to suffer from poverty than those living with both parents. According to the US Department of Health and Human Services (HHS), "Research does show that children living with their married, biological (or adoptive) parents are less likely to be poor, to use drugs, to experience educational, health, emotional and behavioral problems, to be victims of child abuse, and to engage in criminal behavior than their peers with absent fathers."

Though fewer fathers are living with their children, those that do are spending more time with them as compared with previous generations. The amount of time fathers spent per week with their children increased from 2.7 hours in 1975 to three hours in 1985. In the year 2000, fathers spent 6.5 hours taking care of their kids. Based on the economic and social trends, it is safe to assume that that weekly average will increase further.

One of the major sociological trends influencing fatherhood today is the ever-greater number of women entering the workforce. From 1948 through 2001, the percentage of working women in the United States rose from under 33 percent to over than 60 percent. That pattern held steady for the next ten years. Whereas once the jobs women were filling on the whole earned significantly less than those in male-dominated industries, this pattern is changing. According to the Bureau of Labor Statistics (BLS), approximately one quarter of working women in two-income households earn more than their spouses. Meanwhile, women have been outstripping men in educational attainment, thus upping their future earning potential relative to men. In 2010, for example, 36 percent of women between the ages of 25 and 29 had achieved at least a four-year college degree. For men in the same cohort, it was 28 percent.

As women have made these strides, other factors have further reduced the economic influence of men and fathers. During the global financial crisis of 2008 and 2009, for example, approximately eight million jobs were lost in the United States. Of these, 82 percent were held by men, according to the Sphere Trending report, "Women in 2010: The New Mom." Though men have fared better during the subsequent economic recovery, they have not recouped all the lost ground. Indeed, in 1950, the US Labor Participation Rate for men, as compiled by the BLS, was almost 90 percent. In 2011, it was around 70 percent. "The traditionally male industries have been hit hardest by economic change," remarks Jeremy Adam Smith for the *Washington Post*. "The men who refuse or are unwilling or unable to adapt will fall way behind."

Economic and sociological developments have altered the conventional twentieth-century family dynamic: that of the father as breadwinner and the mother as caregiver. In the twenty-first century, men are increasingly embracing the role of caregiver. In 2009, 7.4 percent of married American men with children under eighteen were stay-at-home dads, taking care of the kids and the household while their spouse went to work. Though well outnumbered by stay-at-home moms, stay-at-home dads are growing more numerous.

The evolving role of fathers has not occurred without controversy. Among stay-at-home fathers, in particular, ceding the responsibility of providing for their families to their wives can affect their self-esteem. Furthermore, inasmuch as they are fulfilling a somewhat "nontraditional" role, they run into difficulties that mothers might not experience. "Dads who are taking care of their kids during the weekday are a minority," Smith observed to *US News and World Report.* "They experience all the problems that minorities experience. Gender is an even tougher barrier than other social barriers. Moms meet each other on neighborhood playgrounds and in general, they bond readily. Fathers are more out on their own, and some fathers are made to feel like outsiders."

Nevertheless, as stay-at-home dads grow more and more common, the social stigmas surrounding them are likely ease. "[P]eople need to understand the family unit is different than it was in 1960 or 1970," stay-at-home dad John Amicucci told the *Washington Post.* "You're doing what you need to do to make your family whole, to run properly, and to make sure kids have a place to come home to and feel secure. Whether it is the mother or the father, it's just important that it gets done."

Though large numbers of fathers are absent from the home, a greater number of fathers are the only parents in the home than in the past. As of 2010, according to the US Census, there were 1.8 million single fathers in the United States, making up 15 percent of all single parents, and 8 percent of all households. According to some estimates, there could be nearly 2.8 million single fathers. The 1.8 million figure marks a 27.3 percent increase over 2000. Of these single fathers, approximately 46 percent are divorced, and 19 percent are separated. Another 6 percent are widowers, and 39 percent never married.

The increase in the number of single fathers has also caused a shift in social perspectives. Up until the 1970s, courts generally favored mothers in custody disputes. The underlying assumption was that they were better equipped to raise the children. Gradually, this view has evolved. Family courts have recognized that the mother is not always the best option. As fathers take on caregiving roles, they want to do more than simply provide financial support. "[M]ore men are interested in raising their children in the event of a divorce or the breakup of a relationship," Matthew Weinshenker, a sociology professor at Fordham University, explains to the *New York Times.*

Compared to past generations, fathers are also having children later in life. Widely accessible birth control has allowed couples to delay having children. The decline in marriage rates is also a factor. Many men are having children long after they turn forty. Older fathers have advantages and disadvantages over their younger counterparts. Overall, they are more secure in their careers and their marriages. They are also more inclined to help around the house. However, there are increased health risks. There is evidence that children born to older fathers are at greater risk for autism and schizophrenia, among other disorders.

Changing attitudes towards homosexuality have also influenced the modern perceptions of fatherhood. A number of states have approved gay marriage or civil union initiatives. Though the issue of same-sex marriage remains controversial, many gay couples are starting their own families. According to the 2010 Census, about one in four gay couples are raising children. Gay fathers are a growing demographic in the United States. Many children raised by same-sex parents encounter discriminating attitudes outside the home. Nonetheless, a number of organizations—among them the American Academy of Pediatrics, the American Academy of Child and Adolescent Psychiatry, and the American Psychological Association (APA)—have concluded that, in terms of mental and physical health, children raised by same-sex couples fare just as well as those brought up in households led by a man and woman.

Though the nature of fatherhood is changing, the importance of fathers—and two-parent families, more generally—has remained constant. Children brought up in two-parent households face better odds of leading healthy, successful lives than those brought up by single parents. The 1950s rubric may no longer hold sway, and fathers are taking different roles than their predecessors a half-century ago, but they are as vital as ever in raising the next generation of Americans. "Having a father isn't magic," author Armin Brott commented, "but it does make a difference for the kids."

Remarks by the President at a Father's Day Event

By Barack Obama
Whitehouse.gov, Washington, D.C., June 21, 2010

The President: Hello! Hello, everybody! Thank you so much. Thank you. (Applause.) Thank you very much. Everybody, please have a seat. Thank you very much. (Applause.) Thank you. Let me just begin by making a few acknowledgements. First of all, I've got some outstanding fathers here in the first row who aren't seeing their kids enough because I'm working them all the time—three members of my Cabinet: Secretary of the Treasury Tim Geithner—(applause)—Attorney General Eric Holder—(applause)—and Secretary of Commerce Gary Locke are here. (Applause.)

In addition, we've got one of my heroes and I'm sure one of yours, somebody whose shoulders I stand on and allowed me to become President of the United States, and that's Congressman from the great state of Georgia, John Lewis, is here. (Applause.) A fierce advocate on behalf of the District of Columbia, Congresswoman Eleanor Holmes Norton is here. (Applause.)

I want to acknowledge the Mayor of Washington, D.C., Adrian Fenty in the house. (Applause.) The executive director of ARC, Edmund Fleet, is here. (Applause.) I want to thank all the panel discussion participants who are involved in today's events, and I want to thank Nurney Mason—a Washington, D.C. icon. Nurney founded Mason's Barbershop in 1961. That's the year I was born. It's still going strong. He is here with his children and his grandchildren. Where is he? There he is right there. (Applause.) I could use a little trim. (Laughter.)

One year ago this week, we kicked off a national conversation on fatherhood and personal responsibility, and members of our administration fanned out all across the country to hear from fathers and families about the challenges that they face. Secretary Arne Duncan, our Secretary of Education, held a discussion in New Hampshire about the link between fatherhood and educational achievement. Gary Locke talked to fathers in California about balancing the needs of their families with the demands of their jobs. Secretary Shinseki, of Veterans Affairs, held a town hall for military and veteran dads in North Carolina. And Attorney General Holder traveled to Georgia for a forum about fathers in our criminal justice system.

And in each of these places, each of these leaders posed a simple question: How can we as a nation—not just the government, but businesses and community

From Whitehouse.gov (21 June 2010).

groups and concerned citizens—how can we all come together to help fathers meet their responsibilities to our families and communities?

And we did this because we know the vital role fathers play in the lives of our children. Fathers are our first teachers and coaches—or in my house, assistant teachers and assistant coaches—(laughter)—to mom. But they're our mentors, our role models. They show us by the example they set the kind of people they want us to become.

But we also know that what too many fathers being absent means—too many fathers missing from too many homes, missing from too many lives. We know that when fathers abandon their responsibilities, there's harm done to those kids. We know that children who grow up without a father are more likely to live in poverty. They're more likely to drop out of school. They're more likely to wind up in prison. They're more likely to abuse drugs and alcohol. They're more likely to run away from home. They're more likely to become teenage parents themselves.

And I say all this as someone who grew up without a father in my own life. He left my family when I was two years old. And while I was lucky to have a wonderful mother and loving grandparents who poured everything they had into me and my sister, I still felt the weight of that absence. It's something that leaves a hole in a child's life that no government can fill.

So we can talk all we want here in Washington about issues like education and health care and crime; we can build good schools; we can put money into creating good jobs; we can do everything we can to keep our streets safe—but government can't keep our kids from looking for trouble on those streets. Government can't force a kid to pick up a book or make sure that the homework gets done. Government can't be there day in, day out, to provide discipline and guidance and the love that it takes to raise a child. That's our job as fathers, as mothers, as guardians for our children.

The fact is, it's easy to become a father, technically—any guy can do that. It's hard to live up to the lifelong responsibilities that come with fatherhood. And it's a challenge even in good times, when our families are doing well. It's especially difficult when times are tough, families are straining just to keep everything together.

> *Those family meals, afternoons in the park, bedtime stories; the encouragement we give, the questions we answer, the limits we set, the example we set of persistence in the face of difficulty and hardship—those things add up over time, and they shape a child's character, build their core, teach them to trust in life and to enter into it with confidence and with hope and with determination.*

In a time of war, many of our military families are stretched thin, with fathers doing multiple tours of duty far away from their children. In difficult economic times, a lot of fathers are worried about whether they're going to be able to keep their job, or find a job, or whether they'll be able to pay the bills and give their children the kinds of opportunities that if they didn't have them themselves, at least they wished for their children. And there are a lot of men who are out of work and wrestling with the shame and frustration that comes when you feel like you can't be the kind of provider you want to be for the people that you love.

But here's the key message I think all of us want to send today to fathers all across the country: Our children don't need us to be superheroes. They don't need us to be perfect. They do need us to be present. They need us to show up and give it our best shot, no matter what else is going on in our lives. They need us to show them—not just with words, but with deeds—that they, those kids, are always our first priority.

Those family meals, afternoons in the park, bedtime stories; the encouragement we give, the questions we answer, the limits we set, the example we set of persistence in the face of difficulty and hardship—those things add up over time, and they shape a child's character, build their core, teach them to trust in life and to enter into it with confidence and with hope and with determination. And that's something they'll always carry with them: that love that we show not with money, or fame, or spectacular feats, but through small daily acts—the love we show and that we earn by being present in the lives of our children.

Now, unfortunately, the way we talk about fatherhood in this country doesn't always reinforce these truths. When we talk about issues like child care and work-family balance, we call them "women's issues" and "mothers' issues." Too often when we talk about fatherhood and personal responsibility, we talk about it in political terms, in terms of left and right, conservative/liberal, instead of what's right and what's wrong. And when we do that, we've gotten off track. So I think it's time for a new conversation around fatherhood in this country.

We can all agree that we've got too many mothers out there forced to do everything all by themselves. They're doing a heroic job, often under trying circumstances. They deserve a lot of credit for that. But they shouldn't have to do it alone. The work of raising our children is the most important job in this country, and it's all of our responsibilities—mothers and fathers. (Applause.)

Now, I can't legislate fatherhood—I can't force anybody to love a child. But what we can do is send a clear message to our fathers that there is no excuse for failing to meet their obligations. What we can do is make it easier for fathers who make responsible choices and harder for those who avoid those choices. What we can do is come together and support fathers who are willing to step up and be good partners and parents and providers.

And that's why today we're launching the next phase of our work to promote responsible fatherhood—a new, nationwide Fatherhood and Mentoring Initiative. This is a call to action with cities and states, with individuals and organizations across the country—from the NFL Players Association to the National PTA, to everyday moms and dads—we're raising awareness about responsible fatherhood and working to re-engage absent fathers with their families.

As part of this effort, we've proposed a new and expanded Fatherhood, Marriage and Families Innovation Fund. And we plan to seek out and support the very best, most successful initiatives in our states and communities—those that are offering services like job training, or parenting skills classes, domestic violence prevention—all which help provide the kind of network of support for men, particularly those in vulnerable communities.

We're also going to help dads who get caught up—we want to make sure that they're caught up on child support payments and that we re-engage them in their children's lives. We're going to support efforts to build healthy relationships between parents as well—because we know that children benefit not just from loving mothers and loving fathers, but from strong and loving marriages as well. (Applause.)

We're also launching a new transitional jobs initiative for ex-offenders and low-income, non-custodial fathers—(applause)—because these are men who often face serious barriers to finding work and keeping work. We'll help them develop the skills and experience they need to move into full-time, long-term employment, so they can meet their child support obligations and help provide for their families.

And under Eric Holder's direction, our Justice Department is planning to create its first "Fathering Re-Entry Court" for ex-offender dads—(applause)—and to help replicate this program in courts across the country. The idea here is very simple: to reach fathers right as they're leaving the criminal justice system and connect them immediately to the employment and services they need to start making their child support payments and reconnecting them with their families.

This program was inspired by leaders like Peter Spokes, who was the executive director of the National Center for Fathering—a good friend to many in our administration, all of whom were deeply saddened by his recent passing. And we are honored to have Peter's wife, Barbara, with us here today. Where's Barbara? I just saw her earlier. There she is. (Applause.) Thank you.

So these initiatives are a good start. But ultimately, we know that the decision to be a good father—that's up to us, each of us, as individuals. It's one that men across this country are making every single day—attending those school assemblies; parent-teacher conferences; coaching soccer, Little League; scrimping and saving, and working that extra shift so that their children can go to college. And plenty of fathers—and men who aren't fathers as well—are stepping up to serve as mentors and tutors and big brothers and foster parents to young people who don't have any responsible adult in their lives.

Even when we give it our best efforts, there will still be plenty of days of struggle and heartache when we don't quite measure up—talking to the men here now. Even with all the good fortune and support Michelle and I have had in our lives, I've made plenty of mistakes as a parent. I've lost count of all the times when the demands of work have taken me from the duties of fatherhood. And I know I've missed out on moments in my daughters' lives that I'll never get back, and that's a loss that's hard to accept.

But I also know the feeling that one author described when she wrote that "to have a child . . . is to decide forever to have your heart go walking around outside your body." (Laughter.) Think about that—to have a child is to have your heart walking around outside your body.

I'm sure a lot of fathers here know that same memory that I have, of driving home with Michelle and Malia right after she was born, going about 10 miles an hour. (Laughter.) Your emotions swinging between unadulterated joy and sheer terror. (Laughter.) And I made a pledge that day that I would do everything I could to give my daughter what I never had—that if I could be anything in life, I would be a good father. (Applause.)

And like a lot of the men here, since that time I've found there's nothing else in my life that compares to the pleasures I take in spending time with my girls. Nothing else comes close to the pride I feel in their achievement and the satisfaction I get in watching them grow into strong, confident young women.

Over the course of my life, I have been an attorney, I've been a professor, I've been a state senator, I've been a U.S. senator—and I currently am serving as President of the United States. But I can say without hesitation that the most challenging, most fulfilling, most important job I will have during my time on this Earth is to be Sasha and Malia's dad. (Applause.)

So you don't need a fancy degree for that. You don't need a lot of money for that. No matter what doubts we may feel, what difficulties we may face, we all have to remember being a father—it's not just an obligation and a responsibility; it is a privilege and a blessing, one that we all have to embrace as individuals and as a nation.

So, Happy Father's Day, everybody. God bless you. God bless the United States of America. (Applause.)

How Dads Develop

By Brian Mossop
Scientific American Mind, July/August 2011

When men morph into fathers, they experience a neural revival that benefits their children.

Last year I met my four-month-old nephew, Landon, for the first time. During the weekend I spent visiting him in San Diego, my inner science nerd often got the best of me. I would find myself probing my nephew's foot reflexes and offering unsolicited explanations for why his toes curled this way or that, only to be met by my wife's disapproving looks and the new parents' blank stares. Soon enough I dropped the shoptalk in favor of baby talk.

Having spent my postdoctoral career in neuroscience, I have seen how important early experiences are for a baby animal's health. In the first few days after birth, babies' brains are like sponges soaking up their sensory environment. What to me seemed like inconsequential sights or smells had markedly different impacts on the impressionable newborns, shaping their brains as they tried to make sense of the unfamiliar world around them. But as astonishing as a baby's brain is, on this family visit what struck me was the redevelopment of my 26-year-old brother-in-law.

In my eyes, Jack has always been my wife's kid brother. When I first met him, Jack was a tall, lanky, wet-behind-the-ears 19-year-old kid who enlisted in the U.S. Navy right after graduating high school. As a two-tour Iraq War veteran, he saw more of the world in six years than most of us ever will, and he frequently regaled us with his large repertoire of crazy sailor stories. But in just a few months' time, Jack had managed to permanently ground his sea legs and become a hands-on first-time father.

Even having served in Iraq, Jack will no doubt find raising Landon the biggest challenge he has ever faced. Whether he knows it or not—and whether he likes it or not—things are about to change drastically for him. Not only will Jack be financially and legally responsible for Landon for the next couple of decades, he will form and sustain an unbreakable emotional bond with his son. In the early days after birth, changes occur in the brains of both the dad and the baby. We can now see the mark left on a baby's brain when a father is not around. When he sticks around, a father gains a cognitive edge by virtue of tending to his children. Although many of the findings are still preliminary, scientists are beginning to sketch a neural portrait of the father-child bond.

By the end of the weekend trip, I saw glimpses that Jack was beginning to accept his new identity. After struggling for several weeks to secure Landon's car seat in the back of his souped-up Mazda RX-8, Jack finally broke down and traded it in for a sensible sedan that will let him transport the little guy more easily. In the cellular networks inside his head, a transformation was well under way.

Figuring Out Fatherhood

To unearth the roots of fatherly feelings, scientists had first to figure out where to look. On the surface, the intangible link of fatherhood appears nothing like a mother's connection to her child. During the nine months of a pregnancy, oxytocin and other hormones course through a woman's body, forging a biochemical bond between her and her baby. Even their heartbeats can synchronize while the child is in the womb. Following birth, a mother's lactation serves as a natural food source for the newborn.

What a dad offers is less obvious. Sure, men help out during conception, but afterward we are not exactly crucial to a child's survival. Nevertheless, research shows that the father-child bond makes a major contribution. If a father leaves his children to be raised solely by their mother, they are more likely to suffer a whole host of problems later in life, including emotional troubles, aggression and addiction.

The numbers are actually quite staggering. In 2008 about one in four children lived with only their mothers, whereas only 4 percent lived with just their fathers. A third of the approximately 12 million single-parent families in the U.S. live below the poverty level. Perhaps as a product of struggling to make ends meet, single parents are at a higher risk of raising children with lower academic achievement and self-esteem, as well as difficulties forming social relationships. Until recently, large population surveys were the most effective tool for investigating a father's contribution to the upbringing of a child. But new clues are emerging from deep inside the brain. Neuroscientists are now revealing one critical part of the puzzle—the biological mechanisms that connect a father and his child.

Take the sound of a baby's cry. In 2003 psychiatrist Erich Seifritz of the University of Basel in Switzerland and a team used functional MRI to show that just as in mothers, certain areas in the brains of dads became activated with a signature pattern unlike that of nonparents who heard the same sounds. Although the team could not pinpoint exactly what had changed, the brains of both parents appeared to have adapted to recognize the sounds critical to a baby's comfort and survival.

Brains, after all, are not static. Neurons constantly rewire themselves in response to new experiences and changes in our surroundings. Additional neurons can also materialize, a process called neurogenesis. The mechanisms of neurogenesis are not fully understood, but scientists have connected extra brain-cell growth with learning new things.

Brainpower Boost

Building off these observations, Gloria K. Mak and Samuel Weiss, two neuroscientists at the University of Calgary in Alberta, designed a series of experiments to figure out how offspring might reshape a father's brain. In results published in 2010 Mak and Weiss showed that the brains of mouse dads do not simply rewire, they also sprout additional neurons. The cells form brand-new connection pathways, or circuits, in the days following the birth of the pups. In the olfactory bulb, new neurons developed that responded specifically to the smells of his pups. Another set of neurons grew in the father's hippocampus, a crucial memory center in the brain, which presumably helped to consolidate the smell of his pups into long-term memory.

The mouse father only gained the extra brain cells if he stayed in the nest, though. If he was removed on the day of his pups' birth, his brain remained the same. As Weiss sees it, this study demonstrates that the experience "is not just changing what exists [in the brain] but developing something brand-new to serve the relationship."

In mammals, neurons located in the nose use special odor receptors to detect scents and shuttle the information to the olfactory bulb, which is the integration center for our sense of smell. Simply sniffing his pups, though, was not enough to cause new neurons to spring into existence. When Mak and Weiss placed a mesh screen across a cage to separate a dad from his pups, they saw no additional brain cells appear. This test and other similar ones indicate that neither the birth of the new offspring nor their smells alone change a dad's brain, Weiss says. Rather the hands-on experience of being a father brings about the extra dose of brain cells. Physical contact with the pups, coupled with the experience of their smells, is what makes the neurons grow, the researchers suggest.

But are pups different from pals? A few weeks' separation is usually enough for adult mice to forget all about their former cage mates. Mak and Weiss demonstrated that the parent-child bond indeed stands out. These new neurons formed their own brain circuits, thus helping to form long-term memories and therefore a lasting bond. With distinct memory pathways forged, the mouse fathers easily recognized their offspring by smell even after they had been separated for three weeks. "We still struggle to understand why new neurons are born in the brains of all mammals, including humans," Weiss says. "It certainly appears as though one of the main functions may be to adapt to change, form new circuits, and, in this case, [create] what we call a 'social memory' between the father and his offspring."

Like Mother, Like Father

To solidify social memories, the brain relies on hormones to control the connection of those newly forged neurons. Mak and Weiss found that the father's ability to form new brain cells is at the mercy of a hormone called prolactin—the same hormone responsible for milk production in new mothers. When they disrupted the brain's ability to produce prolactin, they discovered that fathers did not form any offspring-specific brain cells.

Also parallel to how babies and mothers bond, many studies have shown that human fathers with higher levels of oxytocin (the "love hormone") exhibit stronger paternal instincts and motivation in the first months of their child's life. In findings published last December, Atsuko Saito of the University of Tokyo and Katsuki Nakamura of Kyoto University pushed that observation further by studying the food-sharing habits of marmoset father monkeys. Marmoset dads readily feed their youngsters during their first four months. But after six months, the fathers begin to ignore their now adolescent offspring and keep their food for themselves. To test what drives the change in behavior, the team infused oxytocin into the brains of marmoset fathers. Regardless of the dose Saito and Nakamura administered—and with no change in the fathers' appetites—the male marmosets were more likely to indulge their offspring's clamoring for food.

Because prolactin and oxytocin are both heavily tied to social interaction, their involvement in the father-child bond may not be surprising. Nevertheless, new data are providing a broader prospective. As psychologist Elizabeth Gould of Princeton University and her colleagues pointed out in an October 2010 review article, hormones relating to sex and stress have now also been linked to paternal behaviors.

Gould has published numerous papers detailing the connection between the human stress hormone cortisol (corticosterone in rodents) and structural changes in the brain. Although stress usually has a negative connotation, Gould and her colleagues have used experiments with rodents to show that it can be both good and bad for the brain, depending largely on context. For example, bad stressors, such as when animals are briefly submersed in cold water or exposed to a natural predator, have negative effects on the brain, reducing the brain's ability to generate new neurons and rewire itself. But as Gould and her colleagues published last July, stressors such as exercise and sex, which also boost corticosterone levels, actually stimulate new brain cells to grow. The challenges of fatherhood may well fall into the category of good stress.

Although male sex hormones seem to be deeply intertwined with the birth of offspring, other species show that the hormones have inconsistent effects. In certain rodents and fish, fathers produce excess testosterone. They take good care of their young and simultaneously maintain aggressive tendencies that help them to, say, defend the nest against predators. In tropical birds and primates, however, elevated testosterone levels get in the way of good parenting. Human fathers with excess amounts of testosterone may exhibit less sympathy for and desire to respond to a crying baby.

These studies make a strong case for hormones as the brokers of certain paternal behaviors. As Weiss points out, this line of research is "adding a new dimension to the impact that hormones can have on adult brain-cell production."

A Critical Link

Whereas an arsenal of hormones cultivates a father's brain in the presence of a baby, a child may actually be born ready to bond. To test this idea, a research team led by neurobiologist Katharina Braun of Otto von Guericke University of Magdeburg in Germany turned to a rodent with a remarkably familiar nest structure. Degu rat mothers and fathers split the parenting duties. Similar to human fathers, degu dads spend the early days of their pups' lives helping with basic care, huddling over them to keep them warm and bathing them with gentle licks when needed. As the pups get older, the fathers begin to play with their toddler offspring by chasing them, romping and roughhousing around the cage.

Braun and her team reasoned that degu nests lacking fathers would create a social and emotional void for the offspring, just as a missing dad would affect the dynamics of a human family. Indeed, they found that if a rodent father remained in the nest with his pups, his babies' brains developed normally. But if the father was removed from the nest shortly after the birth of his pups, they observed in two regions of the brain that the newborns developed fewer synapses, the short chemical junctions that allow brain cells to communicate with one another.

At a stage of development when most of the brain should be burgeoning with new connections, the pups raised without a father had deficits in the orbitofrontal cortex and the somatosensory cortex. The orbitofrontal cortex is part of the prefrontal cortex, which regulates decision making, reward and emotion. And although it is difficult to extrapolate from rodent studies to effects in humans, it is worth noting that faulty synapses and processing problems in this locale might well explain why we see some kids who grow up without a dad wrestle with occasionally serious behavioral problems.

Taken together, these rat studies suggest a model for why fathers matter. A newborn emerges into the world having spent weeks afloat in amniotic fluid, its senses somewhat deprived and its somatosensory cortex ripe for change. But instead of flourishing in the early postnatal days, the synapses of the somatosensory cortex wither away

> *The mouse father only gained the extra brain cells if he stayed in the nest, though. If he was removed on the day of his pups' birth, his brain remained the same. As Weiss sees it, this study demonstrates that the experience "is not just changing what exists [in the brain] but developing something brand-new to serve the relationship."*

when degus are raised without a father. As a result, the newborns may not process touch as well as they should, which could lead to a number of other developmental problems, such as metabolism issues and irregular hormone production.

A father's brain, it seems, is significantly and beautifully intertwined with his offspring's. "Having two parents is one thing," Weiss points out, "but having effective relationships between parents and offspring is yet something else. It's actually the effectiveness of the relationships [that matters]."

Perhaps my nephew, bolstered by a healthy set of brain connections that formed in response to the simple fact of Jack's touch, has already collected the tools he will need to fend off behavioral and emotional challenges as he grows older. And while I can't exactly probe Jack's brain to see if he is sprouting neurons, I noticed an undeniable change in his focus as his new bond took hold. Small movements and sounds from Landon that went unnoticed by most people mysteriously captured Jack's attention. It is comforting to think that a small set of neurons might be tucked away in Jack's head solely dedicated to his son.

On the surface, the intangible link of fatherhood appears nothing like a mother's connection to her child.

A dad's ability to grow new neurons is at the mercy of prolactin—the hormone that controls milk production in mothers.

Faulty brain connections may explain why children who grow up without a dad often wrestle with behavior problems later.

Mind Matters

Each week in Mind Matters (www.ScientificAmerican.com/mind-and-brain), researchers explain their disciplines' most notable recent findings. Mind Matters is edited by Gareth Cook, a Pulitzer Prize–winning journalist at *The Boston Globe*, where he edits the Sunday Ideas section.

Fast Facts

Symbiotic Brains

1. The brains of babies and fathers alike benefit from one another's influence.

2. A father sprouts supplemental neurons in his brain and experiences hormonal changes after the birth of a child.

3. For a baby, the presence of a father figure early on may be important for developing healthy behaviors later.

4. For a guy to set aside the sports car and man up to a minivan, his brain must surely have revised its circuitry. Indeed, neural modifications nudge him toward nurturing behaviors.

5. A baby's brain appears to be primed for contact with a father. For a dad, interacting with his children gives him a cognitive edge.

6. When children are raised without a father, they are at a greater risk of developing emotional troubles, experiencing aggression and suffering from addiction.

7. The challenges of child care are likely to be good sources of stress. The hormones induced by good stress can stimulate the growth of new brain cells.

8. For a dad, the scent of a child, along with physical contact, appears to be pivotal to making new neurons grow. Those neurons form the foundation of a lasting bond between father and child.

Further Reading

Family Guy. Emily Anthes in *Scientific American Mind*, Vol. 21, No. 2, pages 46–53; May/June 2010.

Hit the Ground Crawling: Lessons from 150,000 New Fathers. Second edition. Greg Bishop. Dads Adventure, 2006.

Parenting and Plasticity. B. Leuner et al. in *Trends in Neuroscience*, Vol. 33, No. 10, pages 465–473; October 2010.

The Role of the Father in Child Development. Fifth edition. Edited by Michael E. Lamb. John Wiley & Sons, 2010.

Brian Mossop holds a Ph.D. in biomedical engineering and has had postdoctoral training in neuroscience. He writes for Wired, Scientific American, Slate, *and* The Scientist *and is the community manager at the Public Library of Science (PLoS).*

Military Dads and Fatherwork

By Jerry Novack
GoodMenProject.com, June 14, 2011

Soldier-fathers have added challenges in maintaining a balanced life at home.

Fathering can start with a paradox—fathering a child is so simple and easy that it frequently happens "by accident," and yet being a daddy can prove one of the most daunting, intimidating, and difficult tasks a man ever faces. While there are millions of involved, nurturing fathers in the world, realities such as poverty and incarceration can contribute to a sense of impossibility about fathering for some men. Additionally, conflicting social expectations (e.g., good fathers provide for their families, *and* good fathers are regularly home spending time with their children) worsen the situation by making "good" fathering a lose-lose proposition.

Most men have the choice between spending time at home, or excelling at work by spending long hours in the office. In some cases, men must work extra hours and pick up overtime just to make ends meet, let alone excel. Few men feel as if they can accomplish both, and choosing one invites criticism and judgment for not doing the other. Studies reveal that even highly motivated fathers feel confused and uncertain about their role. Specific family situations, too, can create even greater barriers to involved fathering. Military fathers frequently experience the confounding effects of general, social obstacles, and specific difficulties related to their service.

Military service does provide several benefits for families, such as economic stability, early retirement, health benefits, and an existing social structure. But there are also costs: frequent moves to new geographic locations, periodic father absence (due to deployment), the potential for injury or death of the father, and a rigid structure. These challenges can interact with the aforementioned situations and expectations to create frustration and discourage involved parenting for some military men.

In the 1990s, David Dollahite and Alan Hawkins proposed a framework intended to facilitate men's healthy involvement with their children. In their book, *Generative Fathering: Beyond Deficit Perspectives*, Dollahite and Hawkins cited research demonstrating that involved fathering provides specific benefits for children (e.g. decreased incarceration, improved academic performance) as well as specific benefits for the men. *Generative Fathering* (GF) is defined by concern for the next generation, and results in improvements on measures of personality development and life-purpose for fathers, which in turn positively impacts their emotional wellness, physical health, and interpersonal relationships. Involved fathering benefits children, men and families.

The GF approach argues that fathering is work—a job to be done. According to the

> *Families with more rigid adherence to traditional gender norms tend to struggle more with deployment and post-deployment reintegration.*

authors, *fatherwork*, a central construct in GF, is the most challenging and the most meaningful job a man can have. Fatherwork consists of identifying the various biological, psychological, and social needs of one's children and helping those children address their needs by maximizing the father's individual strengths and abilities.

Also central in GF is the assumption that children's needs and fathers' abilities exist within the specific contexts of individual families. This attention to context becomes extremely valuable when considering men who need to integrate fathering with serving in the armed forces.

Soldier-fathers and their families must raise their children amidst the realities of long and often dangerous deployments, sometimes without the benefit of regular phone calls or Skype conversations; frequent moves that can take children away from their schools and their friends; and a rigidly structured environment. Staying mindful of specific risk/protective factors that effect military families and adopting a GF perspective can facilitate good outcomes for children and improved quality of life for fathers.

Researchers working with military families have identified factors that have the potential to either ease or exacerbate the stress and difficulty that accompanies deployment. First, the relationship quality between fathers and their children is a powerful predictor of family adjustment to the deployment and post-deployment reintegration. By maintaining a loving, involved relationship with his children, a military father can help ensure family success during and after deployment. Also, an important predictor of family cohesion and adaptability with regards to deployment is gender expression.

Families with more rigid adherence to traditional gender norms tend to struggle more with deployment and post-deployment reintegration. When gender roles are less rigid, a female partner or child can take over some of the family duties and household responsibilities typically expected of men (e.g., automobile maintenance), thus easing some of the stress resulting from his absence. Similarly, a service member willing to participate in some of the more "female" household chores (e.g., washing dishes) can help smooth his transition home. After a woman in the home has spent months performing her regular tasks as well as the "man's work," his returning home and resuming his old responsibilities, but refusing to assist with her work sends the message that, while she is expected to help with his jobs during his absence, he is somehow above helping with her jobs when he returns home.

Finally, finding meaning in military service seems to predict more successful family outcomes during and after deployment. Families who consider military service meaningful and important work tend to cope with stressors related to deployment and reintegration better than those who join the military for pragmatic reasons, but do not find the work meaningful.

Another potential threat to functioning in military families is the frequency with which they tend to move. Military children are often moved away from their friends and forced to change schools, sometimes mid-term. While challenging, military psychiatrist Kay Tooley observes, "moving house seems to improve family adjustment or individual adjustment almost as often as it disturbs it." In fact, military children tend to realize better academic performance, higher scores on IQ and achievement tests, and lower rates of delinquency and incarceration when compared to civilian children. Family attitudes about diversity and long-distance relationships seem the most important factor in predicting adjustment to frequent moves. Families who enjoy new foods, customs, and people tend to thrive from frequent moves, seeing them as an opportunity for adventure and instead of a disruption of the status quo. Families that enjoy maintaining cross-national and international relationships with friends and relatives do even better.

The bottom line? Fathering can be elusive and intimidating for many men. Fathers serving in the armed forces must contend with the challenges of fathering within the context of a soldier's life, which contains its own struggles and difficulties. By helping military fathers to build strong relationships with their children by understanding and addressing their individual needs, understanding the importance of more flexible gender expression, developing an appreciation for diversity and adventure, and find meaning and value in their work, friends and clinicians can help these men foster resilience, health and happiness for themselves and their families. Happy Father's Day.

Jerry Novack is a doctoral student studying counseling psychology at Ball State University (www.bsu.edu). He is a second lieutenant in the U.S. Air Force (www.airforce.com), a husband, and the proud father of a 1-year-old son.

Holidays

By Nick Serpe
Dissent, Winter 2011

My father moved out the summer before I began middle school, just before I turned twelve. The first months of separation were marked by his efforts to reach out to my two sisters and me. He came to all our concerts, helped coach my football team, and when Thanksgiving came around, he was back at our dining room table, sitting across from my mother. Despite the tough few months behind us, the meal passed without fighting, so we decided it was a good pattern to keep up. Dad came back for Christmas the following month and returned for both holidays the next season. Our nascent tradition didn't last long. Within a couple of years, Dad had moved into a new place, with a new woman. He then left the United States, right before I entered the eighth grade, to spend a year-and-a-half in Paris on assignment for the Internet company he worked for. When he returned, it was with a baby boy. A baby girl soon followed. As Dad took on the responsibilities of caring for his young children during my high school years, it became my sisters' and my responsibility to visit him. We saw less of him during most of the year, but for the winter holidays, we always made it to his house.

On both Thanksgiving and Christmas, days began at Mom's by default, since that was our home. We passed our morning eating pancakes and candy, watching the Macy's parade or fiddling with our presents. In the early afternoon we departed for Dad's. Mom cooked by herself during the hours we were away. Our route from Westford into Cambridge, where Dad lived, went along tortuous roads running through old farming towns. The drives to the city passed quickly and with good conversation; on the way home, the three of us seldom spoke, instead hiding from our own thoughts in the fading winter light.

Dad made many small gestures to encourage us to feel at ease at his new home. There was a key under the mat, a parking pass always at the ready, and an open invitation to stay over. But gestures are only necessary when you're a guest, and these overtures never made us feel otherwise. We called ahead whenever we came to visit him, even though we knew we didn't have to. My sisters and I never stayed there for more than a few hours. We talked the way that we'd been trained to speak to extended relatives: asking the courteous questions, avoiding the taboo subjects. We would eventually gravitate toward our half brother and half sister. (They gripped onto our legs the minute we walked in the door, so it wasn't hard to do.) Our fondness for them was always genuine, if a bit self-interested; young children are indelicate, a relief in a carefully worded milieu. One Christmas, my then five-year-old brother asked me, in a state of complete innocence, how it was possible that our fathers were the same person, but not our mothers. There was nothing like it to remind me of the absurdity of the innuendoes the adults had been using all day long.

Thanksgiving is a holiday about and for a meal, but we never ate with Dad. When he, his wife, their kids, and whoever else was over seemed about ready to sit for dinner, we headed toward the door, because Mom's meal was bound to be almost ready by then. Our leaving always began with a weary look from my older sister, and then the hushed voice—"I think we should get going soon, maybe fifteen minutes"—and the consultation and confirmation with our younger sister. The kids would say good-by, sometimes distractedly and sometimes exuberantly; their mother, with the gratitude of a host ("We're so glad you could make it!"); and Dad, in a way that suggested that much remained to be said and done. Those hours at his house passed slowly, but they were never enough. His goodbyes took a long time to finish.

> *One Christmas, my then five-year-old brother asked me, in a state of complete innocence, how it was possible that our fathers were the same person, but not our mothers. There was nothing like it to remind me of the absurdity of the innuendoes the adults had been using all day long.*

On Christmas, the gap between new and old family yawned wider. The first hours of hazy happiness, after waking early in the morning, were spent at Mom's. She picked presents with the quotidian attentiveness that's often mistaken for motherly intuition—how did she know all my socks had holes in them, that I really wanted that book? She never worried about her choices, but Dad worried, and worried about worrying. "Well, I was pretty sure you didn't have this already. . . . I heard someone at work talking about it. . . . It's pretty cool, right?" His gifts betrayed the habits of a busy man. He usually shopped for both sisters and me at the same one or two stores each year, often from the novelty item section of a local record shop. He removed price tags with inconsistency and left holes in the wrapping paper where the pieces he'd cut were too short.

For too long, I took these details as symbols of a deficit of Dad's love. His younger children had more gifts, of a greater variety, chosen with the care of a father deeply involved in their lives. He knew that Mom, whose attention was spread less thin, could pick up the balance, and that his first children had reached an age where they were less materially demanding. So he was able to let go a little more, to expend the energies of the second half of life doing right by the children he would never leave. I was mostly wrong, I think. Looking back, Dad's love for us remained close to what it had always been—sometimes quiet but occasionally strangely fierce, messy and inconstant but always searching. More than once he forgot my friends' names, and sometimes the name of a girlfriend, but when he did forget, it was easy to see the frustration on his face.

Even when my parents were still together, I saw more of Mom—she was the one who stayed at home, who knew our plans, and made plans for us, questioning us about our goings-on with warm concern. The onus placed on her after the divorce was unjust, in terms of the parental division of labor and the precepts of feminism. But for my father to have been a constant presence would have rung false, much the same as Mom's love was rarely spontaneous and carefree. Over the years, my sisters and I undoubtedly gave her more grief than we gave Dad, all too often over slight things, because there was never any Big Thing. Mom stuck with us. Our holiday nights at her (and our) home advanced with quiet decency and regularity. All four of us helped put the last touches on dinner and brought out the good china and crystal. We sat together and told each other how happy we were to be in each other's presence, to be eating such a wonderful meal, to have stepped back from the speed of our separate lives. And then we sat around and mocked bad holiday movies on TV, just as I imagined other families did. And one by one, we went off to bed, like the family von Trapp: so long, farewell, auf Wiedersehen, good night. I was usually the last left awake. As I drifted off to sleep, I always felt content, but also impatient for the return of normalcy. Soon my siblings and parents would retreat to the background of my life, nestled into houses just far enough away.

Tolstoy delivered his judgment of familial dysfunction in the way only a self-assured mystic (with a dysfunctional family) can: "Happy families are all alike; every unhappy family is unhappy in its own way." He was wrong—not because happy families are different too, but because he assumed families are either happy or unhappy, when they are invariably both. Sadness and affection often fit together quite well. My blue-tinged memories of holidays with the family are regularly interrupted by recollections of uncommon love. One recent Christmas, Dad wrote me a message on the inside jacket of a book that I didn't plan on reading: "I never really understood until recently that when Grandma gave me a book that made me say, 'huh?' it was just her way of saying, 'I'm thinking of you always. You are near and dear to my heart. I want happiness for you and for all to be right in your world.'" I didn't discover the note until months after he gave the book to me, but I called him right then, not telling him what I'd just read. We all deserve moments of connection without reason, in the midst of so much trying and falling away.

Father's Day: Why Dads Are More Engaged . . . and More Absent

By Mark Trumbull
The Christian Science Monitor, June 17, 2011

Two distinct trends characterize fatherhood on Father's Day: Educated fathers are spending more time than ever with their kids, but poorer fathers are often absent altogether.

American families will rally around dad this weekend amid a social landscape that is sharply divided: Fathers tend to be more active as parents than their male counterparts a generation ago, but more children than ever are growing up without a father living in their home at all.

These trends—moving in seemingly opposite directions—partly reflect changes that are splitting US society along lines of education and income.

Researchers say the institution of marriage is on much firmer footing among couples with college degrees and higher incomes than among working-class families with lower levels of education.

At the higher end of this demographic, fathers are becoming more engaged. But for a large portion of less-educated Americans, fathers are often absent.

The pattern is not new, but it appears to be continuing to grow. New polling results show the gap, with the Pew Research Center releasing the data this week under the headline, "a tale of two fathers."

"Fathers who live with their children have become more intensely involved in their lives, spending more time with them and taking part in a greater variety of activities," Pew researchers Gretchen Livingston and Kim Parker said in the report. But "more than one-in-four fathers with children ages 18 or younger now live apart from their children."

In 1960, only 11 percent of US children lived apart from their fathers. That share reached 27 percent in 2010, according to data from the National Survey of Family Growth, which the Pew Center analyzed and paired with its own poll results.

Among fathers who never completed high school, 40 percent live apart from their children, versus 7 percent for fathers who graduated from college. Some 44 percent of black fathers live apart from their children, versus 21 percent of white fathers, the poll found.

Key reasons are probably both economic and cultural, says Bradford Wilcox, a sociologist at the University of Virginia who directs a research program called the National Marriage Project.

Mr. Wilcox sees "an erosion of good-paying, stable jobs for less-educated men." This has made many men less capable as family providers, and less attractive to women as a result, he says. The deep recession of 2007–09 only made an existing problem worse, leaving many working-age men on the economy's sidelines.

Socially, attitudes of Americans with moderate education, who have traditionally been conservative on marriage-related matters, appear to have become more socially permissive.

But Wilcox says that, perhaps surprisingly, highly educated Americans appear to be growing "more marriage-minded."

> *Socially, attitudes of Americans with moderate education, who have traditionally been conservative on marriage-related matters, appear to have become more socially permissive.*

Highly educated Americans, he said in a report last year, adhere to an ethos of delayed gratification, in which the goal is a "success sequence" of education, work, marriage, and childbearing. That sequence makes a successful family life more likely.

At the same time, a decline in civic engagement, including things such as churchgoing, has hit poor and working-class neighborhoods particularly hard, Wilcox says.

Whatever the causes behind the recent trends, they have a big impact on children. According to a survey by the National Survey of Family Growth, conducted mostly before the recession, a majority of fathers who live with their children engage multiple times each week in things like ferrying children to activities, talking with them about their day, helping them with homework, and eating meals together.

For fathers living apart from children, the level of involvement plunges. Only 16 percent have several meals a week with their son or daughter, for example.

The good news is that, on average, dads are living with their kids and spending more time with them.

In 1985, the typical father who lived with his children spent about three hours a week on child care, the survey found. By the time the latest recession began in 2007, that number had risen to 6.5 hours per week. By comparison, moms spend about 12.9 hours per week on child care, which is also a rise (from about nine hours in 1985).

Why Antipoverty Efforts Must Not Neglect Fathers

By Leslie Lenkowsky
The Chronicle of Philanthropy, September 9, 2010

Government and philanthropists are seeking new ways to help men become more responsible husbands and fathers.

Speaking in June at an arts and recreation center in Washington, President Obama announced his new "Fatherhood and Mentoring Initiative," designed to help the estimated 24 million children in the United States who do not live with their fathers. He also called on Congress to pass legislation based on an idea he had earlier suggested: a $500-million "Fatherhood, Marriage and Families Innovation Fund," which would make grants to programs that help men become more responsible husbands and fathers.

Not long ago, proposals such as these from most public figures—let alone a President of the United States—would have been controversial. And few in the philanthropic world would have supported programs that sought to enable men to become better fathers. But, as James T. Patterson, the Brown University historian recounts in his new book, *Freedom Is Not Enough*, our understanding of the causes of poverty and other social problems has been changing and now points toward the importance of fostering more stable families.

Mr. Patterson's story begins 45 years ago, when a then little-known U.S. Department of Labor official, Daniel Patrick Moynihan, produced a report asserting that the growing number of female-headed families in the "Negro" community presented a significant obstacle to achieving racial equality. The study, entitled "The Negro Family," helped shape Lyndon B. Johnson's 1965 commencement address at Howard University, during which he called for a new phase of the civil-rights movement, one designed to overcome the social and economic disadvantages faced by African-Americans.

But the "Moynihan report" (as it became popularly known) also attracted vitriolic criticism from prominent civil-rights leaders, scholars, editorial writers, and many others.

They faulted it for "blaming the victim" rather than focusing on the legacy of discrimination, which critics believed was still the fundamental problem. Despite Mr. Moynihan's goal to make "The Case for National Action" (as the report's subtitle put it), the controversy his analysis generated ensured that neither the Johnson administration nor subsequent ones did much, although the Nixon administration, in which Mr. Moynihan served as a domestic-policy adviser, made an attempt.

Much of what the report said was actually hard to dispute. Without adequate support at home, Mr. Moynihan wrote, children will have difficulty succeeding in school, work, and other aspects of American life. Many will be at greater risk of physical or mental illness and imprisonment. As adults, they will be less likely to establish stable families of their own. And government or philanthropic programs to help them overcome or compensate for the disadvantages of their home lives will have a harder time doing so.

> *Just 35 percent of African-American children lived with two married parents in 2006 (compared with 67 percent when the Moynihan report was written and 76 percent of non-Hispanic white children today). As Mr. Moynihan had predicted, whether measured by income, by educational achievement, or in other ways, equality between blacks and whites remains a long way off.*

However, what provoked Mr. Moynihan's critics were two other parts of his argument. First, he said, families headed just by women were apt to confront more problems than did two-parent ones, headed by men. In addition, because of the lingering effects of slavery and other reasons, black families were more likely to be headed by women than white ones were, he said.

Using a mixture of statistics and pointed analysis, he contended that this combination was creating "a tangle of pathology" that was increasing in scope and likely to undermine the opportunities for social and economic progress that the civil-rights movement had created for black Americans.

Mr. Patterson presents a thorough and balanced assessment of the four-decade-long debate that followed. Some scholars, Mr. Patterson notes, took issue with Mr. Moynihan's depiction of African-American families, claiming he had ignored their strengths and, especially, their reliance on extended kinship networks to support children when one or both biological parents were absent.

Others maintained that the lack of progress Mr. Moynihan blamed on the weaknesses of "the Negro family" was really caused by continuing racial discrimination in employment, housing, and other areas. Still others, such as the Harvard professor William Julius Wilson, presented a more nuanced view that acknowledged that the changes occurring among African-American families had not been helpful but attributed them to social, economic, and public-policy causes more than racial ones.

Mr. Patterson seems inclined toward Mr. Wilson's position, as do a growing number of other scholars today. Moreover, the fragile condition of African-American families that concerned Mr. Moynihan in 1965 has subsequently become even more worrisome.

Just 35 percent of African-American children lived with two married parents in 2006 (compared with 67 percent when the Moynihan report was written and 76 percent of non-Hispanic white children today). As Mr. Moynihan had predicted, whether measured by income, by educational achievement, or in other ways, equality between blacks and whites remains a long way off.

Increasing numbers of prominent black Americans are also now willing to talk or write forcefully about the connection between black family structure and socioeconomic progress.

Even before he became president, Barack Obama observed in his book *The Audacity of Hope* that "in their urgency to avoid blaming the victims of historical racism," policy makers and civil-rights leaders "tended to downplay or ignore evidence that entrenched behavioral patterns among the black poor really were contributing to intergenerational poverty."

Thus, the Obama administration's support for pro-fatherhood efforts should not have come as a surprise. Yet apart from their small scale and deference to Washington's current political fashions (the president's speech stipulated a child could benefit from having two fathers, too), the question is whether either government or philanthropy really knows how to achieve the goal of encouraging more-stable families.

Past efforts to do so or to help lower-income men overcome the multiple obstacles they often face to becoming more responsible parents have had mixed, and some might even say disappointing, results. Although the 1996 welfare overhaul changed a public-assistance program that most believed weakened two-parent families, improvements in the ability of families to support themselves, care for their children, and avoid nonmarital births have been less noticeable than sharp reductions in the numbers of recipients.

Mentor programs have proven their effectiveness, but maintaining their quality, while expanding them to reach the large numbers of children in need, will be a major challenge.

Nonetheless, the willingness of national leaders to address the importance of strengthening family life is a major development—and potentially a watershed for government and philanthropic efforts to reduce poverty. As Mr. Moynihan understood, getting the real nature of the problem right is an essential step toward figuring out what to do about it.

Leslie Lenkowsky is professor of public affairs and philanthropic studies at Indiana University and a regular contributor to The Chronicle of Philanthropy. *His e-mail address is llenkows@iupui.edu.*

Fatherhood 2.0

By Lisa Takeuchi Cullen and Lev Grossman
Time, October 15, 2007

As dads have begun to act more like moms, old notions of masculinity have come into question.

Does being more of a father make you less of a man? To a group of committed dads assembled one night in a New Jersey diner, the answer is obvious. Sort of. Paul Haley, 38, a father of two, says women look at him when he walks down the street with his kids. "I think it's admiration," he says. Adam Wolff, also 38—with two kids and one on the way—ponders what it means to be a man. "Is my man-ness about being the breadwinner or being a good father to my kids or something else?" Michael Gerber, 36, father of a 7-month-old, asks, "Do you mean, Do we feel whipped?"

"I'm probably a little whipped," shrugs Lee Roberts, 45. He's a part-time copy editor, married to a full-time journalist, who has stayed home for nine years to raise their two children. "There are definitely some guys who look at me and think, 'What's up with him?' Do I care? Well, I guess I do a little because I just mentioned it," he says. Haley speaks up to reassure him: "Kids remember, man. All that matters is that you're there. Being there is being a man."

But what does it mean, exactly, to be a man these days? Once upon a Darwinian time, a man was the one spearing the woolly mammoth. And it wasn't so long ago that a man was that strong and silent fellow over there at the bar with the dry martini or a cold can of beer—a hardworking guy in a gray flannel suit or blue-collar work shirt. He sired children, yes, but he drew the line at diapering them. He didn't know what to expect when his wife was expecting, he didn't review bottle warmers on his daddy blog, and he most certainly didn't participate in little-girl tea parties. Today's dads plead guilty to all of the above—so what does that make them?

As we fuss and fight over the trials and dilemmas of American mothers, a quiet revolution is occurring in fatherhood. "Men today are far more involved with their families than they have been at virtually any other time in the last century," says Michael Kimmel, author of *Manhood in America: A Cultural History*. In the late 1970s, sociologists at the University of Michigan found that the average dad spent about a third as much time with his kids as the average mom did. By 2000, that was up to three-fourths. The number of stay-at-home fathers has tripled in the past 10 years. The Census counts less than 200,000, but those studying the phenomenon say it's probably 10 times that number. Fathers' style of parenting has changed too. Men hug their kids more, help with homework more, tell kids they love them more. Or, as sociologist Scott Coltrane of the University of California, Riverside, says, "Fathers are beginning to look more like mothers."

Many dads are challenging old definitions of manliness. "Masculinity has traditionally been associated with work and work-related success, with competition, power, prestige, dominance over women, restrictive emotionality—that's a big one," says Aaron Rochlen, an associate professor of psychology at the University of Texas who studies fatherhood and masculinity. "But a good parent needs to be expressive, patient, emotional, not money oriented." Though many fathers still cleave to the old archetype, Rochlen's study finds that those who don't are happier. Other research shows that fathers who stop being men of the old mold have better-adjusted children, better marriages and better work lives—better physical and mental health, even. "Basically," says Rochlen, "masculinity is bad for you."

So are sugar doughnuts and beer bongs, and men hate to let go of those too. Women forced the revolution by staging one of their own: in the 1970s they began storming into the workforce, making it harder for men to shirk child care. What's more, they showed their sons that it's possible to both work and parent. Economic forces were at work as well: for the entire 20th century, every successive generation of American men could expect to do better financially than their dads—that is, until Generation X. According to a study by the Pew Charitable Trusts, the median income for a man in his 30s in 2004 was 12% lower than it was in 1974, once adjusted for inflation. Men were forced to relinquish sole-breadwinner status for their households to stay afloat.

But how to forge a new idea of manhood for this brave new two-income world? Hollywood hasn't been much help. From Michael Keaton in the 1983 movie *Mr. Mom* to Adam Sandler in *Big Daddy* (1999) to Eddie Murphy in *Daddy Day Care* (2003), the sight of a man caught in the act of parenting has been a reliable laugh getter—always a good indicator of what the culture considers uncomfortable material. For every *Pursuit of Happyness*, there's a movie like this summer's *Knocked Up*, which plays not so much as a tribute to fatherhood as an effort by men to convince themselves that fatherhood is all right—and the movie's happy ending is the least plausible thing about it. One show at least managed to capture the tension: What were those seven seasons of *The Sopranos* about if not a man fighting to reconcile the tender pangs of a caring, new-style father with the old-school masculine ideals of violence and stoicism—not to mention the psychological damage wreaked on him by his own old-school father?

Society hasn't made it easy for newly evolved dads to feel manly either. In Rochlen's study of stay-at-home dads, those who scored low on measures of traditional masculinity professed higher degrees of happiness in their roles—as well as in their marriages, with their children and with their health. But even they worried about how the rest of the world viewed their choice—with some reason. "There's definitely a stigma out there," says Rochlen. "The dads tell stories about mothers on the playground looking at them like they're child molesters or losers."

Ironically, dads who take on parenting roles once considered emasculating may simply be responding to nature. Studies have shown that men experience hormonal shifts during their female partner's pregnancy. A man's testosterone level drops after settling down to marriage and family, perhaps in preparation for parenthood, as the male hormone is thought to be incompatible with nurturing behavior. In one study, for example, men with lower amounts of testosterone were willing to hold baby dolls for a longer period of time than those with a higher count. In another, the very act of holding dolls lowered testosterone.

More evidence of nature's intent to design men as active parents might be seen in the effects of involved fathering on children. Given the politically charged debates over same-sex unions and single parenting, it is perhaps not surprising that the richest area in the nascent field of fatherhood research is in the results of fathers' absence. David Popenoe of Rutgers University has pointed to increased rates of juvenile delinquency, drug abuse and other problems among children raised without a male parent present. Research on the unique skills men bring to parenting is sparse but intriguing. Eleanor Maccoby of Stanford University has found that fathers are less likely than mothers to modify their language when speaking to their children, thus challenging their kids to expand vocabulary and cognitive skills. Fathers also tend to enforce rules more strictly and systematically in reaction to children's wrongdoing, according to educational psychologist Carol Gilligan. "Having a father isn't magic," says Armin Brott, author of seven books about fatherhood, "but it really does make a difference for the kids."

When men take on nontraditional roles in the home and family, it also makes a difference to the marriage. Coltrane of UC Riverside and John Gottman at the University of Washington found in separate studies that when men contribute to domestic labor (which is part and parcel of parenting), women interpret it as a sign of caring, experience less stress and are more likely to find themselves in the mood for sex. This is not to say that more involved fathering has erased marital tensions or that it hasn't introduced new ones. Dads admit they get fussed over for things moms do every day. "Sometimes you're treated like a dog walking on its hind legs—'Oh, look, he can do laundry!'" says Jim O'Kane, 47, a father of two in Blackstone, Mass. And some women resent ceding their role as top parent. When her daughter fell down at a birthday party, Amy Vachon, 44, of Watertown, Mass., recalls that the girl ran crying all the way across the room—to her husband Marc. "I admit it hurt at the time," she says, "mostly because I wondered what everyone thought. There's such a high standard in society for the good mother."

> *More evidence of nature's intent to design men as active parents might be seen in the effects of involved fathering on children. Given the politically charged debates over same-sex unions and single parenting, it is perhaps not surprising that the richest area in the nascent field of fatherhood research is in the results of fathers' absence.*

It's a slippery slope: a recent Pew survey found that increasingly, parents rank their relationships with their kids as more important than their relationship with their spouse. Just as interesting, they rank their job dead last. That most masculine of traits—the ability to go out into the world and bring home a buck—is receding in importance for the men of Generation X. Men's rates of labor-force participation have dropped from just above 90% in 1970 to just above 80% in 2005. Almost a third of young fathers (32%) say they dedicate more time to their children, while 28% say they devote more time to their jobs.

Big employers are beginning to catch on. Deloitte & Touche, Pricewaterhouse-Coopers, Xerox and IBM are urging family-friendly benefits for their male employees and touting them to male recruits. California recently became the first state to guarantee paid time off for new dads. But the U.S. still lags far behind other countries: only 12% of U.S. corporations offer paid leave for fathers of new babies (the U.S. Family and Medical Leave Act enables workers in large companies to take up to 12 weeks off, but that time is unpaid), while dads in 65 other countries are guaranteed paid paternity or parental leave; 31 countries offer 14 weeks of it or more. At companies that offer and encourage paternity leave, participation is high. KPMG reports that 80% of eligible workers have taken paternity leave since it was first offered in 2002. Still, more than half of working men say they would not take paternity leave even if it was offered, most saying they could not afford it, others fearing it would harm their careers—the same complaints long made by working women.

Today's fathers aren't the men their own fathers were but only if you insist that the nature of masculinity doesn't change—that it's a biological fact and not a mutable cultural construct. The new fathers are creating a new ideal of masculinity. It's not as Mad Men cool, but it is healthier. "The emerging and evolving norms of fatherhood and masculinity challenge men to be a different kind of guy," says Rochlen. "But on the positive side, it gives them new opportunity to embrace and enact these dimensions that are good for them and good for their families." It's even good for their emotional health. Coltrane says fatherhood is proving a "safe pathway" for men to develop and explore their nurturing side. "It's not considered wimpy or gay to hug your daughter," he adds. That's something we can all embrace.

4

Adoption and the Changing Face of Families

(Getty Images)

Jamie Lieberman (left) of New York City, cries as she holds her adopted son Theo, 2, an orphan originally from Ethiopia, after he received American citizenship on November 18, 2010, at the US Citizenship and Immigration Services offices in New York City. Eighteen children, originally from Haiti, Ethiopia, China, and other countries, were sworn in as citizens with their American adopted parents standing by in a ceremony at the New York headquarters of USCIS.

Multiple Approaches to Adoption and Building Families

By Paul McCaffrey

In 2007, according to statistics compiled by the US Department of Health and Humans Services (HHS), out of the 73.76 million children under the age of eighteen living in the United States, a total of around 1.78 million—almost 2.5 percent—were adopted. Though each of these children has a unique story as to how they came to their new families, most adoptions fall into one of three major categories. In 2007, about 38 percent of adoptees were placed through private/independent domestic adoption. In this variation, American children are adopted through a private, nongovernmental agency. Another 37 percent of adoptions occurred through the foster care system. These involve American children who were orphaned or removed from their homes, made wards of the state, and found a foster family willing to care for them. Finally, about 25 percent were international adoptions, in which US families take in children from overseas.

There are two principal types of private/independent domestic adoptions: "open" and "closed." Throughout much of the twentieth century, closed adoptions predominated. The central features of a closed adoption are the metaphorical wall that separates the birth mother and the larger birth family from the adoptive family throughout the process, and the wall that is erected between the birth mother and the child once the former gives up custody. In a closed adoption, the identities of the birth mother and the adoptive family are kept from one another and only the most basic information is exchanged. The birth mother rarely has any influence in determining who will adopt her child, and matching children to prospective families is left largely to social workers employed by the adoption agencies. Upon relinquishing the child, the birth mother in large measure gives up all ties to that child. Often the adoption records are sealed so that even when children reach adulthood, they may not be able to track down their birth families.

Since approximately the 1980s, closed adoptions have fallen out of favor and open adoptions have become the norm. Open adoptions are mostly arranged between birth mothers and adoptive families. They are regulated by the state and federal governments, and facilitated by private attorneys and adoption agencies. Open adoptions are not a recent innovation, but rather are something of a return to form. During the 1920s, for example, some women ran ads in newspapers searching for parents to raise their children. In the modern era of open adoptions, the birth mother tends to determine who will adopt the child, often after sifting through applications from prospective parents. Once the adoption goes through, the birth mother and the larger birth family may or may not maintain a relationship with the child and the adoptive family in the years ahead.

The shift from closed to open adoptions reflects changes in both numbers and attitudes. Thanks to accessible birth control and evolving family structures—the rise in single motherhood, for example—fewer newborns are being put up for adoption. In 1970, 175,000 newborn babies were given up. In 2002, by contrast, that number had declined to less than seven thousand. Newborns are the most sought-after demographic among prospective adoptive parents, and the high demand coupled with the diminished supply has created a seller's market that serves to empower the birth mother.

Thanks to such developments, American birth mothers have had much more influence in adoption proceedings in the 2010s than in the past, and in certain cases are even given the prerogative of changing their minds. The adoptive family, on the other hand, is responsible for covering the cost of the process and, since many adoption agencies are for-profit concerns, frequently pays a premium. This is a change from foster child adoptions, which are handled through government agencies and are much less expensive.

In terms of attitudes, the various stakeholders in a given adoption—the birth family, the adoptive family, and adoption officials—have come to recognize that the child may have an interest, both psychologically and otherwise, in knowing his or her genetic and familial history and even in forging bonds with blood relatives. That is not to say, however, that there is a consensus in favor of open adoptions. Indeed, many prospective adoptive parents, wary of a potentially intrusive birth family and the complications such lingering attachments could cause, opt instead for international adoptions, where there are fewer prospects for such entanglements.

There are numerous variations on both open and closed adoptions, so there is not one typical model. Sometimes, the adopting family is not composed of strangers. According to 2007 statistics, in a good many cases—about 41 percent of private domestic adoptions—the adopting parents included a relative of the adoptee. Hence, a sizeable proportion of private/independent domestic adoptees are brought up by relatives if not their birth family.

In a foster care situation, the foster parents are not the child's legal guardians. That role is played by the state. In exchange for caring for the child, the foster family receives a stipend from the government. In general, an orphan's stay with a foster family is a temporary one, rarely lasting longer than five years and often far less. In 37 percent of American adoptions in 2007, the foster parents decided to officially adopt the child. This is accomplished through public agencies rather than private ones. On the whole, the average age of foster care adoptees skews older than other forms of adoptions. As with other domestic adoptions, relatives of the child are members of a large share of the adopting families. About 23 percent of foster children adopted in 2007 were related to their new parents.

Historically speaking, international adoption in the United States is a recent innovation that only commenced in earnest at the conclusion of World War II. Faced with thousands of war orphans in Europe and Asia, American authorities began airlifting many back to the United States to be adopted by American families. Similar airlifts occurred during the Korean War, Fidel Castro's communist take-over of Cuba, and the Vietnam conflict. The situation in South Korea, in particular, proved an important moment in the growing prominence of international adoption. Inspired by a 1955 presentation about the plight of Korean orphans of American military personnel, Bertha and Harry Holt, a couple from Oregon, adopted eight children from South Korea. The publicity they generated persuaded others to in-quire about adopting themselves, and soon the Holts were flying back planeloads of Korean orphans to unite with families in the United States.

At the time, such forms of international adoption ran counter to the accepted wisdom of adoption professionals. Up until that point, the social workers respon-sible for facilitating adoptions believed it was important to match children with families from similar religious, cultural, and ethnic backgrounds. Efforts were even made to find adoptees who "looked" like members of their prospective families. Commenting on such attitudes against the people like the Holts, the Nobel Prize–winning author Pearl Buck remarked, "The real barrier to adoption of mixed-blood children was not that no one wanted them, but that adoption practice demanded child and adoptive parents [should] match."

As such selection criteria fell somewhat out of favor in the post–World War II era, fewer and fewer American children were being put up for adoption. So while the headlines generated by the warzone airlifts may have been short-lived and the publicity only temporary, there still existed a demand for adoptees that could not be filled domestically, and prospective parents were inclined to expand their search overseas.

In the years since, the tide of overseas adoptions has ebbed and flowed, reaching its high mark in 2004, when 22,884 children, hailing from more than ninety differ-ent countries, were taken in by American families. As the global economy soured, that number fell considerably, with fewer than ten thousand international adop-tions counted in 2011. Since the 1950s, Asia has continued to play a major role in overseas adoptions, with China and South Korea, and to a lesser extent Cambodia and Vietnam, taking center stage. Beginning in the 1980s, Latin American children became a larger presence, with Guatemalans growing especially numerous in the 2000s. Following the lifting of the Iron Curtain in Eastern Europe and the subse-quent demise of the Soviet Union in the late 1980s and early 1990s, children from those nations started coming to the United States. Children from Haiti and Ethio-pia, too, have featured prominently in international adoptions.

One of the main criticisms leveled against international adoptions is the poten-tial for corruption and abuse. The overseas adoption industry is not well regulated and oversight tends to be lax, opening the door to malfeasance. As John Seabrook observed in the *New Yorker* (10 May 2010), "Over the years, both a legal and an underground economy have sprung up around international adoption. The dividing line between an ethical adoption and a baby-buying scam generally falls on the issue of whether the birth mother has been coerced into giving up her child." A common pattern has recurred in a number of countries, wherein, according to Seabrook, "A nation opens its borders; adoptions proliferate; corruption creeps in; there is a scandal; the borders close." Not all incidents develop in the sending nation either. In 2010, for example, Russia suspended adoptions to the United States over concerns about the treatment Russian-born orphans were receiving in the United States.

Many overseas adoptions—and many domestic ones—are transracial in composition, pairing parents with children from different racial backgrounds. The 2000 US Census projected that about one in six adopted children were being raised in a transracial environment. The overwhelming majority of transracial adoptions involve placing a child of color with white parents.

Adoption professionals worried about such arrangements in past generations, and while their thinking has fallen out of favor, their concerns were not entirely unjustified. Though US adoption law stipulates that the adoption process must be colorblind, studies show that adoptive children, especially those of African descent who are raised by families from different racial backgrounds, report struggling with feelings of alienation more so than their nontransracial peers. An analysis conducted by the Evan B. Donaldson Adoption Institute found that "minority children adopted by white parents are likely to express a desire to be white, and black transracial adoptees have higher rates of behavioral problems than Asian or Native American children adopted transracially; they also exhibit more problems than biracial or white adoptees, or the biological children of adoptive parents," Jeninne Lee-St. John commented in *Time* (27 May 2008). The concerns raised by such studies suggest that transracial families would do well to acknowledge the underlying racial complexity and build structures and relationships that keep the adopted child connected to his or her heritage.

US Census data from 2010 revealed an emerging trend in American adoptions: despite considerable prejudice in some quarters and legal barriers in many states, same-sex couples are adopting children in growing numbers. According to these figures, of the 115,064 same-sex households with children, about 16 percent, or 18,400, were bringing up one or more adopted children. Though the statistics vary somewhat from one source to another, indications are that the rate of adoption among same-sex couples tripled between 2000 and 2009.

The ease with which same-sex couples can adopt varies from state to state. Though Utah and Mississippi are the only two states to prohibit these adoptions outright, most other states give preference to married couples, and since most states do not permit or recognize same-sex marriage or civil unions, it is much harder for same-sex couples to adopt domestically, leading many to look overseas. The majority of domestic adoption agencies do accept applications from homosexual couples, however, and about four out of ten have facilitated same-sex adoptions. Of domestic same-sex adoptions, about one-third were open, meaning the birth mother or family approved the match.

A fairly new development of the twenty-first century, adoption by same-sex couples is controversial in many sectors, with large segments of the population opposed to the practice. Much of the resistance has a religious basis, with many objecting to the violation of traditional values represented by same-sex couples adopting children. However, over the past generation, opposition to same-sex couples adopting—and to same-sex marriage—has been declining rapidly. As it is a relatively new development, there is not a wealth of data analyzing adoption by same-sex couples and its impact on their children over the course of their lives. Nevertheless, though families consisting of same-sex couples face elevated levels of discrimination, most research thus far suggests that children raised in same-sex households fare just as well as those brought up in more traditional environments.

Adoption in the United States covers a broad array of relationships and demographics. Domestic and overseas, open and closed, foster care, interfamily, and same-sex adoptions—all compose a broad and complex spectrum. Further adding to the nuance is a form of adoption that is exceedingly common but not generally counted in the statistics—stepparent adoptions. In these cases, a stepmother or stepfather officially becomes a legal guardian of the spouse's child. Though in its composition and complications, each adoption is singular, they are all motivated by the desire to form a family. Thus, even with their differences, all adoptions have that element in common.

Modern Family

By Meryl Gordon
Ladies Home Journal, August 2010

After the death of her husband, Marilyn Berger found happiness in a surprising new role. The 74-year-old, who never had kids of her own, is raising Danny, an 8-year-old orphan from the streets of Ethiopia.

Veteran journalist Marilyn Berger is not by nature an impulsive person. Her friends describe her as "measured," "very thoughtful," "an intellectual." Yet Berger, now 74, has fallen deeply, passionately—and instantly—in love twice in her life, with two strong-willed males who could not be more different from each other.

The first time around the magic moment happened when Berger, then a globe-trotting diplomatic correspondent for NBC, found herself fixed up with Don Hewitt, the brash creator and executive producer of CBS's *60 Minutes.* They hit it off from the moment he called to make a first date—to the point where Hewitt inquired, "If it works out on Thursday, can we have dinner on Friday and Saturday, too?" By the end of that 1976 weekend Berger had found her life's companion. "He was a really good-looking guy, full of vitality—he laughed a lot," Berger recalls. "We went out for Chinese food and my fortune cookie read: 'You are doomed to be happy in marriage.'"

And indeed she was. Berger, who had been based in Washington, quit her job to be with him. She moved back to New York City, her hometown, and found a new career anchoring public affairs programs. She was 43 when the couple wed (Hewitt was 56), in 1979, a period before the advent of today's fertility technology. "I wanted to be a mother but never connected with the right guy," she says. "By the time I connected it was too late."

She put aside those maternal yearnings for nearly three decades. But a chance encounter far from home—on a dusty Ethiopian street populated by vendors and beggars—upended her well-ordered, adult-centered life. Berger had gone to Addis Ababa in January 2008 to research a magazine article on Rick Hodes, MD, an American physician who works in Mother Teresa's Mission caring for desperately sick children. Chloe Malle, the daughter of Berger's friend Candice Bergen and then a Brown University senior, tagged along on the trip and one afternoon suggested walking from the clinic to their hotel—a mile away.

During that walk they saw a little beggar holding his hand out. "He was looking up, as dirty as he could be in a green T-shirt, with these long eyelashes," Berger recalls. But what really got her attention was the child's back, which was curved in a bizarre hump. Dr. Hodes, an internist now familiar with many third-world illnesses, would later explain to Berger that this deformity signified tuberculosis of the spine. Fatal if left untreated, it is common in Ethiopia but virtually unknown in America. As they walked away, Berger remembers, "I was just haunted by this little boy." Says Malle, "Marilyn had created this entire connection between her and that boy in her mind."

> *Under Ethiopian law, Berger is considered too old to legally adopt the boy, who is believed to be 8 and is now in second grade. But he will live with Berger—permanently.*

Finding Her Son

Back at the mission, Berger immediately told Hodes about the homeless boy with the ill-formed back, which prompted a search. Thanks to word of mouth the boy, Danny, was located and agreed to be examined at the clinic. He told them that he had fled his abusive stepfather and impoverished mother for the streets.

Danny was named a legal ward of Mother Teresa's Mission. Hodes, a single man who has adopted five Ethiopian children, eventually took Danny into his home and made arrangements for him to have spinal surgery in Ghana. "Marilyn saved Danny's life," Hodes says. "Without surgery he'd have died."

Berger, en route to Ethiopia on a reporting trip, stopped over in Ghana to visit Danny after the operation. "I saw him for a few hours and he was very thin," she says. "He had malaria. He was lying there like a sick puppy."

By then she was emotionally hooked. Several months later, when she heard that Hodes was coming to New York City on a fund-raising trip, she asked him to bring Danny for an extended visit with her and Hewitt. Fate then dealt another odd twist: A week after Danny's arrival, Hewitt, who had not been well, went to see a doctor and received a terrible diagnosis: pancreatic cancer.

The summer of 2009 was a trying time for the threesome. Hewitt was dying but opted for upbeat denial, refusing to acknowledge his illness. The couple's friends looked on in wonderment at this strange confluence of events. "We were back and forth to their house as Don got sicker," recalls Joan Ganz Cooney, a friend of Berger's for 30 years. "Marilyn was so happy as a mother. Don was proud of them, looking at the two of them and smiling as they played together. He liked Danny and he'd say, 'What a boy!'"

Hewitt died in August 2009. A grieving Berger buried him, then set about finding a local school that would take Danny. "It was such an incredible blessing to have Danny at a time when there was an enormous hole," says her friend Arlene Alda. Still, Berger agonized over whether she was doing the right thing for Danny, given her age. "I began to think, what would it mean to take in a child? My friends said, 'You're too old!' But my mother lived until she was 101. I feel good. If I can give him 10 years, he'll be 18. I hope I'll live longer than that."

These days Berger has a full household. Robert Fishman, her 24-year-old nephew and a Columbia Journalism School graduate, now lives with them. She has also hired a male student as a "manny" to come in at least twice a week so Danny has men in his daily life.

Raising Danny

Rick Hodes has been designated Danny's legal decision maker and Danny has taken Hodes as his last name. (With D.H. as his initials, Berger notes, he can use Don Hewitt's monogrammed possessions.) Under Ethiopian law, Berger is considered too old to legally adopt the boy, who is believed to be 8 and is now in second grade. But he will live with Berger—permanently. "Danny is still in my life," Hodes explains. "But Marilyn is able to give him such opportunities. I could give him half a mattress. He's in a different world now."

Indeed, Berger took Danny skiing this winter in Aspen and later on a trip to Los Angeles, where he attended a private screening of *How to Train Your Dragon* and he played with Julia Roberts's twins. "I tried to tell him American people don't all live this way," says Berger, "but there he was in a plush screening room eating frozen custard."

A small, lively boy, Danny is grumpy this afternoon when Berger retrieves him from school. His teacher has just chastised him for being too boisterous during a baseball game in Central Park. He loves baseball so much that he has been sleeping with his mitt under his pillow. Berger hugs and comforts him and Danny takes her hand while crossing the street. Soon he is mischievously kicking a ball down the sidewalk. If he bears psychic wounds from his traumatic past, they are not visible. "He never asks, 'What if I had been left there?'" says Berger. "I've offered to take him back to Ethiopia to visit, but he says he wants to stay here."

Berger is keenly aware that Danny came along at a time when she would otherwise be bereft. "I read somewhere that mourning comes in waves," she says. "I have a feeling it's still coming—sometimes I'll see Don's keys, his eyeglasses. We'll be having dinner and I'll think, without Danny I'd be having dinner alone."

Yet life with Danny astonishes her every day with moments of joy. "I am blissed out," says Berger, who transformed Hewitt's old office into a bright bedroom adorned with a Spider-Man comforter and matching rug. "Danny said he wants to call me mom. I told him I can't replace his mother, but I can be his American mother."

Formerly a late sleeper, Berger is now up at 7:30 a.m. to wake Danny. Afternoons find her supervising his piano lessons or playing catch in the park. And rather than go to the opera at night with widowed friends, she's at his bedside reading out loud. She shows me the book of jokes they have been giggling over of late. Her face turns incandescent when she talks about Danny. "Danny is a little Don," she says, "a very large personality even if he is a tiny figure. He does as much for me as I do for him. They say I saved his life, but he has also saved mine."

Berger is the author of This Is a Soul, *a book about Rick Hodes that was published this past April by William Morrow.*

About a Boy

By Adam H. Graham
Advocate, July 15, 2008

Irish actor Johnny O'Callaghan went to Africa to help a friend make a documentary about AIDS orphans—but what he found was his son.

Though neither of them sees it anymore, the visual contrasts between 6-year-old Odin and his adoptive father, Johnny, couldn't be more stark. I'm sitting on the lawn of the Grove, an outdoor Los Angeles shopping center, on a Sunday in May with the two, their friend Jackie, and Charlie, the family dog. Odin has dark brown skin, dangling cornrows, and big eyes that shine like black onyx. He's dressed in cargo shorts, red Crocs, and a matching red checkered shirt. Like many boys his age, he's constantly bounding about, blowing bubbles, petting dogs, and occasionally dancing to the live band playing oldies covers. Tall, with wavy blond hair and cerulean eyes, his dad, Johnny O'Callaghan, is an Irish-born actor who has a recurring role on SciFi Channel's Stargate Atlantis. As Johnny finishes off an ice-cream cone, struggles with Charlie's leash, and keeps one eye on Odin, he talks with me about being a single gay adoptive father. "You learn to multitask pretty quick with this job," he chuckles in his singsong Irish accent.

Johnny adopted Odin from Uganda three years ago when Odin was just 3 and living in the House of Hope Orphanage in Kasese, a village in the foothills of the misty Rwenzori Mountains, which are sometimes called the Mountains of the Moon. Though Johnny had no intentions of ever adopting—particularly without a live-in significant other—the events that brought him to Odin just kind of fell into place. "Going to Uganda was very much last-minute," he said over breakfast at a Hollywood café a week before our trip to the Grove. "My friend Ellen-Ray Hennessy told me she was working on a documentary in Uganda and asked if I'd like to come. I got 10 vaccinations the next day," he recalls, adding that they left on the following Saturday, landed the following Monday, and drove 10 hours to get to the orphanage.

What awaited Johnny would change his life forever. It would also make him question everything he knew about raising kids and force him to confront the idea of what really makes a family. "I always wanted kids but thought I would do it with someone . . . that perfect other person," he says, fiddling with his napkin but never losing eye contact with me. "But I'm a big believer that there's never a right time for anything. You get opportunities, and you either live life or you don't."

Seeing Odin for the first time was one of those opportunities, and, like many adoptive parents, Johnny relied on an instinctive hunch about Odin rather than paperwork or medical records. "I just had this feeling like, God, this is my son. I know it sounds ridiculous, but I instantly had this connection I can't explain," he says.

During a short break from our breakfast interview, Johnny and I walk to the car to let his dog, Charlie, out. "Cute dog," I say. O'Callaghan beams and rolls his eyes. "Charlie here was recently approached by an agent who wanted to cast him in a film," he says, chuckling before finishing his sentence. "They offered to pay us all sorts of money, but it meant Charlie being away from me and Odin for three months. I just couldn't do it because I want Odin to experience family stability."

This kind of loving, tight-knit family-management style—described by Johnny's best friend, actress Caraid O'Brien (another Irish transplant), as "very old-school"—is evident the minute you meet Johnny. You immediately understand his desire to protect Odin (and perhaps Charlie too) from the bad of the world by fostering the individual good within. "Johnny is a thoughtful, kind, generous, and loving parent, and he sees Odin as a reflection of himself," continues O'Brien. "He also believes the quantity of time you spend with your kid is just as important as the quality, so the two meditate together and pray before every meal. Johnny, Odin, and Charlie the dog are an incredibly beautiful and endearing family, and people are struck by that unique beauty. They're head-turners, the three of them."

O'Callaghan had spent time with other kids in the orphanage before he met and "fell in love" with Odin—but none of them spoke to him in the same way. "This one kid, Danny, was a bag of bones left on the doorstep," he says back in the café, periodically turning his head to check up on Charlie, who's happily tied up in the shade outside, greeting each new customer with a spunky little jump. "This kid at the orphanage had serious food issues and did things like eat bananas with the skin on," he continues. "I noticed that Odin would share his food with

Seeing Odin for the first time was one of those opportunities, and, like many adoptive parents, Johnny relied on an instinctive hunch about Odin rather than paper-work or medical records.

him, which I thought was incredible. Here was this little boy who had nothing himself but was able to recognize that others were in need too. And he was only 3."

That selflessness clearly struck O'Callaghan, who began the adoption process shortly after his first encounter with Odin. Adopting the boy involved the Uganda High Court, international lawyers, the FBI, and the U.S. Embassy, and it took nine months to complete, but surprisingly, O'Callaghan's sexuality didn't affect the process. There was no law in Uganda against a single father adopting, and O'Callaghan was never asked about—nor did he disclose—his sexual orientation. Back in the States he was out to the social worker assigned to Odin, and that was no problem either—not that any adversity would have dissuaded him. "Odin shares many traits with his father," says O'Brien. "He has Johnny's generosity, his inner strength, his beauty, his impishness, his charisma, and his determination of spirit. It's obvious that Odin and Johnny are father and son. Their body language and the way they interact clearly show how they are related."

And she's right. It's hard not to feel a certain warmth when watching the two interact on that sunny Sunday afternoon. Their affection is evident to the curious onlookers as Odin tumbles in and out of his dad's arms with an ease rarely seen in biological families, let alone adoptive ones.

Before Johnny came along, Odin was named Benson and spoke only Rwandese. He was born in a village called Kasinga in Uganda along the border of the Congo and Rwanda. "I had to piece together a lot of the information about Odin's family," explains Johnny. "His family or tribe was Tutsi, and I believe his biological mom died of HIV-related causes while giving birth to him. The father [still living] is also HIV-positive. Odin is a little miracle because he's HIV-negative." Like most children born in AIDS-stricken areas of Africa, Odin had his mother's antibodies for the first 18 months of his life and then developed his own and tests HIV-negative.

A lot of people in the orphanage assumed he was HIV-positive, but he hadn't been tested, and O'Callaghan didn't know when he first met him what Odin's serostatus was. "Of course, it wouldn't have mattered to me," he says, "but looking back, it would've been complicated due to the U.S.'s strict visa and immigration policies. As far as I know, America would not have allowed me to bring Odin into the country if he'd been HIV-positive, which is wrong really, because so many kids in the world need better access to medicine."

Though Uganda is one of the few countries in Africa where HIV infections have declined, largely because of the President's Emergency Plan for AIDS Relief's "ABC" approach ("abstinence, be faithful, use condoms"), antiretroviral treatments still reached only about 41% of Ugandans needing them in 2006, according to the World Health Organization.

Johnny is currently in a relationship with the Australian actor Jaason Simmons, who formerly played a lifeguard hunk on Baywatch. Simmons is close to Odin but not exactly a second father. "I tell Odin he has a mom and dad rolled up into one," says Johnny. "Some people have a dad and a dad, or a mom and dad, but Odin got a two-for-one special with me. I joke about it now, but I just don't want people coming in and out of his life," Johnny says, turning serious. "You know, sometimes we go to these really big houses on play dates where they spend hundreds of thousands of dollars on parties, and in the beginning Odin would look at me and say, 'Daddy, I'm OK here. You can leave me now,'" he continues, laughing again. "But seriously, I don't think he quite grasped the concept that a daddy is someone for life and that a family is something that doesn't change. So, yeah, Jaason and I would love to adopt together someday, and if we get there, that's great."

For now, the couple seems to be enjoying the slow pace of things. "It's interesting watching us all adjust," says Simmons, who hadn't really thought about adoption until his 30s but is enjoying creating little traditions with Odin, like going out for pot pies at KFC (their first meal together). "Stability for Odin is the main focus, so we are in no rush with our relationship," he continues. "I know next to nothing about parenthood, but Johnny is a wonderful reference, so I feel I'm on the right track."

Though Johnny and Odin live in a small house in posh Nichols Canyon now, Johnny grew up in the working-class suburbs of Dublin, the third of four children in a mixed Protestant and Catholic household. He always wanted a lot of kids, which is something he remembered during a recent trip to Ireland to have Odin christened. "It was really an excuse to celebrate him in Ireland in a way that my family could understand," explains Johnny. "It was beautiful, and they all fell in love with him straightaway." In many ways it was harder for Johnny's family to accept his sexuality than it was for them to support his adoption. "You know, it took some time, but now my family is very comfortable and supportive of my sexuality. I think my mom and dad are the generation that's been educated by Oprah Winfrey. That woman has had a huge impact throughout the world, even in Ireland. They all watch it, and they learn," he says. "Now, as a gay parent, I want to talk more about it, because we need more stories to normalize the experience of being gay. It's important to Odin and me that we're connecting with other gay families to accomplish this."

Johnny and Odin are involved in a variety of community activities, such as soccer practice and church. "Sometimes being a gay parent in the U.S. makes you feel like you're being observed and have a lot to measure up to," he says. "And when you adopt a child, people seem to think they can say anything they want to about it. I don't understand that. They see brown and white and automatically assume there's no way he's yours. People talk to you like you're doing some random kid a favor. I used to get a lot of 'Where's that kid's mama?' And a few complete strangers came up to me in the grocery store and asked if they could give him a hug or give him some chocolate, which I thought was just weird.

"But sometimes you can look into these things too much or overanalyze the situation," he admits, leaning back in his chair and taking a deep breath. "For me, Odin is my son, not an accessory or a kid that I've helped out in life. He's not an orphan anymore."

Perhaps the most common misconception is that Odin was the only one to benefit from this adoption. "In many ways, I feel like Odin saved me as much as I saved him," Johnny says. "So many people live their lives for themselves only, and I could see myself heading down that same unfulfilling track. Especially being an actor in L.A., the business can make you so self-obsessed," he says, laughing. "It's much more interesting to hear and talk about Odin than it is to hear people tell you for the 20th time about when they worked with Elizabeth Taylor."

The American Adoption Family I Know Of

By Meixin Dai
Translated by Sheng-Wei Wang
ChinaUSFriendship.com, January 11, 2011

In the United States when you see a White couple with a child that has black hair and yellow skin, you need not ask as you know that the child was adopted from the Orient. Our friends Bob (Robert) and Anna adopted before 2004 a baby girl Daniella from Sichuan, China. They were deeply impressed with the smartness, sweetness and cuteness of this Chinese daughter. They felt that she was so lovely that they decided to adopt a second daughter as Daniella's sister for companionship. So, again, they sent in an application to the Ministry of Civil Affairs of the People's Republic of China through the relevant department of the United States and then waited patiently. They often could not contain their excited mood and told us the joy of being parents again. Daniella also prepared herself well to become an elder sister by saying that her sister Sofia was about to come. Well, even a name was chosen.

During the days of this long waiting, the Bob couple became very anxious and worried because they did not receive any information from the adoption agency. They could not help but asking whether there had been any change of China's adoption policy and why it took so long. They recalled that when Daniella was adopted, they waited for only eight or nine months. Indeed, since 2006, the Chinese Government has adjusted the adoption policy of Chinese children by foreign families and imposed more stringent requirements for the qualifications of the adoption families. People with obesity, older than 50 years of age, and unmarried families do not meet the qualifications for adoption; there is also a new requirement for annual income. So, the review time becomes longer.

At the end of 2007, Anna emailed us Sofia's photos. Her childlike look was very cute; the pair of big eyes was just like two black jewels embedded in her tender face and that innocent look in her eyes was as if it was waiting for a mother's embrace. This was the baby girl from Dianjiang Orphanage near Chongqing in the Sichuan Province. American families that adopt Chinese children establish their first impressions and feelings with the children through the photos provided by the Chinese adoption agencies. Before Sofia was taken away to the United States, Bob had already hung the child's magnified photo on the wall at home. The children room of Daniella was also freshly decorated in the expectation of the arrival of the new family member.

Every time they looked at Sofia's sweet little face in the photo, the Bob couple could not wait to lovingly get her home. Finally, after the Spring Festival last year, they received a notice to go to China to complete the formalities. The whole family carried a full set of luggage, flew happily to Sichuan and brought back the eight-month-old little Sofia.

Taking this opportunity, they brought the then four-year-old Daniella back to the Liangping Orphanage in Chongqing, her old home before she was adopted. This orphanage turned the visit into a big happy event, because it was the first time that an adopted child who lived abroad returned to the orphanage for a visit. The yard of the orphanage was decorated with lanterns and streamers, and even personnel who had been transferred out of the orphanage came back especially to see this previous orphan who paid the return visit from the other side of the ocean. The lovely and gracious Daniella showed off her Chinese dance, sang many Chinese and foreign songs, which delighted everyone. It was an exciting and spectacular international party.

Bob and Anna have made videos of the two adoption trips to China, which recorded the birth of the two daughters and were filled with joy and passion. When we were invited to their home as guests, we saw a big map of China hanging on the wall of the living room; they had made a special mark at Chongqing in Sichuan as a significant area. When we were watching the videos, Daniella herself became a narrator; she was very familiar with the subject and made the talk very impressive.

Anna with motherly kindness introduced the different characters of her two daughters. In comparison with finicky, self-willed, sensitive Daniella, Sofia seemed kind of easy-going and independent. Anna said affectionately that she could no longer do without these two girls. Bob said he was very lucky to have two daughters, and his life was satisfied. He said this was their life's work. I listened to them and understood tacitly. Oh, yes, when these adopted Chinese girls became Americans, they left the orphanage

According to reports, in recent years, the total number of Chinese children adopted by American families exceeds 50,000. The New York area alone has about 10,000.

and entered into the warm family of a different country. From being helped to being loved like princesses, the living conditions underwent huge differences. These children were born in China, but lived in the mainstream society as soon as they entered the United States. At the same time their foreign parents accompanied them and came out tirelessly from the mainstream society to participate in various learning activities, such as Chinese language classes on weekends. They have really given much thought to these matters. Thanks to his insistence, today, Bob very impressively can actually read and write Chinese. It is really not an easy job. Anna then gave up her position at the bank and became a full-time mother who with Sofia sends Daniella to school and picks her up every day.

When Daniella told us in a childish tone that she was from Sichuan and adopted to the United States, I did not know why my heart felt some pain while listening to her. Once I went to their home, Daniella pulled a small toy trunk and told us that she was about to take a flight to Chongqing. She held a piece of paper as the ticket and acted as if she was hailing a taxi, entering into the airport, finding the gate; she was as serious as the real thing. I was surprised to see this while I was next to her. Anna called me to the kitchen and told me that a few days ago, Daniella cried and asked why her own mother did not come to see her, or want her. Anna said emotionally: "We had thought about the problem that the kids would care about their biological parentage, but did not expect it to come so early." Ah, a five-year-old young child already started looking for her roots! In the future, there would be a longer way to go and more difficult questions to answer. These would often test the adoptive family. I thought that fortunately the adoptive parents were open-minded, started from love and respected the child's independent personality and free will; this kind of problems would not daunt a happy adoptive family.

In fact, adoptive families having kids like Daniella and Sofia are far from rare. According to reports, in recent years, the total number of Chinese children adopted by American families exceeds 50,000. The New York area alone has about 10,000. Last May, we went with the whole Bob and Anna family to the Liberty State Park by the side of the Hudson River in New Jersey to participate in the yearly Chinese Culture Day organized specifically for adoptive families. The event had a variety of programs and activities like traditional Chinese folk dancing, calligraphy, arts and crafts displays, story-telling and tug-of-war competitions. American parents were all happy and almost all adopted children were girls. They dolled themselves up and it was like a holiday scene. Among them there were some mothers who held dearly their disabled girls they adopted and participated in various activities. Strolling in the park, I watched the yellow-skinned, black-eyed children enjoying and playing heartily under the sunshine of the early summer. Their loveliness matched brilliantly the affectionate and happy smiling faces of their American parents. When these little children sang Chinese children's songs and danced under the leadership of the teacher, their parents in the audience eagerly clapped their hands to add to the fun. Seeing the scene at that time, I was deeply moved by this true love in the world that knows no borders.

Daniella who loved singing and dancing was also a performer on the stage. Her parents were busily taking pictures of her and videoed her. It just happened that a Xinhua News Agency reporter came for an interview at this time. Anna introduced her two daughters and said how sad their families felt that the Wenchuan earthquake occurred five days before. Sofia was still young and did not understand what had happened. But Daniella looked at the TV screen; seeing the catastrophe of the homeland, she wept sadly. Hearing the story, we were much moved.

Bob and Anna have always been grateful for the tremendous joy brought by the children to the family. They seemed to have endless love and energy. Bob said that they would like to adopt a disabled child, but the queue was very long; he also said that they intended to adopt another child aged 12 or 13. He heard that the orphans in the orphanage would be placed in the community to make a living on their own when they became fifteen years old; this was very dangerous: what if they encountered bad guys or ran into a triad and learned to do bad things? He said that his ability was limited, but the adoption of a child was to help a child. Daniella interrupted on the side saying: "Why not adopt one younger than Sofia and then I will be the big sister." I did not know what the rules required, but I admired their spirit.

Both Bob and Anna are devoted Christians. Recently they told me that their church activities have switched to a Chinese church. They often prepare presentations and strive to speak in Chinese. Naturally they have also made more Chinese friends. Every time we met, Bob often took out the big Chinese-English dictionary brought back from China and asked many questions trying to understand how to check the difficult words and the precise meanings of the phrases that had special Chinese characteristics. Sometimes it was really not easy to answer them. They fell in love with China and learned Chinese culture not due to professional or business needs, but entirely because of the two daughters from China. They themselves are already half Chinese.

Bless you, the children from China in the American adoption families and the American parents who adopted Chinese orphans!

January 11, 2009

Meixin Dai was born in Suzhou, China. She made accounting her profession. She went to the United States in 1986 to study and often lived in New York City. In recent years, she has published her observations and thoughts based mostly on true stories in a series of essays on the Chinese media located in China and the US. She uses her simple and exquisite writings to reflect the customs abroad, the colorful life and her care and love. They are extolled by readers. "The American adoption family I know of" published this month is one of her many touching essays that would help to enhance the nice friendship between the people at the two ends of the global village.

Same & Different

By Rosetta Eun Ryong Lee
Independent School, Winter 2011

Supporting Transracially Adopted Asian Americans

"Transracial adoption is a reality of contemporary American life," note the authors of a recent landmark study. "Since 1971, parents in this country have adopted nearly a half-million children from other countries, the vast majority of them from orphanages throughout Asia, South America, and, most recently, Africa. Additional tens of thousands of multiracial families have been formed during this period with boys and girls adopted from foster care, with the rate of such adoptions from the domestic system growing from 10.8 percent in 1995, when there were about 20,000 total adoptions, to 15 percent in 2001, when there were over 50,000. In the vast majority of these cases—domestic and international—children of color have been adopted by Caucasian parents."

Given these numbers, it's no surprise that a significant and increasing number of transracially adopted children are enrolled in independent schools. And yet, there is very little in the research and literature that specifically addresses how schools can help these individuals form a positive identity. Of particular concern is how schools work to support children adopted from Asian countries. Since nearly half of all foreign-born adopted children in 2009 are from Asia, and one in ten Korean American citizens entered the United States through adoption, transracial adoption is an increasingly significant Asian American issue.

In 2009, the Evan B. Donaldson Adoption Institute published its study of identity development in adults who were adopted as children. Previous research involving identity development of adopted individuals focused primarily on the experiences of children and youth. The institute's study offers us a more complete perspective of how these adults have integrated "adoptedness" and race/ethnicity into the whole that comprises their sense of identity. The study included 468 adults—179 of whom were born in South Korea and adopted by white parents, and 156 of whom were U.S.-born whites adopted by white parents. Comparing the responses of these two groups resulted in important findings and recommendations that specifically address the challenges and opportunities faced by individuals transracially adopted from Asia—and included some clear lessons for schools.

The School Experience of Transracially Adopted Children from Asia

The central findings of the Donaldson Adoption Institute's study add macroscopic understanding to existing research and literature about racial/ethnic identity development and transracial adoption. These resources combined provide a significant window into the struggles transracially adopted students of Asian origin face in school.

Adoption is an increasingly significant aspect of identity for adopted people as they grow up, and remains significant even when they are adults

Regarding their adoption status, Asian-born students who have white parents don't have the same privilege of invisibility as white students who are adopted. Rather, they face an immediate reminder of their adopted status every time they enter a new school or new environment within a school. Peers, and even teachers, often ask questions that have a profound impact on these students. These questions, such as—Are you adopted? Is that your real mom/dad? Where are you from? What are you? How do you speak English so well?—may be asked out of a sense of innocent curiosity. But for transracially adopted children, they are more often than not injurious.

These micro-aggressions are brief and commonplace verbal, behavioral, or environmental indignities that communicate hostile, derogatory, or negative slights and insults, whether intentional or unintentional. They serve to remind youth that they are adopted and foreign-born, and imply that their relationship to their parents may not be legitimate.

In addition to the impact of innocent but damaging questions, transracially adopted students of Asian origin face a host of other school-related issues. For instance, they are more often than not subject to unfairly high academic and social expectations stemming from the myth of the model minority and the quiet and submissive Asian. At some point in their school careers, they are given assignments that require background information and connection to biological roots (family tree, ancestors, genetics, baby pictures, etc.). In addition, in independent schools, they are subject to admissions materials that presume the same race of parents and children.

Race/ethnicity is an increasingly significant aspect of identity for those adopted across race and culture

Although the Korean-born participants in the Donaldson Adoption Institute study reported a stronger sense of ethnic identity than their white counterparts, they were also less likely to have a strong sense of belonging to their ethnic group. Other research describes the "between two worlds" status of many transracially adopted Asians. Many report not feeling a part of the white world as a result of the physical attributes that make them stand out as different, and thus they were compelled to connect with their "Asianness." And yet, many also report not being part of the Asian world because they do not have the same language and cultural knowledge necessary to feel a full sense of belonging or worth. Indeed, many transracially adopted individuals report feeling a full sense of belonging only with other transracially adopted people.

Schools inadvertently create uniquely awkward or painful situations when lessons of Asian history or culture are not facilitated with proper sensitivity. Transracially adopted students of Asian origin report feeling "stared at" by peers or asked to corroborate or refute "the Asian perspective." As a young woman in one study stated: "It's always when they're talking about Korea. If [classmates] say something wrong, they would ask 'Michelle, is that right?' And I'd answer, 'I don't know.' It's like I'm ashamed. . . . I'm Korean [by birth] but I grew up in this white society. . . . I just feel really ashamed that I can't answer their questions."

The all-too-common stress of isolation and difference compounded by the burden of being a "spokesperson" for one's group is difficult for any student of color. When the student shares little to no cultural, historical, or language background with his/her racial/ethnic group, there are additional feelings of inadequacy and shame.

Coping with discrimination is an important aspect of coming to terms with racial/ethnic identity for adoptees of color

In the Institute study, 80 percent of Korean-born respondents reported racial discrimination from strangers; 75 percent reported racism from classmates; 48 percent reported negative racial experiences due to interactions with childhood friends; and, sadly, 39 percent reported race-based discrimination from teachers.

Quite often, especially when transracially adopted youth live in mostly white communities, much of the racial discrimination isn't directed toward the individuals. Nonetheless, the individuals experience negative self-construal as a result. Sometimes, negative stereotypes and jokes arise about Asians in general or other people of color. When individuals protest or express discomfort, perpetrators often explain, "It's not directed towards you. We're just talking about Asians." Although the intention of these responses is to profess to seeing the person as an individual, to transracially adopted youth, these comments are an affirmation of two debilitating facts: they do not fully belong to their racial/ethnic group, and the community around them believes the same negative racial stereotypes portrayed by much of the media.

> *Regarding their adoption status, Asian-born students who have white parents don't have the same privilege of invisibility as white students who are adopted. Rather, they face an immediate reminder of their adopted status every time they enter a new school or new environment within a school.*

An additional problem is that transracially adopted youth often find little comfort or training in how to cope with these racial assaults from their white parents, teachers, or peers. Most parents of color train their children to recognize, cope with, and respond to racial stereotypes and harassment. At the very least, these parents can speak from experience about what racial encounters are like, thus giving legitimacy to the strategies they suggest to their children. But white parents, teachers, and peers attempting to help adopted children in such situations generally don't have the resources or experience to be of help. In fact, the typical approach to comforting transracially adopted youth in these situations—saying, for instance, "Just ignore them," or "I totally understand what you're going through"—tends to silence youth into thinking racial discrimination is something to be dealt with on one's own—and, therefore, further increases the feelings of difference and isolation.

What Schools Can Do to Help

These basic findings make it clear that transracially adopted children need our concerted effort in order to thrive in schools. There are many steps schools can take, including the following.

Acknowledge the realities of adoption

As with any important issue in school, the first step is to acknowledge the issue. To this end, schools need to help teachers, administrators, parents, and students understand the realities of adoption—for all adopted children, but especially for transracially adopted children. The next step is to work together as a community to erase stigmas and stereotypes, minimize discrimination, and provide adopted children with more opportunities for positive development.

Consciously support the positive racial/ethnic identity of students

In particular, the Donaldson Adoption Institute study highlights how, for transracially adopted children, "positive racial/ethnic identity development is most effectively facilitated by 'lived' experiences such as travel to [their] native country, attending racially diverse schools, and having role models of their own race/ethnicity." The study's respondents appreciated cultural celebrations and other opportunities to learn about their racial and ethnic heritage, but these are singular events and do not offer a wholesale solution to the struggles transracially adopted people face.

As one youth states in a different study: "What's hard for me is that [Korean Culture Camp] takes place only once a year! I finally get to go to a place where I feel safe, where I feel comfortable, where I feel like I'm around people who understand me. . . . If I had been able to grow up that way, and if I always had those role models to say, 'You're Korean—be proud of yourself,' instead of always feeling 'I'm American—I don't know what that means,' I think I would be a little more confident."

Identify and confront micro-aggressions

All educators need to understand that transracially adopted students constantly face micro-aggressions. Since the research reveals that most adults and students in school are not even aware of this fact, it behooves schools to raise awareness. For instance, teachers can be trained on the accumulated impact created when students are repeatedly asked to represent "their group" in the classroom. They can also be trained to facilitate the conversations that arise when peers ask a student to speak as a representative of his or her group.

The goal is not only to help reduce these micro-aggressions, but also to help transracially adopted students deal with them. In addition, they need support as they seek to negotiate difficult situations in schools so that their identity as an adopted person is neither ignored nor highlighted as a deficit.

Psychologist April Harris-Britt describes training to deal with the realities of race and racism as "Parental Race Socialization." Schools can augment this parental effort by providing "School Race Socialization." Harris-Britt's studies suggest that a certain amount of this training is necessary to ensure resilience through painful encounters of prejudice and discrimination. At the same time, her research also suggests that too much of this training—defensive by definition—could result in youth approaching life in a white-majority society with fatalism and suspicion. Racial pride, on the other hand, is something that can be taught in abundance without negative side effects. Whether by parents or role models of the same race/ethnicity, this socialization is clearly a necessity in the transracially adopted youth's life.

Provide affinity group space that's welcoming to transracially adopted students

As diversity in schools increases, more and more schools find value in offering affinity groups for students. Students adopted from Asian countries can benefit from an Asian American affinity group. It is also important to ensure that this group welcomes everyone, regardless of cultural or language knowledge or access to a parent with such knowledge. Better yet, schools can provide a space specifically for students who are transracially adopted.

Focus on developing a welcoming, diverse culture in the school

Schools can—and should—provide support, role models, information, and the understanding that, when it comes to race/ethnicity and discrimination, they need to supplement parental efforts and provide a safer climate for all. A diverse student body and faculty/staff population can provide mirrors of experience and positive role models for transracially adopted students. Affinity groups can offer a space where experiences and strategies are shared and discussed. Beyond diversity and safe spaces, however, schools must help raise the critical consciousness for all. The discussion must go beyond how people of color can cope with prejudice and discrimination and venture into what these acts of prejudice and discrimination are and how so many of us perpetrate them overtly or implicitly. When there is a common community understanding and commitment to undo bias, transracially adopted students no longer carry alone the burden of needing to know how to recognize and combat acts of racial/ethnic aggression. Rather, these actions become a community charge.

Consider school publications from the perspective of adopted students

Admission brochures and other school publications are designed to accurately put forth the best possible image of the school. But if there are no images of transracially adopted children and no references to such families in any publication, an unintended message of indifference is being sent to such students and their families.

One Educator's Perspective

I am a teacher and Asian and Pacific Island Affinity Group co-facilitator at Seattle Girls' School (Washington). We have 117 girls, over 40 percent of whom are girls of color, and many of these girls are Asian American. A vast majority of these Asian American students are multiracial or transracially adopted. As a Korean-born immigrant with two Korean parents, I attempt to provide students with a positive role model, create a safe space where they can openly discuss challenges, and teach them a little about what it is to be a confident Asian woman in a society that does not always make it easy. I will never know what it's like to have white parents and navigate the world with this compass, but I can show them full acceptance for exactly who they are: Asian, adopted, culturally white, and more. With the school's anti-bias core belief that "it is fundamental to understand and address issues of difference and oppression," we attempt to have dialogue in the classroom and as a whole school about the realities of the world as well as provide students critical thinking skills and practical tools to change the world for the better.

Given this context—and given the location of Seattle, Washington, a racially diverse city with a large transracial adoption community—the transracially adopted students at my school have a better shot at establishing positive self-identity. As one of my students said to me, "I like it here—you don't get stereotyped. . . . I like being Asian, and I like being adopted. . . . I like that my parents aren't the same race as me, because it's like we're special."

Not every transracially adopted student will attain this enlightened state of self-awareness, and the school and I will continue to stumble and make mistakes as we try to support these girls well. However, doing right by them is a critical challenge and opportunity we welcome. I invite your schools to continue to do great work as you open your approach and practices to include as fully as possible these vibrant, truly multicultural, multiethnic, and multiracial families that constitute a growing part of the norm of the American family.

Rosetta Eun Ryong Lee is a teacher, professional outreach specialist, and Asian and Pacific Island Affinity Group co-facilitator at Seattle Girls' School (Washington).

References

"Adoption Statistics." Child Welfare Information Gateway. Web. 10 Sept. 2010. www.childwelfare.gov/systemwide/statistics/ adoption.cfm#inter.

Gay, G. (1999). "Ethnic Identity Development and Multicultural Education." In R. Sheets, E. R. Hollins (Eds.), *Racial and Ethnic Identity in School Practices: Aspects of Human Development*. Mahwah, NJ: Lawrence Erlbaum Associates.

Harris-Britt, A., Valrie, C. Kurtz-Costes, B., & Rowley, S. J. (2007). "Perceived Racial Discrimination and Self-Esteem in African American Youth: Racial Socialization as a Protective Factor," *Journal of Research on Adolescence,* 17.

Kim, J. (1981). *Processes of Asian American Identity Development: A Study of Japanese American Women's Perceptions of Their Struggle to Achieve Positive Identities as Americans of Asian Ancestry.* Unpublished doctoral dissertation, University of Massachusetts.

Lee, S. J. (1996). *Unravelingthe "Model Minority" Stereotype: Listening to Asian American Youth.* New York and London: Teachers College Press.

McGinnis, Hollee et al. *Beyond Culture Camp: Promoting Healthy Identity Formation in Adoption.* 2009 November. New York, NY: Evan B. Donaldson Adoption Institute.

Mullen, M. (1995). "Identity development of Korean Adoptees." In W. L. Ng, S. Chin, J. S. Moy, & G. Y. Okihiro (Eds.), *Reviewing Asian America: Locating Diversity.* Pullman, WA: Washington State University Press.

Palmer, J. D. (2001). "Korean Adopted Young Women: Gender Bias, Racial Issues, and Educational Implications." In C. C. Park, A. Lin Goodwin, & S. J. Lee (Eds.), *Research on the Education of Asian Pacific Americans.* Greenwich, CT: Information Age Publishing Inc.

Born Identity

By Kelley Christin
Hyphen Magazine, December 20, 2012

A growing number of Asian adoptees are choosing to adopt children from their birth countries as a way to reclaim their culture.

When Rebecca Eun Hee Viot speaks of her daughter Ruby, her tone expresses a love that clearly transcends words.

"She has basically done what no husband or therapist or boyfriend or girlfriend has ever been able to do," Viot said. "She's basically quieted my heart."

Viot, a Korean adoptee, grew up in the Midwest feeling a disconnect between her US life and her culture of origin. But, through Ruby, her adopted Korean daughter, Viot has filled a void within herself.

Over a half-million children in the United States are adopted, and 60 percent of Americans have either been through the adoption process or know someone who has, according to the Evan B. Donaldson Adoption Institute, a New York–based nonprofit devoted to improving adoption policy and practice.

Once a hushed issue, adoption has become more commonly accepted and practiced over time. Between 1971 and 2001, US citizens adopted 265,677 children from other countries. In the last decade of that period, international adoptions more than doubled from 9,050 to 19,237; girls dominated those adoptions over boys, 64 percent to 36 percent.

The first documented transracial Asian adoptions in the United States date back to the 1900s, but only after World War II did they become more pervasive. Between 1971 and 2001, 156,591 children were adopted from Asia, making it the most popular global region to adopt from (Europe came in a distant second, with less than a third of that figure). In 1990, South Korea dominated US international adoptions; and in 2001, China took the lead.

Today, a growing number of adoptees are adopting children from their birth countries, according to a 2009 study released by the Donaldson Adoption Institute titled "Beyond Culture Camp." Of adoptees polled in the study, 30 percent reported that they had adopted at least one child. In comparison, 3.7 percent of households in 2003 included at least one adopted child, as reported by the US Census Bureau.

These figures may indicate a potential trend: "No one's done that kind of work so we don't know for sure, but if you look at the study, there was a stunning percentage

(Photo by Baii Nguyen)

Korean adoptee Rebecca Eun Hee Viot adopted her daughter, Ruby, from her birth country as a way to connect with her heritage.

of adoptees who adopted," said Adam Pertman, executive director of the Donaldson Adoption Institute.

Asian adoptees can benefit from an expedited adoption process depending on the adoption agency and country they choose. A Korean adoptee, for instance, is still considered a national and, therefore, granted preference in adopting a child from Korea.

When Viot was 6, she left South Korea, her birth country, to live with her adoptive white family in St. Paul, MN. Growing up in the Midwest in the '70s was difficult. Viot and her biological brother, part of an early wave of Korean adoptees in the United States, were the only people of color in her neighborhood. Their family lacked access to resources to learn more about the children's birth country and any relevant cultural differences. Viot's adoptive parents raised her as though she shared their history and experiences.

When Viot was ready to start her own family, adoption wasn't her first choice. But when complications moved Viot and her husband to adopt, Viot naturally looked to Korea: She felt she could better understand an adopted child from her country of origin.

Ruby arrived at Viot's St. Louis Park, MN, home in 2008 as a 9-month-old baby. Since then, Ruby has brought peace to Viot's life and tightened Viot's bonds to her birth country. "I never took a pride in being Korean," Viot said, though she wasn't necessarily ashamed. "I was often confused and sad because I knew I didn't fit in. I just didn't know who I was."

Motivated by her daughter, Viot has begun to explore Korean food (she can now cook kaktugi, bulgogi, japchae and kimchi jigae) and the Korean language (she has learned to read Hangul and aspires to speak it with her biological family). She is also interested in learning Korean drumming and dance through the Korean Heritage House, which recently opened in the Twin Cities; Ruby will be enrolled when she turns 4.

"We're learning together," said Viot, who has founded an Internet forum for parents undergoing the adoption process. I have to stop myself from thinking that just because [Ruby and I] look alike that is enough. I'm still learning about the traditions. I have to do my homework, just like my [friends who are] Caucasian adoptive parents.

Looking alike eliminates one complication that often accompanies international adoption: Most people assume Ruby is Viot's biological child. But Viot anticipates that Ruby may still grapple with cultural and identity issues. She hopes to expose Ruby to her Korean heritage from the outset—something Viot's parents were unable to do for their adopted children.

> *Looking alike eliminates one complication that often accompanies international adoption: Most people assume Ruby is Viot's biological child. But Viot anticipates that Ruby may still grapple with cultural and identity issues.*

"I want my daughter to know from the beginning who she is and why she does some of the things she does and thinks the way she does," Viot said. "There are a lot of things my parents didn't do that I am going to do. I am going to make every effort to learn the language. As her mother, I want her to have less holes to fill in when she's older than all the holes I had."

But Viot knows she cannot shield Ruby from everything: Ruby will grow up with the label of "adoptee." "The day she totally intellectually understands that she is adopted is the day that her self-view will change."

In 1961, at 15 months old, Melinda Matthews met her adoptive family in New Jersey. Despite some challenges, Matthews views her experience as a Korean adoptee in a white family as positive. Unlike Viot, Matthews always had a desire to adopt from her birth country.

"Adopting my daughter didn't feel like baby-buying to me," Matthews said. "It was, ironically, the sole thread from my own adoption that I felt compelled to continue. I absolutely needed to pass on my adoptive heritage; it meant far more to me than continuing my genetic heritage."

An adopted child was someone Matthews could relate to completely, someone she could guide and understand. "Most importantly, I could love full-heartedly and unreservedly, without passing along the twin specters of guilt and gratitude that have haunted me," she said.

Matthews now lives in Plantation, FL, with her three children: two biological children and her youngest daughter, Kimmy, who was adopted from Korea as a 5-month-old.

Like Viot, Matthews believes that her physical similarity to her adopted daughter, now 11, goes a long way. "I don't think she is impacted much by her adoption,"

Matthews said. "She doesn't stand out as physically different so she doesn't draw the questions and stares that I did. She's never singled out as an adoptee."

In fact, strangers often remark on Kimmy's resemblance to her, especially compared with her biological children who are half-Korean and half-white.

Matthews has fostered the same relationship with Kimmy as with her biological children. "I have not emphasized our adoption connection," she said, though she is always alert and open to that topic being raised. "I want her to be aware of her adoption and mine, but I don't want her pegged as the 'adopted one.'"

Kimmy, whom Matthews calls a very social "all-American girl," occasionally asks about her biological parents, but for now she doesn't dwell on the topic. Kimmy has not yet shown much interest in Korean culture or in seeking out her roots. But Matthews is preparing for the time when that changes. "That is when I hope I can step up and support her the way she needs to be supported. I just hope if anything comes up that I can give her perspective or that I can at least understand."

"Her experience is really different than mine," Matthews said. "She does not seem to be the oddity that I was growing up."

Kelley Christine Blomberg is a Korean adoptee who grew up in the Midwest and now lives in San Francisco.

For Adoptive Parents, Questions Without Answers

By John Leland
The New York Times, September 18, 2011

In almost any adoption, the new parents accept that their good fortune arises out of the hardship of the child's first parents. The equation is usually tempered by the thought that the birth parents either are no longer alive or chose to give the child a better life than they could provide.

On August 5, this newspaper published a front-page article from China that contained chilling news for many adoptive parents: government officials in Hunan Province, in southern China, had seized babies from their parents and sold them into what the article called "a lucrative black market in children."

The news, the latest in a slow trickle of reports describing child abduction and trafficking in China, swept through the tight communities of families—many of them in the New York area—who have adopted children from China. For some, it raised a nightmarish question: What if my child had been taken forcibly from her parents?

And from that question, inevitably, tumble others: What can or should adoptive parents do? Try to find the birth parents? And if they could, what then?

Scott Mayer, who with his wife adopted a girl from southern China in 2007, said the article's implications hit him head on. "I couldn't really think straight," Mr. Mayer said. His daughter, Keshi, is 5 years old—"I have to tell you, she's brilliant," he said proudly—and is a mainstay of his life as a husband and a father.

"What I felt," he said, "was a wave of heat rush over me."

Like many adoptive parents, Mr. Mayer can recount the emotionally exhausting process he and his wife went through to get their daughter, and can describe the warm home they have strived to provide. They had been assured that she, like thousands of other Chinese girls, was abandoned in secret by her birth parents, left in a public place with a note stating her date of birth.

But as he started to read about the Hunan cases, he said, doubts flooded in. How much did he—or any adoptive parent—really know about what happened on the other side of the world? Could Keshi have been taken by force, or bought by the orphanage in order to reap the thousands of dollars that American parents like him donate when they get their children?

In his home in Montclair, N.J., Mr. Mayer rushed upstairs to re-examine the adoption documents.

According to the news reports, the children were removed from their families when they were several months old, then taken to the orphanages. "The first thing I did was look in my files," he said, speaking in deliberative, unsparing sentences. According to his paperwork, his daughter had been found on a specific date, as a newborn.

He paused to weigh the next thought.

"Now, could that have been faked?" he said. "Perhaps. I don't know. But at least it didn't say she was 3 months old when she was left at the orphanage."

According to the State Department, 64,043 Chinese children were adopted in the United States between 1999 and 2010, far more than from any other country. Child abduction and trafficking have plagued other international adoption programs, notably in Vietnam and Romania, and some have shut down to stop the black market trade.

But many parents saw China as the cleanest of international adoption choices. Its population-control policy, which limited many families to one child, drove couples to abandon subsequent children or to give up daughters in hopes of bearing sons to inherit their property and take care of them in old age. China had what adoptive parents in America wanted: a supply of healthy children in need of families.

As Mr. Mayer reasoned, "If anything, the number of children needing an adoptive home was so huge that it outstripped the number of people who could ever come."

This narrative was first challenged in 2005, when Chinese and foreign news media reported that government officials and employees of an orphanage in Hunan had sold at least 100 children to other orphanages, which provided them to foreign adoptive parents.

Mr. Mayer was not aware of this report or the few others that followed. Though he knew many other adoptive families, and was active in a group called Families With Children From China—Greater New York, no one had ever talked about abduction or baby-selling.

"I didn't even think that existed in China," he said.

Again he paused.

"This comes up and you say, holy cow, it's even more complicated than you thought."

"Adoption is bittersweet," said Susan Soon-Keum Cox, vice president for public policy and external affairs at Holt International, a Christian adoption agency based in Eugene, Ore., with an extensive program in China. The process connects birth parents, child and adoptive parents in an unequal relationship in which each party has different needs and different leverage. It begins in loss.

Adoptive parents and adoption agencies have powerful incentives not to talk about trafficking or to question whether a child was given up voluntarily, especially given how difficult it is to know for certain. Such talk can unsettle the children or anger the Chinese government, which might limit the families' future access to the

Adoptive parents and adoption agencies have powerful incentives not to talk about trafficking or to question whether a child was given up voluntarily, especially given how difficult it is to know for certain.

country or add restrictions to future adoptions. And the possible answer is one that no parent wants to hear.

Most parents contacted for this article declined to comment or agreed to speak only on the condition of anonymity. Several said they never discussed trafficking, even with other adoptive parents. To a query from *The New York Times* posted on a Web forum for adoptive parents, one parent urged silence, writing, "The more we put China child trafficking out there, the more chances your child has to encounter a schoolmate saying, 'Oh, were you stolen from your bio family?'"

Such reticence infuriates people like Karen Moline, a New York writer and a board member of the nonprofit advocacy group Parents for Ethical Adoption Reform, who adopted a boy from Vietnam 10 years ago. "If the government is utterly corrupt, and you have to take an orphanage a donation in hundred-dollar bills, why would you think the program was ethical?" she said. "Ask a typical Chinese adoptive parent that question, and they'll say, my agency said so. My agency is ethical. People say, the paperwork says X; the paperwork is legitimate. But you have no idea where your money goes.

"Now you have to give $5,000 as an orphanage fee in China. Multiply that by how many thousand adoptions. Tens of millions of dollars have flowed out of this country to get kids, and you have no accounting for it."

Agencies say that cases of child abduction are few compared with the number of abandoned Chinese babies who found good homes in America. The abductions reported in August were of 16 or more children taken from their parents between 1999 and 2006. According to the investigation, population-control officials threatened towering fines for couples who violated the one-child policy because they were too young to be married or already had a child, or because they had themselves adopted the child without proper paperwork. When the parents could not pay, the officials seized the children and sent them into the lucrative foreign adoption system.

"The incident when it happened was resolved quickly by the Chinese in a way that was drastic and made very clear that the Chinese would not tolerate trafficking," said Ms. Cox, of Holt International. "I'm not saying there are not any other incidents, but people can be assured that the process in China is a good one."

A 2010 State Department report said there were "no reliable estimates" of the number of children kidnapped for adoption in China, but cited Chinese news media reports that said the figure might be as high as 20,000 children a year, most of whom are adopted illegally within the country, especially boys.

But it is hard to know, said David Smolin, a professor at the Cumberland School of Law at Samford University in Birmingham, Ala., who has written extensively about international adoption and trafficking. Changes in China in the early 2000s—a rising standard of living, an easing of restrictions on adoption within the country, more sex-selective abortion—meant that fewer families abandoned healthy babies, Professor Smolin said.

"Orphanages had gotten used to getting money for international adoption," he said, "and all of the sudden they didn't have healthy baby girls unless they competed with traffickers for them."

Professor Smolin has two daughters, whom he and his wife adopted from India as teenagers. Within six weeks the girls disclosed that they had been kidnapped from their birth parents. But when Professor Smolin and his wife tried to find the girls' biological parents, he said, no one wanted to help.

When he started to speak publicly about his experience, he met other parents in the same situation—hundreds of them, he said. "They all said they felt abandoned by adoption agencies and by various governments," he said. "There's a sense that other people in the adoption community did not want to hear about these circumstances. People were told that it was not a good thing to talk about. So you're left alone with these practical and moral dilemmas, and that is overwhelming." In the end, it took more than six years for the couple to find their daughters' birth parents, by which time the girls were young adults.

Susan Merkel, 48, who with her husband adopted their daughter, Maia, at 9 months old in August 2007, said that even within their own home, her husband did not like to talk about the possibility.

"My husband really feels like it's something that we don't know whether that's the case and would rather not think about it," she said at her home in Chesterfield, N.J.

But for Ms. Merkel, who is studying social work at Rutgers University, the uncertainty is haunting. Her daughter's orphanage, in Hubei Province, which is immediately north of Hunan, is near an area known for strict enforcement of the one-child policy, and Ms. Merkel said she could not shake the possibility that a population-control official had seized her and turned her over to the orphanage.

Ms. Merkel was adopted as a child, and said that meeting her birth mother had helped her understand her past and herself. What, then, was her responsibility as a parent—to find Maia's birth parents, who might make a valid claim for her return? How could Ms. Merkel, who got so much out of meeting her own birth mother, not want that for her child? "What I do know is that she's my daughter and I love her," she said. "We're giving her the best family and life that we can. And if she has questions someday, we'll do all we can to help her find the answers."

Ms. Merkel said that she would support Maia's meeting her birth parents if it was possible, but that she would not willingly return her to them, even if there was evidence that she had been taken.

"I would feel great empathy for that person," she said. "I would completely understand the anger and the pain. But I would fight to keep my daughter. Not because she's mine, but because for all purposes we're the only family she's ever known. How terrifying that would be for a child to be taken away from the only family she knows and the life that she knows. That's not about doing what's right for the child. That's doing what's right for the birth mother."

Brian Stuy, an adoptive father of three in Salt Lake City, runs a service called Research-China.org to help adoptive families learn about their children's origins. When he has managed to contact birth parents, he said, most were content to learn that their children were alive, that they were healthy and in good homes. "Unfortunately, the reaction of most adoptive parents is to go into hiding," Mr. Stuy said. "When they have suspicions, they don't want to come forward."

Many parents simply never have suspicions. Tony X. Tan, an associate professor of educational psychology at the University of South Florida whose research specialty is adoption, surveyed 342 adoptive parents of Chinese children last month. Two-thirds said they "never" suspected that their children might have been abducted, and one in nine said they thought about it "sometimes." Several said the paperwork from the orphanages was inconsistent or suspicious.

One mother, who adopted two girls from different provinces, wrote, "My Guangxi daughter was adopted with a group of 11 other infants, all roughly the same age, and came home with an extremely detailed description of her first 11 months of life in her orphanage. Yet 'her' information was word-for-word the same as the info given the families of the other 11 children adopted at the same time—making it all too specific to be believable."

Judy Larch, a Macy's executive who lives in Pelham, N.Y., said she adopted two girls from China, in 2001 and 2007, because she had heard good things about the program, and because she could adopt as a single woman. Though she has read about trafficking, she said, "I've never had any doubts or concerns about their adoptions." She said she had faith in the adoption agency, Holt International.

Such faith is small comfort to a woman named Ms. Chen, who said population-control officials in her hometown, Changle, in Fujian Province, took her daughter in 1999. Ms. Chen, who is in the United States illegally, applied for asylum as a dissident this year, but was denied. She declined to speak to *The Times*, but gave permission for a reporter to watch a videotaped interview conducted by a Christian group in Flushing, Queens, called All Girls Allowed, which works with women's rights groups in China and maintains a database of photographs of missing children. Her story could not be corroborated.

In the interview, Ms. Chen said that her first child, born in 1997, was a girl, and that she was under great pressure from her in-laws to produce a son. She became pregnant soon afterward, but this child, too, was a girl. Ms. Chen was in violation of the one-child law, which in her area allowed parents to have a second child after six years. Officials came to her with a choice: give up the second child—then 5 months old—or undergo tubal ligation.

"I was holding my daughter and crying," she said on the video. The official told her that if she gave up the child, in six years she could try again to have a son, she said. "I was afraid for my marriage," she said. "Of course I didn't want to give up the child. But I was afraid that without a boy my marriage wouldn't last."

She said, "I handed her over meekly."

Mr. Mayer in Montclair, who also has an adopted son from Ethiopia, has accepted that he may never know the full truth about his daughter's beginnings.

After absorbing the revelations about trafficking, he said, he took a step back. "O.K., what does this mean to my life today? And how does it change my life today?" he said he asked himself. "And today it changes absolutely nothing about my life with Keshi. If I want Keshi to be able to question and to come to terms with the issues of why she would have been put up for adoption in the way she was, she's going to ask these questions. This is just another one of those questions to which I don't have a concrete answer. That's my role as a dad."

In the future, families like his may have better answers. Parents or children may be able to search online databases of children whose birth parents say they were taken. For now, though, is it the parents' duty to ask those questions? Or is it for children to decide, in time, how much they want to know?

"I can't change the past or change whatever anybody has done in China," Mr. Mayer said. "What's most important to me is there are real significant issues for my daughter coming of age and understanding her birth story. And I'm committed to supporting her in that and making sure that it's as honest and truthful and supportive as possible. And that's a scary thing."

Adoption 2.0: Finding Mom on Facebook

By Belinda Luscombe
Time, August 16, 2010

Dana Lowrey has known she was adopted for as long as she can remember. And for almost as long—about 30 years—she had been looking for what she calls her "first family." She combed through county records, searched the online adoption registries and enlisted the help of reunion experts. On Jan. 10, she set up a Facebook page and asked the friends she had made in the adoption community to help her search. Within 24 hours, she was in touch with her birth mother, Mary Stark. And by Jan. 15, she had made contact with her biological dad, Kenny Morse.

In retrospect, Lowrey, a 41-year-old nurse who is raising two kids of her own in Roseville, Calif., is not sure why it took her so long to use social-networking sites to trace her birth parents. In 2008 she used MySpace to connect with the son, Tim Daugherty, she'd given up for adoption 19 years earlier.

Of all the relationships that are being changed by Facebook and other sites that trade on bringing people together, the thorny, delicate bonds that connect what's known in adoption circles as the triad—the biological family, the child and the adoptive parents—may be the most profoundly altered.

For older adoptees like Lowrey, who were raised in an era when talking about birth parents was generally verboten, social networks are a boon, another way to put together the puzzle of their backgrounds. But the methods Lowrey used could just as easily be employed by a curious adopted teenager or a birth mother who regrets giving up her child. This is raising concern among some adoptive parents and agencies. "We have not yet begun to wrap our mind around what the implications are," says Adam Pertman, executive director of the Evan B. Donaldson Adoption Institute, a research and policy organization in New York City.

Most kids and adult adoptees have been told or can find out the names of their birth parents—and that's the starting point for their Facebook searches. Contact can be made, often suddenly, without the guidance of parents or adoption professionals. And since teenagers' Web savviness is often light-years ahead of their emotional maturity, it can all head south pretty fast. "Even in the best of cases, you want a little knowledge first," Pertman says of reuniting with birth parents. "You want to do this thoughtfully and methodically. With Facebook, you don't have any of that."

In some ways, Lowrey was lucky. "I promised I wouldn't contact my son until he was 18," she says. "When I first thought of trying to find him, it would have been a bad time, because his mom had significant health issues." She held off for a couple of years and then sent a message through MySpace. He replied within a week.

Most agencies encourage some form of communication, and most birth mothers demand—as a condition of the adoption— such things as e-mailed pictures, annual letters or a frequently updated website. But social networks are throwing wide open a door that used to be merely ajar.

Two months later, they met face to face.

Some people are not ready for this kind of contact and never will be. "Biological parents have called me in tears and in fear" about being discovered, says Chuck Johnson, acting CEO of the National Council for Adoption in Alexandria, Va. "They don't know what to do." Social networking's implications for children whose birth parents' rights have been terminated are even more serious. In the U.K., where adoptions are more often contested, birth mothers were reported to be using Facebook to contact kids who had been taken away from them by child-protection officials.

In standard adoption cases, it's become less common over the past 20 years for newly adoptive families and birth parents to have no contact at all. Most agencies encourage some form of communication, and most birth mothers demand—as a condition of the adoption—such things as e-mailed pictures, annual letters or a frequently updated website. But social networks are throwing wide open a door that used to be merely ajar.

"I want my son to meet his birth mother," says an adoptive parent who lives in a New York City suburb and who asked that we not print her name. "When he's old enough, we'll all go on a road trip." Every year, she sends a letter and photos to the birth mother, but she worries that a birth-family member will contact her 12-year-old on Facebook before she decides he's mature enough to handle it. "None of us are ready yet," she says.

Mindful of what can go wrong, several adoption agencies have issued advisories on how to handle social networking. The worst thing to do, they say, is to try to keep kids off the Web. A smarter strategy is to keep an eye on children's online activities and help them understand the ramifications of finding their birth parents, says Martha Henry, director of the office of foster care and adoption at the University of Massachusetts Medical School. "Parents should figure out what steps they can take to join that journey and try to create an environment where their kids feel safe to talk about it."

Henry says it helps to understand why a child is looking for his or her birth family. Some parents fear being replaced in their child's affections, particularly during the relentless tussles of adolescence. Others think their child will be overwhelmed. But whatever the reason, the situation is better faced, like Thanksgiving, as a family, with professional help if necessary. "The search for the birth parent is not just about the child," says Henry. "It's about all of you."

In January, when Lowrey discovered her birth father's identity, an intermediary ended up making the first contact. "I was torn. I said, 'I'm going to have to pass on it,'" says Morse, a former musician and truck driver. "I called the guy back five minutes later."

"I'm glad this came out to be a good thing," he says. Lowrey is still in touch with all three of her recently located family members. Mostly she talks to them on the phone, although Daugherty has made a couple of surprise visits. And thanks to Facebook, now they all know exactly where to find each other.

5

Families Across Cultures

(Getty Images)

An Arab-American family poses for a photograph in a public park during the Muslim Eid al-Fitr prayers and celebrations at the end of Ramadan on August 30, 2011, in the Brooklyn borough of New York. The three-day Eid holiday marks the end of the Islamic month of fasting, prayer, and reflection. Eid al-Fitr begins after the sighting of a new crescent moon.

Bicultural and Multilingual Families

By Paul McCaffrey

On October 3, 1965, President Lyndon Baines Johnson came to Liberty Island in New York Harbor to sign the Immigration and Nationality Act. Standing before the Statue of Liberty, the president addressed the crowd assembled to mark the occasion. "Our beautiful America was built by a nation of strangers," Johnson declared. "From a hundred different places or more they have poured forth into an empty land, joining and blending in one mighty and irresistible tide." More than any other measure, the Immigration and Nationality Act transformed US immigration and ushered in a period of demographic transformation that continues to play out in the twenty-first century and is reflected in the changing face of the American family.

Though a nation of immigrants, the United States has long had an ambivalent relationship with foreign-born newcomers. This ambivalence has manifested itself in both the shifting immigration regulations put in place by the state and federal governments and by the complicated and fluid attitudes towards these recent arrivals among natural-born citizens. Indeed, in the nearly two centuries leading up to the passage of the Immigration and Nationality Act, immigration policy was often a reaction to public concerns about the practice. When settling the frontier was a national priority, an "open door" policy was embraced. As much of the population grew wary of the economic and cultural influence of new immigrants, restrictions were put in place, some of them explicitly discriminatory.

In 1790, the country took an exclusionary approach to immigration. That year, Congress passed the Naturalization Act, which placed strict limits on just who could qualify for citizenship. According to the law, the only immigrants who could be naturalized were "free white person[s]" of "good character" who had lived in the country for at least two years. This statute would not be the last to limit citizenship based on ethnicity. In 1882, for example, the Chinese Exclusion Act banned immigration from China and outlawed Chinese settlers from becoming naturalized. This measure was not repealed until the 1940s.

Motivated by economic factors and antipathy to the influx of newcomers from southern and eastern Europe, further immigration restrictions were imposed in 1921 and 1924 that capped annual immigration at 350,000 and 300,000, respectively, and established a National Origins Formula limiting the number of newcomers allowed from particular countries. The 1921 Emergency Quota Act restricted immigration from individual countries to 3 percent of what the foreign-born US population from that nation was in 1910; the 1924 law, seeking to further restrict immigration from southern and eastern Europe, adjusted the quota to 2 percent based on the foreign-born population of 1890 and outlawed immigration from much of Asia and the Middle East. As the Great Depression commenced in 1929, the government permitted even fewer newcomers.

A common theme emerges in these various immigration statutes: the central motivation was not only to reduce immigration overall, but to give preference to certain types of newcomers—northern and western Europeans, in particular—over others. With the repeal of the Chinese Exclusion Act in 1943 and the removal of ethnic preferences in naturalization procedures in 1952, that began to change, and with President Johnson's Immigration and Nationality Act, the door was opened for a more diverse and multicultural nation.

The naturalization of immigrants from Africa and Asia was now permitted. Instead of complicated formulas based on national origins, immigration visas—green cards—would be allotted on a first-come, first-serve basis, and naturalized citizens could sponsor their relatives from overseas, making it easier for them to immigrate to the United States. Despite the far-reaching changes instituted by Johnson, their effect was not immediately felt. In 1970, for example, the percentage of the US population that was foreign-born was a mere 4.7 percent, the lowest level ever recorded and less than a third of the peak rate of 14.8 percent in 1890. Thereafter, however, a nearly forty-year immigration boom commenced.

In the years after 1970, the flow of American immigration shifted from Europe to Asia, Africa, and especially Latin America. By 2009, the full effects of Johnson's reform were readily apparent. According to the US Census, the foreign-born population measured more than 38.5 million, 12.5 percent of all US residents. Of these, 43.7 percent had obtained their citizenship through the naturalization process while the rest were divided among permanent legal residents, undocumented immigrants, and those on temporary visas. The plurality—29.8 percent—came from Mexico. The Philippines, India, and China, contributing 4.5 percent, 4.3 percent, and 3.7 percent, respectively, rounded out the top four.

Given the diversity among American immigrant families, generalizations can obscure as much as they reveal. The experience of an Arab American family from Yemen living in Dearborn, Michigan, may not, on the surface, have much in common with a Mexican American family residing in El Paso, Texas, for example. Nevertheless, amid this striking array of cultures, all such families confront the perennial immigrant's dilemma: how to adapt to a new culture and language and how much of the old ways to preserve and pass on to the next generation. Beyond that, there is the demographic profile, the hard numbers that reveal the underlying dynamics of the American immigrant family, its structure, strengths, and challenges.

A 2010 analysis by the Urban Institute found that about 23 percent of the roughly 70 million children under the age of eighteen in the United States were being raised by at least one immigrant parent. Twelve percent lived with two foreign-born parents, 6 percent resided with a single immigrant parent, and 5 percent lived with one foreign- and one native-born parent.

As a group, immigrant families diverge from natural-born ones in several crucial ways. On one hand, they adhere to the structure of a nuclear family to a greater degree than American-born households; the Urban Institute found that 76 percent of immigrant families were headed by two parents compared to only 62 percent of natural-born families. With 26 percent having at least three children as opposed to only 14 percent among native-born American households, families with foreign-born parents skewed larger as well. Mothers in foreign-born households were also less likely to work outside the home.

On average, immigrant parents were also found to have less formal education than their US-born counterparts. Among foreign-born mothers and fathers, 27 percent never completed high school, 36 percent graduated but did not go on to college, 7 percent earned an associate's degree, 17 percent a bachelor's degree, and 14 percent a master's degree. Among parents in native-born families, on the other hand, only 7 percent never finished high school, while 46 percent earned just a high school diploma, 11 percent an associate's degree, 22 percent a four-year degree, and 15 percent a graduate degree.

The difference in educational attainment is accompanied by a language barrier. The Urban Institute found that six in ten children of immigrants had at least one parent who qualified as Limited English Proficient (LEP)—speaking, reading, or writing little or no English. In 26 percent of immigrant families, no one over the age of fourteen qualified as adept in English. These language and education deficiencies are correlated with greater poverty rates.

Immigrant parents have outpaced American-born mothers and fathers in one key area: hours worked. According to the Urban Institute, in 92 percent of immigrant families, the parents worked at least 1,800 hours in the previous year, the equivalent of a year's worth of full-time labor. In natural-born families, it was only 89 percent. The striking thing about the 92 percent figure was its consistency. Unlike marriage rates, family size, and educational attainment, which varied somewhat depending on the household's country of origin, the 92 percent held true for all immigrant groups, regardless of where they hailed from and where they lived in the United States.

The Immigration and Nationality Act was not President Johnson's only revision of the immigration system. The year before, he ended the Bracero Program, a controversial guest worker initiative started in the 1940s that recruited Mexican laborers to help with the American harvest. This aspect of Johnson's immigration policy had unforeseen ramifications. Many blame the end of the Bracero Program, in part, for the increased number of undocumented immigrants that entered the country in the decades after the Johnson administration. The elimination of Bracero, Siobhan Gorman wrote in *National Journal*, "inadvertently reinvigorated illegal immigration."

According to 2008 estimates by the Pew Hispanic Center, there were 11.9 million unauthorized immigrants in the United States—up from 3.5 million in 1990—who composed about 4 percent of the US population and, in 2009, about 28 percent of the foreign-born population. In terms of their origins, an estimated 59 percent were Mexican and more than three quarters were Hispanic. Of these 11.9 million, about 8.3 million participated in the labor force and accounted for 5.4 percent of all workers in the United States.

Unauthorized and LEP immigrants are less likely to learn English and are comparatively less educated than legal immigrants. Their uncertain legal status further exacerbates these deficits, keeping them from fully integrating into American society. Deportation can tear families apart and therefore many undocumented newcomers lead circumscribed lives, avoiding contacts outside their immediate communities to avoid the authorities. As a result, these immigrants have fewer economic opportunities. The cost of this social and economic insecurity is especially steep for families with children. In 2008, 47 percent of undocumented households included children. According to estimates by the Pew Hispanic Center, there were about 5.5 million minors with at least one parent who was an undocumented immigrant currently living in the United States. Of these children, about 4.5 million were born in the United States and thus had American citizenship. Another million children were born elsewhere and lacked proper documentation. In total, these 5.5 million children made up about 6.8 percent of all students in American schools, from kindergarten through high school.

Though families of illegal immigrants are more likely than either documented immigrant or native-born ones to have two parents, they suffer from poverty to a greater extent than their counterparts. About one-third of illegal immigrant children live in poverty, a rate twice as high as among the children of American-born parents. They are also more likely to lack health insurance coverage. A study published in the *Harvard Educational Review* in 2011 found that these children are "at risk of lower educational performance, economic stagnation, blocked mobility and ambiguous belonging."

Along with such challenges, immigrant families, whether documented or otherwise, must confront anti-immigrant sentiment. Such attitudes have taken on many forms since the formation of the United States, but the focus has usually been on a particular group's religion or culture and the stereotypes that are associated with them. In the nineteenth century, Irish Catholic, Chinese, Italian, Eastern European, and Jewish immigrants all had particular vices attributed to them. Based on these prejudices, many immigration skeptics concluded that these groups and American culture and values were not compatible. Today, many newcomers face similar attitudes. Arab and Muslim immigrants endure increased discrimination based on their religion and on fears related to terrorism. Newcomers from Latin America are frequently suspected of being undocumented immigrants. Other criticisms of immigrants, regardless of their country of origin, are that they are not assimilating fast enough or are abusing government services. How to endure and overcome such negative perceptions is a perennial dilemma for immigrant families.

By relying on family and hard work, today's Asian, African, and Latin American newcomers are following the pattern set by previous waves of immigrants in confronting these challenges. One of the lessons of American history—one that motivated President Johnson to sign the Immigration and Nationality Act—is that immigrant families do eventually transcend poverty, discrimination, and educational deficits, and in the course of a generation or two become fully integrated into American society, in Johnson's words, "joining and blending in one mighty and irresistible tide."

Dearborn in the USA

By Sohrab Ahmari
Tablet Magazine, November 14, 2011

The new TLC reality show All-American Muslim *doesn't do enough to display the theological and intellectual diversity of Islam in the U.S.*

If you've recently started a new job or embarked on a graduate degree, chances are you've had to engage in some sort of cultural-sharing exercise designed to promote diversity and inclusion. You know the drill: Sitting in a circle, each person tells his or her story—or, to use the proper nomenclature, offers his or her narrative. Participants from "subaltern" backgrounds are expected to tell stories of repression and exclusion; those who come from the "dominant culture," meanwhile, must "unpack" their own privileges and wicked biases in front of the group.

Over the years, I've had to sit through many such sessions, be it at Teach For America, where new recruits are required to complete a grueling regimen of diversity training, or during my first year at law school. It didn't take me long to realize that, as a Shia-born Iranian-American in the post–Sept.11 era, I have anecdotes aplenty that, told correctly, can place me right in the sweet spot of the race-gender-class matrix. I could recount how on that dreadful September day a high-school classmate of mine in rural northern Utah yelled out, "Hey, Sohrab, I heard your people bombed New York!" Or I could mention how I've learned to preemptively take the tension out of the room when I sense that my Iranian background might be an issue. ("I come from the heart of the axis of evil," I say.)

In some ways, *All-American Muslim*, TLC's new reality TV show documenting the lives of five families in the Arab enclave of Dearborn, Mich., is this culture-sharing exercise writ large. As the title suggests, the show aims to expose a broad audience to the day-to-day lives of American Muslims who, while assimilated into the culture, must nevertheless balance the various aspects of their identities. The cast of characters includes Fouad, the (literally) all-American coach of the local high-school football team; Jeff, an Irish Catholic preparing to convert to Islam, and Shadia, the heavily tattooed, self-described Muslim redneck engaged to him; Samira, Shadia's sister, and her husband Ali, who struggle with infertility; Nina, the strong-willed wedding planner who dresses far too provocatively for Dearborn and is fed up with the town's parochialism; Nawal, the hijab-clad, pregnant newlywed, and her Homer Simpson–esque husband, Nader; and Mike, a policeman, and his wife, Angela, a marketing executive in the auto industry.

The show's central conceit lies in its use of standard-issue reality-television tropes to frame a community that many viewers might otherwise consider alien. The interplay between the familiar plot developments, musical cues, and confessional interviews—how will Jeff's mom react to his conversion to Islam? Stay tuned to find out!—and the insular world of American Islam helps normalize the community.

The show deserves praise for capturing at least some of the internal debates within Western Islam, including those on marriage and conversion, head-covering, drinking, and sexuality. "If a girl is going to wear a scarf or a *hijab*, it is a choice that I think every Muslim woman has the right to make and does make," Angela, the marketing executive, dressed in a tight-fitting skirt and knee-high boots, argues at one point. Nina, the spunky blond wedding planner, agrees: "Nobody can tell that I'm Muslim. I don't wear *hijab* and I don't wear a T-shirt that says, 'I am Muslim.'" The more devout Nawal—who reminded me of a character straight out of the daytime Islamic guidance shows I had to endure as a child in Iran—clearly doesn't approve of Angela and Nina opting out. "What about the people that were born into [Islam]?" she asks during a group discussion about Jeff's conversion. "*They don't have to do it right?*" Her sarcastic question is clearly directed at the liberal Nina, suggesting that she is insufficiently pious. Nina shoots her a piercing look in response.

> *One could easily forgive this narrow sectarian snapshot of Islam in the United States were it not for the fact that Dearborn is also home to large numbers of Sunni-Arab Muslims.*

Such exchanges reflect the very lively—and very real—tensions within American Islam, and bringing them to the cultural foreground is a valuable contribution. But the show does not go nearly far enough in terms of exposing American-Muslims' ethnic, theological, and intellectual diversity. For one thing, most of the show's characters are Lebanese Shia. And just as *The Real Housewives of D.C.* intercuts the ladies' drama with shots of the Capitol and the White House, so does *All-American Muslim* establish its setting by repeatedly cutting to the Islamic Center of America, a Shi'ite place of worship—in effect implying that the mega-mosque is American Islam's capital. The clerics who advise the characters on doctrinal matters, too, are invariably Shi'ite.

One could easily forgive this narrow sectarian snapshot of Islam in the United States were it not for the fact that Dearborn is also home to large numbers of Sunni-Arab Muslims. That *All-American Muslim* eschews showing these divisions could be chalked up to the nature of the medium: Explaining Islam's centuries-old schisms on a reality TV show is not an easy task. It is nevertheless a troubling move, one that reinforces the notion of a monolithic Islam. (This sort of cultural whitewashing and oversimplification has been a misstep in the work of the Iranian-American writer Reza Aslan—who, along with filmmaker Mahyad Tousi, cofounded Boomgen Studios, which is helping to promote *All-American Muslim*. Earlier this year, Aslan published *Tablet and Pen*, a massive anthology of 20th-century Mideast literature that deliberately omitted Jewish authors and modern Israeli literature. (*Tablet Magazine*'s Adam Kirsch took him to task for this startling omission.)

More troubling still is the show's overemphasis on theological matters and its overly deferential editorial attitude toward the Shia clerical class. Consider a painful scene in the second episode in which the hitherto unveiled Samira visits two imams seeking spiritual advice on her inability to get pregnant. "Of course there is no physical link between *hijab* and pregnancy," the more senior cleric explains. "But according to Islam, when you have *hijab* . . . God will cooperate more with you." The junior cleric chimes in: "So, that's the goodness of the faith—the spirit and the body and the brain functioning together."

If these men were, say, Catholic priests, the editors surely would have mocked them endlessly, Luis Buñuel–style. Instead, a soothing melody is heard as the superstitious hokum spills forth from these fonts of clerical wisdom. (Samira, we later learn, cannot afford in vitro fertilization. And since artificial insemination has been prohibited for her by clerical edict, she returns to the *hijab* in the hope of conceiving a baby.)

All-American Muslim's drama is set against the larger backdrop of a supposedly rabid, anti–Muslim American culture. Indeed, the show seems to have been conceived as a reaction to rising Islamophobia in the United States "[We're called] 'towelheads,'" Shadia says in the pilot's opening sequence. "They say we're Muslim, we're barbaric, we're terrorists," her brother complains. Later, we see news footage of far-right protesters howling "Muhammad was a pedophile!" at Muslims attending a business conference in Dearborn.

Yet put into a proper perspective, such grievances form less than half the picture. Indeed, perhaps despite itself, *All-American Muslim* showcases the many ways in which the American experience has allowed Muslims to thrive—a testament to a heritage of religious freedom that has liberated Muslims as never before. In Dearborn, New York, Los Angeles, and beyond, generations of American Muslims—from the pious to the secular-minded—have found safe and open spaces in which to explore and shape their own identities in ways that would be unthinkable for their counterparts trapped in the repressive pressure-cookers of the Mideast.

The Latino Crescent

By Lyndsey Matthews
The Brooklyn Rail, September 2009

A woman wearing a hijab rushes up the stairs of a mosque in Union City, New Jersey. She is frantically murmuring, "Empanadas, empanadas, empanadas!" as if to remind herself to pick up the savory Latino pastries for the crowd waiting inside. The sixth annual Hispanic Muslim Day event is about to begin.

More than 60 percent of Union City's population is Latino, and the storefronts in this neighborhood proudly display flags from Puerto Rico, Mexico, and the Dominican Republic. This stately columned building used to house the city's Cuban community center, once a popular venue for traditional Hispanic celebrations like *quinceañeras*. For 17 years, it's been the Islamic Educational Center of North Hudson.

Unlike churches and synagogues, mosques do not keep rosters of their worshippers. Where one goes to pray is more fluid in the Islamic tradition. Shinoa Matos, one of the young women in attendance, estimates that of the thousands of people who pray at the Union City mosque in any given week, more than a hundred are Latino. "Just like how there are Albanian mosques in Albanian neighborhoods," she explains, "we are a Latino mosque because we are in a Latino neighborhood." Islam, however, discourages differentiation among ethnic groups, she says, so Muslims try not to do it.

Inside the mosque the aromatic scent of steaming empanadas, spiced beef stuffed inside shells of puffed pastry, inundates the first floor auditorium. About a hundred people of various ages mingle around a dozen round tables covered with white plastic cloths and topped with cream-colored ceramic vases holding bouquets of purple silk pansies. Grandmothers coo over infants while a group of young men plug a laptop into the sound system to play *nasheed*, a traditional form of Islamic music. There are more women than men, and only a few women are not veiled. By what seems like an act of natural separation, the men sit on the left of the auditorium, the women on the right, with a few scattered in between.

Eventually Ramon Omar Abduraheem Ocasio comes to the front of the auditorium to give the keynote speech. He is a family man who found Islam in Harlem in the 1970s and reared his six children as Muslims. He describes what it was like in those days to be ostracized in the neighborhood's mosques, which members of the Nation of Islam dominated.

Ocasio is one of the 44 million Latinos living in the United States who constitute the nation's largest minority population, according to 2007 U.S. Census estimates. This, plus the rapid growth in the number of adherents of Islam in the United States, has given rise to the relatively new demographic of American Latino Muslims. In 1997 the American Muslim Council identified some 40,000 Hispanic Muslims in the country, a number that had swelled nine years later to a reported 200,000. A 2008 study by the Pew Forum on Religious and Public Life put the number of Latino Muslim U.S.

> *Although Islam has not permeated Latino culture to the extent that it has permeated black culture—24 percent of Muslim Americans are black— its influence is evident.*

residents at 4 percent of all Muslim U.S. residents. The figure represents a tiny minority within a tiny minority—just over half of 1 percent of the U.S. population— and a somewhat surprising one. Latinos have long been associated with the Roman Catholic Church and, more recently, with the evangelical Christian traditions. All the same, it is not unusual for Americans to change faith for another denomination, an entirely new religion, or no religion at all. For example, of the nearly one in three Americans raised as Catholics, fewer than a quarter still consider themselves Catholic.

Although Islam has not permeated Latino culture to the extent that it has permeated black culture—24 percent of Muslim Americans are black—its influence is evident. Characters in the Spanish-language telenovela *El Clon* (*The Clone*) often discuss Islam and the prerequisites for becoming a Muslim. The appeal, Latinos who have converted say, comes from their search for a simpler and more intimate experience of God. They find the Muslim emphasis on family and conservative values familiar and, beyond that, Latinos often share neighborhoods with black and immigrant Muslims, and in turn develop strong ties as neighbors, friends, and co-workers.

The pale blue balloons floating on strings above the tables match Alex Robayo's baby-blue collared shirt. As the Hispanic Muslim Day emcee, he speaks in both Spanish and English and directs his remarks primarily to the non-Muslims in the crowd.

"Are there any Catholics in the room?" he asks. A young dark-haired woman with a copy of El Coran, the Koran in Spanish, resting on the table in front of her quietly raises her hand and cringes slightly under the attention that turns in her direction.

Repeatedly, Robayo stresses the similarities between Christianity and Islam— the belief in one God and the many common prophets, including Jesus. Many converts say that they find the Christian idea of the Trinity complicated and that the monotheistic simplicity of the Islamic concept of *tawheed*—the "one true oneness of God"—has great appeal.

Robayo shares a story about his mother, a Roman Catholic, whom he picks up after Mass most weeks. He admires the beauty of the Catholic statues of Jesus and the saints but appreciates that in Islam there are no images. He likes the Islamic notion of a direct, unmediated conversation with God, a straightforward approach that appeals to many converts to Islam.

"You may say in Spanish *dios*, in English God, in Arabic *Allah*," Robayo tells the crowd. "Are *dios* and *God* different?"

"Dios es grande," he says.

Chinese or American? Or Both?

By Amy Ku
ChinaUSFriendship.com, April 1, 2010

Because I grew up in white affluent neighborhoods, I never had any Asian friends until I went away to college where the majority of the friends I made were Chinese. For a really long time, before college, I did not want to have anything to do with being Chinese at all. I wanted so desperately to be American, and only American. One may ask, what does it mean to be American?

Throughout high school, I remember attributing "American" to Caucasian, and that was all it was. However, as I grew up a bit, and lost a bit of my ignorance, I realized that being American does not mean being Caucasian. A lot of what is considered as American culture is derived from the Western religion brought over from the Europeans when they first came over to the "New World." American culture, due to the population and society that we are in now, has become a mesh of different cultures combined into one. A lot of the Caucasian Americans that I know take different aspects of other cultures that they like and adopt them as their own. The American culture, it seems, has become one that is generalized and left up to interpretation. On the other hand, the Chinese culture is one that is defined more clearly by the Buddhist religion and from traditions handed down through generations upon generations. It is a culture that is focused on family, honor, and respect and much more centralized and specific.

In my young 25 years, I have realized that a huge difference between the American culture and the Chinese culture is the concept of Individualism versus Community. As an American, I am very individualistic. I have no problem doing things on my own, without others. My thoughts and plans for the future are very much centered on myself. However, as a Chinese, I feel an obligation towards the family. Thus, as a Chinese-American, I worry about my family; yet at the same time, my plans are still about myself.

One thing I have come to realize is the fact that I am constantly re-evaluating where I stand on things due to the Chinese and American culture differences. I realize that sometimes I am much more opinionated on certain things due to the influences of the American culture, and other times, I am much more subdued and respectful due to the influences of the Chinese culture. As I go through life, I realize that I will never really be able to fully complete the process of combining the two cultures. However, it is a process that will be ongoing and I will have to make choices of whether I want to think with the Chinese part or the American part of me, daily.

> *In my young 25 years, I have realized that a huge difference between the American culture and the Chinese culture is the concept of Individualism versus Community.*

What help me with these daily decisions are the influences of my Chinese friends. Through them, I have seen the positives of being Chinese-American, and mixing the Chinese culture, that I had so abhorred, into the American culture, that I had so revered, while growing up. In high school, I would see the small group of Asians who only associated with each other and nobody else. I remember thinking they were discriminating against anybody who was not Asian because they had so much pride in their culture. However, as I sat around with a few close friends from college, I realized that I had become one of "those." I have come to realize that it is not so much pride in the culture, but it is more about who can understand what you have been through and the way you think.

The majority of my close friends now, are not only Asian, but Chinese. I have come to realize that being Chinese and American is not so bad after all. Spending time with my close friends from college, I realize that they have (somewhat) successfully figured out what it means to be Chinese-American. They have taken the honor and respect of the Chinese culture and combined it with the individualism of the American culture and developed it into something I am encouraged and inspired by. They have managed to take the love for the Chinese language and integrated into our daily English language jokes. For example, due to my shyness around large groups, one of my friends would call me "wallflower" in Chinese; but instead of using the actual terminology, he would say qiang2 hua1 (literally translated— "wall" "flower").

Just because I consider myself Chinese, does not mean I do not consider myself American. I am very proud to be an American. However, I am also very proud of being Chinese. Only those of multiple cultures will ever understand the pride that I have in being Chinese-American.

I Just Came Out to My 80-Something Father

By Prumsodun Ok
Salon.com, December 30, 2011

After my sister called me a homophobic slur, I felt overwhelmed by hatred. And I dialed our dad in angry tears.

I don't even remember how it began.

My eldest sister is in my apartment, screaming and yelling at me with a nonsensical fury. There is something about my not going to work. There is something about my going out late at night. Is this woman crazy? I shut down her every attack with calm but assertive responses, revealing the faults in her strange accusations. The exchange is escalating wildly, but she is unable to faze me. Finally, in an angry, spiteful resignation, she says, "You're just a faggot."

The shit was about to hit the fan. And, seeing this, everyone who intruded into the apartment with her—her husband, my brother—tries to pull her out of my path.

Growing up, I've always been the black sheep of my family. I was ripped away from my refugee parents when I began kindergarten, English gaining importance over the Khmer I spoke at home. My mother once threatened to disown me if I pursued the predominantly female art form of Cambodian classical dance. And, in line with the combination of my youthful independence and my family's inability to guide me through American society, I defied my parents and left to study experimental filmmaking at the San Francisco Art Institute.

And now here I am, crying my eyes out in angry confusion, back with the family that my path has torn me from—back in my sleepy hometown of Long Beach—that has been nothing but cycles of poverty, ignorance and violence.

What the hell was I doing here? And how in the world did so much hatred come from my own family?

I grab my phone. I dial the number to my father's house, and he picks up with his voice of aged calm. It is a calm that comes from having lived for 82 years, from living at the mercy of the land, sun and water in rural Cambodia. It is a voice that has lived through French colonialism, the atrocities of the Khmer Rouge genocide, and now, displacement and alienation in America. I begin in tears, speaking in Khmer, "Pa, guess what your daughter did? Who the fuck does she think she is?!"

"What's going on?"

"Pa, I'm gay! I don't care if you don't approve. I don't need your love if you don't respect me! I don't need it!" I am crying uncontrollably, and there is no response on the other line.

"Prum . . . Prum," my father says after what feels like an eternity of drowning in my emotions. "Calm down. You are my son. And you'll always be."

My heart lifted. Surprise began to mix with the chaotic flowing of emotions. I think I just came out to my 80-something father, and he was OK with it. And it wasn't the last time.

> **"Prum . . . Prum," my father says after what feels like an eternity of drowning in my emotions. "Calm down. You are my son. And you'll always be."**

Things seemed to happen quickly after that. I was creating a visible place for myself as an artist in California through shows, fellowships and public talks.

Looking back at the incident, I'm perplexed at how it happened that way. First off, in the context of Cambodian classical dance—the epitome of Cambodian culture—there is a space for those who don't conform to heteronormative molds of man and woman. During the height of Cambodian dance ritual, a lone Brahmin who is half male and half female appears to act as a messenger between heaven and earth. This sacred, divine sanction of queer is echoed in contemporary Cambodia, where men can have wives and boyfriends, and female pop stars enact homosexual romances.

My sister's attack came off as an erasure of cultural memory, perhaps at the hands of colonialism and the fear-driven Puritanism of American society. As a result, my original dance works became increasingly political, and I was preparing to present one of them at REDCAT, the premier venue for experimental performance in Los Angeles.

At this time, a reporter from the *LA Times* was interviewing me (for a story that never ran). She wanted to speak with my father. We met at the dance studio where I was teaching. After questions about my father's life, she asks me, "So what does your father think about your being gay?"

"Pa, she wants to know how you feel about my being gay."

"You're gay?"

Oh dear. "Yes, Pa, I'm gay! Don't you remember? I was crying on the phone and I was telling you." The reporter is obviously wondering what is going on, as both my father and I seem confused. "I'm sorry. He's old. And he's forgotten that I told him that I was gay," I say to her in English.

I ask in Khmer, "Well, Pa?"

"What is there to say? You are my son. I love you no matter what. As long as you are a good person, nothing else matters."

My father, Sem Ok, passed away two years later, on Jan. 20, 2011. It was my 24th birthday. May he be remembered for his love.

❖

Prumsodun Ok is an artist, teacher, curator, writer and organizer. His interdisciplinary performance works explore the tradition of Cambodian classical dance to address contemporary LGBT and social issues. He is a 2011 TED Fellow. He lives in Long Beach, Calif., where he is executive editor of VoiceWaves, a youth-led journalism project of New America Media.

I Am Chinese American

By Ray Kwong
Forbes, May 30, 2011

I read a very good essay today over at the excellent LoveLoveChina blog, which I found extraordinarily honest and a poignant reminder of how people are sometimes (mis)characterized. Authored by a young lady identified only as Louisa, from what I gather a relatively recent NYU grad, her words moved me (and made me laugh). I share her post with you in full (and without comment) with the hope that it might move you, too.

In the eyes of most of the world, I am solely a Chinese girl.

"Where are you from" is a common conversation starter with random strangers, who, when I give them a true, but unsatisfactory answer, shake their heads and say "no, where are you REALLY from?" Sometimes, they skip this question all together and ask me why I don't speak English tinged with an accent (preferably something ching-chongy). Otherwise, they just take one look and scream "NI HAO" or "KON-NICHIWA" at me.

Hey guess what? I was born in America. I'm a Chinese American girl.

Yes, I do speak Mandarin, but no, I can't tell you what that calligraphy says. Yes, my parents do value education and a good job, but no, they are not Amy Chua "tiger parents." Yes, I am a good "Chinese" daughter and listen to my parents, but no, I don't follow blindly. No, I will not give you a sensuous massage. No, my soul is not crushed from my "misogynistic heritage."

I am not the exotic, petite Chinese girl you see on television (when they have Chinese people on television that is). I have huge feet. I am taller than the average white girl.

I am horrible at math. I'm allergic to pastels and most pop music. I pop the "fob sign" (the victory sign) facetiously. I use SAT words in my everyday conversations. I think in English (once in a while in Chinglish).

Amy Tan does not represent me, my experience, or any of my friends' experience. And definitely definitely, I am NOT a banana/twinkie, AZN, American Chinese, Chinese-American, or ABC (American Born Chinese), thank you very much.

What's the difference you may ask? Let me break it down for you:

- Banana/Twinkie: This is the Chinese American who completely rejects his/her Chinese heritage. They pretend to be white. They only associate with whites. They dye their hair blond in some futile attempt to look white. They may even bleach their skin. They hate that they look "ethnic." They are ashamed of themselves. We use this term derogatorily. No one, not even the banana would wear this label proudly.

- AZN: This is a Chinese (or Asian in general) American who is a little too proud of their Chinese heritage. They drive "rice rockets," blasting their hip hop out of speakers too big for their souped up cars with giant spoilers. The boys tend to emulate hip hop artists; the girls the latest Asian pop star. They're loud about their "Chinese-ness", but more than likely have no idea what being "Chinese" means and are probably embarrassments to their family.

- American Chinese/ABC: A term given to Chinese Americans, usually by Chinese people. My parents called me American Chinese, because they thought that having the "American" before the "Chinese" meant I was American first. But grammatically speaking, American Chinese and ABC (American born Chinese) emphasize the fact that the person is first and foremost Chinese. American becomes the adjective that describes the Chinese noun. For those of us who were born in America, this term gives off the impression that we are not American. We are foreigners in the land that gave birth to us.

- Chinese-American: Peter Feng, in his essay "In Search of Asian American Cinema," explains why Asian Americans, including Chinese Americans, decided to drop the hyphen: the hyphen represents a persistent discourse which suggests that Asians will never be fully accepted as Americans. Grammatically speaking, the hyphen makes 'Asian' and 'American' into two nouns, suggesting that Asian-Americans are caught between two distinctive cultures.

Again a question of grammar. In order for us to be accepted as Americans, we dropped the hyphen so that the Chinese became the adjective describing the American. In short, instead of being Chinese (noun) and American (noun), we are American who happen to be ethnically Chinese.

Of course, no one is actually conscious of these terms unless they really looked into it, so I'll let it slide.

So I am a Chinese American girl. Apparently, we don't get a good rep in many circles. Here are some of the things I've heard over the years:

- We only date other Asians (Asians from Asia and Asian Americans)
- We only date non-Asians
- We hate our Asian features and so dye our hair blonde and bleach our skin white
- We love our Asian features and so exploit them because it makes us exotic
- We are innocent lotus blossoms

- We are dragon ladies who will rip your heart out and eat it for breakfast (along with your little puppy dog too)
- Our parents wish we were boys
- Our parents want us to be submissive
- Our parents control every facet of our lives and have squashed out individuality
- We are quiet and timid
- We are loud and skanky
- We are virgins
- We know some secret Chinese sex act that is supposed to be amazing

I am not the exotic, petite Chinese girl you see on television (when they have Chinese people on television that is). I have huge feet. I am taller than the average white girl.

Quite frankly, if we were all these things I don't know how we're actually functional.

My favorite out of that partial list is the perception that being female and Chinese means that you are automatically treated as a second class citizen. A second class citizen in your family no less. It may have been true in the past. It may still be true in some Chinese families. But it is not true of all Chinese American families. The Chinese American families that I know, the Chinese American family that I grew up in, value their daughters. My female Chinese American friends with brothers tell me that their parents see their daughters as the success stories of the family. They are their parents' pride. They, in one friend's words, are ALPHA. I once asked my dad if he wished I were a boy or that he had a son. He told me that I was being stupid.

Maybe that's just because after America lifted the immigration ban on Asians in 1965, more and more educated Chinese immigrants came to America, many of whom were from the cities. They may have brought a different mindset than their rural, apparently "backwards" predecessors (I honestly don't know).

Then again, my parents were the product of the Cultural Revolution. Most of my friends' parents never went to college or have almost illiterate grandparents. Our families all started out as working class, working their way up to a middle or upper middle class life.

But one thing's for sure, they sure do love their daughters.

What does this all mean? I have no idea. Sometimes I wake up and feel like I'm a girl, or a metalhead, or a nerd. Sometimes I wake up feeling Chinese-American, forced to straddle two cultures by some invisible hand. Sometimes I wake up Chinese American, proud to say I'm an American and proud to have the adjective in front of it.

But usually I wake up feeling like me. I am a person. I am not, cannot, and will not, be lumped into a category because of what I look like. I am more than the color of my skin.

And I think that's what all Chinese Americans want.

My Life as an Undocumented Immigrant

By Jose Antonio Vargas
The New York Times, June 22, 2011

One August morning nearly two decades ago, my mother woke me and put me in a cab. She handed me a jacket. *"Baka malamig doon"* were among the few words she said. ("It might be cold there.") When I arrived at the Philippines' Ninoy Aquino International Airport with her, my aunt and a family friend, I was introduced to a man I'd never seen. They told me he was my uncle. He held my hand as I boarded an airplane for the first time. It was 1993, and I was 12.

My mother wanted to give me a better life, so she sent me thousands of miles away to live with her parents in America—my grandfather (*Lolo* in Tagalog) and grandmother (*Lola*). After I arrived in Mountain View, Calif., in the San Francisco Bay Area, I entered sixth grade and quickly grew to love my new home, family and culture. I discovered a passion for language, though it was hard to learn the difference between formal English and American slang. One of my early memories is of a freckled kid in middle school asking me, "What's up?" I replied, "The sky," and he and a couple of other kids laughed. I won the eighth-grade spelling bee by memorizing words I couldn't properly pronounce. (The winning word was "indefatigable.")

One day when I was 16, I rode my bike to the nearby D.M.V. office to get my driver's permit. Some of my friends already had their licenses, so I figured it was time. But when I handed the clerk my green card as proof of U.S. residency, she flipped it around, examining it. "This is fake," she whispered. "Don't come back here again."

Confused and scared, I pedaled home and confronted Lolo. I remember him sitting in the garage, cutting coupons. I dropped my bike and ran over to him, showing him the green card. *"Peke ba ito?"* I asked in Tagalog. ("Is this fake?") My grandparents were naturalized American citizens—he worked as a security guard, she as a food server—and they had begun supporting my mother and me financially when I was 3, after my father's wandering eye and inability to properly provide for us led to my parents' separation. Lolo was a proud man, and I saw the shame on his face as he told me he purchased the card, along with other fake documents, for me. "Don't show it to other people," he warned.

I decided then that I could never give anyone reason to doubt I was an American. I convinced myself that if I worked enough, if I achieved enough, I would be rewarded with citizenship. I felt I could earn it.

I've tried. Over the past 14 years, I've graduated from high school and college and built a career as a journalist, interviewing some of the most famous people in the country. On the surface, I've created a good life. I've lived the American dream.

But I am still an undocumented immigrant. And that means living a different kind of reality. It means going about my day in fear of being found out. It means rarely trusting people, even those closest to me, with who I really am. It means keeping my family photos in a shoebox rather than displaying them on shelves in my home, so friends don't ask about them. It means reluctantly, even painfully, doing things I know are wrong and unlawful. And it has meant relying on a sort of 21st-century underground railroad of supporters, people who took an interest in my future and took risks for me.

Last year I read about four students who walked from Miami to Washington to lobby for the Dream Act, a nearly decade-old immigration bill that would provide a path to legal permanent residency for young people who have been educated in this country. At the risk of deportation—the Obama administration has deported almost 800,000 people in the last two years—they are speaking out. Their courage has inspired me.

There are believed to be 11 million undocumented immigrants in the United States. We're not always who you think we are. Some pick your strawberries or care for your children. Some are in high school or college. And some, it turns out, write news articles you might read. I grew up here. This is my home. Yet even though I think of myself as an American and consider America my country, my country doesn't think of me as one of its own.

My first challenge was the language. Though I learned English in the Philippines, I wanted to lose my accent. During high school, I spent hours at a time watching television (especially "Frasier," "Home Improvement" and reruns of "The Golden Girls") and movies (from "Goodfellas" to "Anne of Green Gables"), pausing the VHS to try to copy how various characters enunciated their words. At the local library, I read magazines, books and newspapers—anything to learn how to write better. Kathy Dewar, my high-school English teacher, introduced me to journalism. From the moment I wrote my first article for the student paper, I convinced myself that having my name in print—writing in English, interviewing Americans—validated my presence here.

The debates over "illegal aliens" intensified my anxieties. In 1994, only a year after my flight from the Philippines, Gov. Pete Wilson was re-elected in part because of his support for Proposition 187, which prohibited undocumented immigrants from attending public school and accessing other services. (A federal court later found the law unconstitutional.) After my encounter at the D.M.V. in 1997, I grew more aware of anti-immigrant sentiments and stereotypes: *they don't want to assimilate, they are a drain on society.* They're not talking about me, I would tell myself. I have something to contribute.

To do that, I had to work—and for that, I needed a Social Security number. Fortunately, my grandfather had already managed to get one for me. Lolo had always taken care of everyone in the family. He and my grandmother emigrated legally in 1984 from Zambales, a province in the Philippines of rice fields and bamboo houses, following Lolo's sister, who married a Filipino-American serving in the American military. She petitioned for her brother and his wife to join her. When they got here, Lolo petitioned for his two children—my mother and her younger brother—to follow them. But instead of mentioning that my mother was a married woman, he listed her as single. Legal residents can't petition for their married children. Besides, Lolo didn't care for my father. He didn't want him coming here too.

But soon Lolo grew nervous that the immigration authorities reviewing the petition would discover my mother was married, thus derailing not only her chances of coming here but those of my uncle as well. So he withdrew her petition. After my uncle came to America legally in 1991, Lolo tried to get my mother here through a tourist visa, but she wasn't able to obtain one. That's when she decided to send me. My mother told me later that she figured she would follow me soon. She never did.

The "uncle" who brought me here turned out to be a coyote, not a relative, my grandfather later explained. Lolo scraped together enough money—I eventually learned it was $4,500, a huge sum for him—to pay him to smuggle me here under a fake name and fake passport. (I never saw the passport again after the flight and have always assumed that the coyote kept it.) After I arrived in America, Lolo obtained a new fake Filipino passport, in my real name this time, adorned with a fake student visa, in addition to the fraudulent green card.

> *There are believed to be 11 million undocumented immigrants in the United States. We're not always who you think we are. Some pick your strawberries or care for your children. Some are in high school or college. And some, it turns out, write news articles you might read.*

Using the fake passport, we went to the local Social Security Administration office and applied for a Social Security number and card. It was, I remember, a quick visit. When the card came in the mail, it had my full, real name, but it also clearly stated: "Valid for work only with I.N.S. authorization."

When I began looking for work, a short time after the D.M.V. incident, my grandfather and I took the Social Security card to Kinko's, where he covered the "I.N.S. authorization" text with a sliver of white tape. We then made photocopies of the card. At a glance, at least, the copies would look like copies of a regular, unrestricted Social Security card.

Lolo always imagined I would work the kind of low-paying jobs that undocumented people often take. (Once I married an American, he said, I would get my real papers, and everything would be fine.) But even menial jobs require documents, so he and I hoped the doctored card would work for now. The more documents I had, he said, the better.

While in high school, I worked part time at Subway, then at the front desk of the local Y.M.C.A., then at a tennis club, until I landed an unpaid internship at *The Mountain View Voice*, my hometown newspaper. First I brought coffee and helped around the office; eventually I began covering city-hall meetings and other assignments for pay.

For more than a decade of getting part-time and full-time jobs, employers have rarely asked to check my original Social Security card. When they did, I showed the photocopied version, which they accepted. Over time, I also began checking the citizenship box on my federal I-9 employment eligibility forms. (Claiming full citizenship was actually easier than declaring permanent resident "green card" status, which would have required me to provide an alien registration number.)

This deceit never got easier. The more I did it, the more I felt like an impostor, the more guilt I carried—and the more I worried that I would get caught. But I kept doing it. I needed to live and survive on my own, and I decided this was the way.

Mountain View High School became my second home. I was elected to represent my school at school-board meetings, which gave me the chance to meet and befriend Rich Fischer, the superintendent for our school district. I joined the speech and debate team, acted in school plays and eventually became co-editor of *The Oracle*, the student newspaper. That drew the attention of my principal, Pat Hyland. "You're at school just as much as I am," she told me. Pat and Rich would soon become mentors, and over time, almost surrogate parents for me.

After a choir rehearsal during my junior year, Jill Denny, the choir director, told me she was considering a Japan trip for our singing group. I told her I couldn't afford it, but she said we'd figure out a way. I hesitated, and then decided to tell her the truth. "It's not really the money," I remember saying. "I don't have the right passport." When she assured me we'd get the proper documents, I finally told her. "I can't get the right passport," I said. "I'm not supposed to be here."

She understood. So the choir toured Hawaii instead, with me in tow. (Mrs. Denny and I spoke a couple of months ago, and she told me she hadn't wanted to leave any student behind.)

Later that school year, my history class watched a documentary on Harvey Milk, the openly gay San Francisco city official who was assassinated. This was 1999, just six months after Matthew Shepard's body was found tied to a fence in Wyoming. During the discussion, I raised my hand and said something like: "I'm sorry Harvey Milk got killed for being gay. . . . I've been meaning to say this. . . . I'm gay."

I hadn't planned on coming out that morning, though I had known that I was gay for several years. With that announcement, I became the only openly gay student at school, and it caused turmoil with my grandparents. Lolo kicked me out of the house for a few weeks. Though we eventually reconciled, I had disappointed him on two fronts. First, as a Catholic, he considered homosexuality a sin and was embarrassed about having "*ang apo na bakla*" ("a grandson who is gay"). Even worse, I was making matters more difficult for myself, he said. I needed to marry an American woman in order to gain a green card.

Tough as it was, coming out about being gay seemed less daunting than coming out about my legal status. I kept my other secret mostly hidden.

While my classmates awaited their college acceptance letters, I hoped to get a full-time job at *The Mountain View Voice* after graduation. It's not that I didn't want to go to college, but I couldn't apply for state and federal financial aid. Without that, my family couldn't afford to send me.

But when I finally told Pat and Rich about my immigration "problem"—as we called it from then on—they helped me look for a solution. At first, they even wondered if one of them could adopt me and fix the situation that way, but a lawyer Rich consulted told him it wouldn't change my legal status because I was too old. Eventually they connected me to a new scholarship fund for high-potential students who were usually the first in their families to attend college. Most important, the fund was not concerned with immigration status. I was among the first recipients, with the scholarship covering tuition, lodging, books and other expenses for my studies at San Francisco State University.

As a college freshman, I found a job working part time at *The San Francisco Chronicle*, where I sorted mail and wrote some freelance articles. My ambition was to get a reporting job, so I embarked on a series of internships. First I landed at *The Philadelphia Daily News*, in the summer of 2001, where I covered a drive-by shooting and the wedding of the 76ers star Allen Iverson. Using those articles, I applied to *The Seattle Times* and got an internship for the following summer.

But then my lack of proper documents became a problem again. *The Times's* recruiter, Pat Foote, asked all incoming interns to bring certain paperwork on their first day: a birth certificate, or a passport, or a driver's license plus an original Social Security card. I panicked, thinking my documents wouldn't pass muster. So before starting the job, I called Pat and told her about my legal status. After consulting with management, she called me back with the answer I feared: I couldn't do the internship.

This was devastating. What good was college if I couldn't then pursue the career I wanted? I decided then that if I was to succeed in a profession that is all about truth-telling, I couldn't not tell the truth about myself.

After this episode, Jim Strand, the venture capitalist who sponsored my scholarship, offered to pay for an immigration lawyer. Rich and I went to meet her in San Francisco's financial district.

I was hopeful. This was in early 2002, shortly after Senators Orrin Hatch, the Utah Republican, and Dick Durbin, the Illinois Democrat, introduced the Dream Act—Development, Relief and Education for Alien Minors. It seemed like the legislative version of what I'd told myself: If I work hard and contribute, things will work out.

But the meeting left me crushed. My only solution, the lawyer said, was to go back to the Philippines and accept a 10-year ban before I could apply to return legally.

If Rich was discouraged, he hid it well. "Put this problem on a shelf," he told me. "Compartmentalize it. Keep going."

And I did. For the summer of 2003, I applied for internships across the country. Several newspapers, including The *Wall Street Journal*, *The Boston Globe* and *The Chicago Tribune*, expressed interest. But when *The Washington Post* offered me a spot, I knew where I would go. And this time, I had no intention of acknowledging my "problem."

The *Post* internship posed a tricky obstacle: It required a driver's license. (After my close call at the California D.M.V., I'd never gotten one.) So I spent an afternoon at The Mountain View Public Library, studying various states' requirements. Oregon was among the most welcoming—and it was just a few hours' drive north.

Again, my support network came through. A friend's father lived in Portland, and he allowed me to use his address as proof of residency. Pat, Rich and Rich's long-time assistant, Mary Moore, sent letters to me at that address. Rich taught me how to do three-point turns in a parking lot, and a friend accompanied me to Portland.

The license meant everything to me—it would let me drive, fly and work. But my grandparents worried about the Portland trip and the Washington internship. While Lola offered daily prayers so that I would not get caught, Lolo told me that I was dreaming too big, risking too much.

I was determined to pursue my ambitions. I was 22, I told them, responsible for my own actions. But this was different from Lolo's driving a confused teenager to Kinko's. I knew what I was doing now, and I knew it wasn't right. But what was I supposed to do?

I was paying state and federal taxes, but I was using an invalid Social Security card and writing false information on my employment forms. But that seemed better than depending on my grandparents or on Pat, Rich and Jim—or returning to a country I barely remembered. I convinced myself all would be O.K. if I lived up to the qualities of a "citizen": hard work, self-reliance, love of my country.

At the D.M.V. in Portland, I arrived with my photocopied Social Security card, my college I.D., a pay stub from *The San Francisco Chronicle* and my proof of state residence—the letters to the Portland address that my support network had sent. It worked. My license, issued in 2003, was set to expire eight years later, on my 30th birthday, on Feb. 3, 2011. I had eight years to succeed professionally, and to hope that some sort of immigration reform would pass in the meantime and allow me to stay.

It seemed like all the time in the world.

My summer in Washington was exhilarating. I was intimidated to be in a major newsroom but was assigned a mentor—Peter Perl, a veteran magazine writer—to help me navigate it. A few weeks into the internship, he printed out one of my articles, about a guy who recovered a long-lost wallet, circled the first two paragraphs and left it on my desk. "Great eye for details—awesome!" he wrote. Though I didn't know it then, Peter would become one more member of my network.

At the end of the summer, I returned to *The San Francisco Chronicle*. My plan was to finish school—I was now a senior—while I worked for *The Chronicle* as a reporter for the city desk. But when *The Post* beckoned again, offering me a full-time, two-year paid internship that I could start when I graduated in June 2004, it was too tempting to pass up. I moved back to Washington.

About four months into my job as a reporter for *The Post*, I began feeling increasingly paranoid, as if I had "illegal immigrant" tattooed on my forehead—and in Washington, of all places, where the debates over immigration seemed never-ending. I was so eager to prove myself that I feared I was annoying some colleagues and editors—and worried that any one of these professional journalists could discover my secret. The anxiety was nearly paralyzing. I decided I had to tell one of the higher-ups about my situation. I turned to Peter.

By this time, Peter, who still works at *The Post*, had become part of management as the paper's director of newsroom training and professional development. One afternoon in late October, we walked a couple of blocks to Lafayette Square, across from the White House. Over some 20 minutes, sitting on a bench, I told him everything: the Social Security card, the driver's license, Pat and Rich, my family.

Peter was shocked. "I understand you 100 times better now," he said. He told me that I had done the right thing by telling him, and that it was now our shared problem. He said he didn't want to do anything about it just yet. I had just been hired, he said, and I needed to prove myself. "When you've done enough," he said, "we'll tell Don and Len together." (Don Graham is the chairman of The Washington Post Company; Leonard Downie Jr. was then the paper's executive editor.) A month later, I spent my first Thanksgiving in Washington with Peter and his family.

In the five years that followed, I did my best to "do enough." I was promoted to staff writer, reported on video-game culture, wrote a series on Washington's H.I.V./AIDS epidemic and covered the role of technology and social media in the 2008 presidential race. I visited the White House, where I interviewed senior aides and covered a state dinner—and gave the Secret Service the Social Security number I obtained with false documents.

I did my best to steer clear of reporting on immigration policy but couldn't always avoid it. On two occasions, I wrote about Hillary Clinton's position on driver's licenses for undocumented immigrants. I also wrote an article about Senator Mel Martinez of Florida, then the chairman of the Republican National Committee, who was defending his party's stance toward Latinos after only one Republican presidential candidate—John McCain, the co-author of a failed immigration bill—agreed to participate in a debate sponsored by Univision, the Spanish-language network.

It was an odd sort of dance: I was trying to stand out in a highly competitive newsroom, yet I was terrified that if I stood out too much, I'd invite unwanted scrutiny. I tried to compartmentalize my fears, distract myself by reporting on the lives of other people, but there was no escaping the central conflict in my life. Maintaining a deception for so long distorts your sense of self. You start wondering who you've become, and why.

In April 2008, I was part of a *Post* team that won a Pulitzer Prize for the paper's coverage of the Virginia Tech shootings a year earlier. Lolo died a year earlier, so it was Lola who called me the day of the announcement. The first thing she said was, "*Anong mangyayari kung malaman ng mga tao?*"

What will happen if people find out?

I couldn't say anything. After we got off the phone, I rushed to the bathroom on the fourth floor of the newsroom, sat down on the toilet and cried.

In the summer of 2009, without ever having had that follow-up talk with top *Post* management, I left the paper and moved to New York to join *The Huffington Post*. I met Arianna Huffington at a Washington Press Club Foundation dinner I was covering for *The Post* two years earlier, and she later recruited me to join her news site. I wanted to learn more about Web publishing, and I thought the new job would provide a useful education.

Still, I was apprehensive about the move: many companies were already using E-Verify, a program set up by the Department of Homeland Security that checks if prospective employees are eligible to work, and I didn't know if my new employer was among them. But I'd been able to get jobs in other newsrooms, I figured, so I filled out the paperwork as usual and succeeded in landing on the payroll.

While I worked at *The Huffington Post*, other opportunities emerged. My H.I.V./ AIDS series became a documentary film called "The Other City," which opened at the Tribeca Film Festival last year and was broadcast on Showtime. I began writing for magazines and landed a dream assignment: profiling Facebook's Mark Zuckerberg for *The New Yorker*.

The more I achieved, the more scared and depressed I became. I was proud of my work, but there was always a cloud hanging over it, over me. My old eight-year deadline—the expiration of my Oregon driver's license—was approaching.

After slightly less than a year, I decided to leave *The Huffington Post*. In part, this was because I wanted to promote the documentary and write a book about online culture—or so I told my friends. But the real reason was, after so many years of trying to be a part of the system, of focusing all my energy on my professional life, I learned that no amount of professional success would solve my problem or ease the sense of loss and displacement I felt. I lied to a friend about why I couldn't take a weekend trip to Mexico. Another time I concocted an excuse for why I couldn't go on an all-expenses-paid trip to Switzerland. I have been unwilling, for years, to be in a long-term relationship because I never wanted anyone to get too close and ask too many questions. All the while, Lola's question was stuck in my head: What will happen if people find out?

Early this year, just two weeks before my 30th birthday, I won a small reprieve: I obtained a driver's license in the state of Washington. The license is valid until 2016. This offered me five more years of acceptable identification—but also five more years of fear, of lying to people I respect and institutions that trusted me, of running away from who I am.

I'm done running. I'm exhausted. I don't want that life anymore.

So I've decided to come forward, own up to what I've done, and tell my story to the best of my recollection. I've reached out to former bosses and employers and apologized for misleading them—a mix of humiliation and liberation coming with each disclosure. All the people mentioned in this article gave me permission to use their names. I've also talked to family and friends about my situation and am working with legal counsel to review my options. I don't know what the consequences will be of telling my story.

I do know that I am grateful to my grandparents, my Lolo and Lola, for giving me the chance for a better life. I'm also grateful to my other family—the support network I found here in America—for encouraging me to pursue my dreams.

It's been almost 18 years since I've seen my mother. Early on, I was mad at her for putting me in this position, and then mad at myself for being angry and ungrateful. By the time I got to college, we rarely spoke by phone. It became too painful; after a while it was easier to just send money to help support her and my two half-siblings. My sister, almost 2 years old when I left, is almost 20 now. I've never met my 14-year-old brother. I would love to see them.

Not long ago, I called my mother. I wanted to fill the gaps in my memory about that August morning so many years ago. We had never discussed it. Part of me wanted to shove the memory aside, but to write this article and face the facts of my life, I needed more details. Did I cry? Did she? Did we kiss goodbye?

My mother told me I was excited about meeting a stewardess, about getting on a plane. She also reminded me of the one piece of advice she gave me for blending in: If anyone asked why I was coming to America, I should say I was going to Disneyland.

Mideast Meets Midwest

By James Poniewozik
Time, November 14, 2011

When I was growing up in Monroe, Mich., one of our biggest football games each season was against the Fordson High Tractors, from the Detroit suburb of Dearborn—a perennially tough team and Monroe's rival since 1928. I knew, vaguely, that Dearborn had the largest Arab-American population in the U.S., but all I saw were beefy guys in football helmets. It's not as if they called themselves the Fordson Crescents.

What never occurred to me until I watched *All-American Muslim* (debuting Nov. 13 on TLC) was that the Tractors face a training challenge unlike most schools in the football-loving Midwest. Those years when the holy month of Ramadan lands in football season—and Muslims abstain from food and drink during daylight—players risk dangerous dehydration. So for a month, the Tractors practice at night, from 10 p.m. until 5 a.m. In the first episode of *All-American*, coach Fouad Zaban calls a meeting and tells the team his plan to sacrifice sleep for safety. Then they go out onto the practice field to knock some heads.

It is at this intersection, where *Friday Night Lights* meets the Friday call to prayer, that the fascinating All-American Muslim lives. Reality shows are not known for ethnic nuance; see the spicy-meatball Italian stereotypes of *The Real Housewives of New Jersey* and *Jersey Shore*. But this eight-part series takes a people that pop culture has spent a decade making sinister and exotic and recasts them as refreshingly ordinary.

TLC was developing the show at a time when Muslim bashing erupted like some kind of delayed stress reaction to 9/11. Protesters screamed against an Islamic center planned near Ground Zero. (Sarah Palin, a TLC star herself last fall, enjoined "peaceful" Muslims to "refudiate" the project.) Fox and NPR analyst Juan Williams was nervous seeing Muslims on airplanes. And Nevada Senate candidate Sharron Angle charged that Muslims were implementing Shari'a in Dearborn, a claim shot down by its non-Muslim mayor, Jack O'Reilly.

TV used to integrate our living rooms with sitcoms about American minorities, from *The Goldbergs* in 1949 to *The Cosby Show* and *Will & Grace*. (After the Ground Zero flap, a *Daily Show* sketch imagined a sitcom that could combat stereotypes about Muslims titled *The Qu'osby Show*.) But today, that's more the role of reality TV. TLC specializes in family stories that open a door on subcultures: *Sister Wives*, about polygamy; *Little People, Big World*, about dwarfism; and the fecund Duggars' *19 Kids and Counting*, which is as much about conservative Christian culture as it is about raising a family the size of a church choir.

Unlike TLC's past family shows, *All-American Muslim* focuses on not one family but several to capture a broader swath of Dearborn. Besides Zaban, there's Nina Bazzy, an independent-minded businesswoman whose ambition of opening a nightclub runs up against the community's ideas of female propriety; Mike Jaafar, a family man and deputy sheriff; and Nader and Nawal Aoude, a young couple expecting their first baby.

Like many family stories, it opens with a wedding. Shadia Amen, 31, a divorced mom with tattoos and a thing for country music ("I'm a hillbilly at heart"), is getting remarried to Jeff McDermott, a Catholic who has agreed to convert to Islam. Jeff serves as a kind of surrogate for the non-Muslim viewer. (Watch Jeff get cranky when he has to fast for his first Ramadan! Watch Jeff's Irish Catholic family find out the reception has no alcohol!) But All-American points out the nuances of the situation instead of amping up the conflict. For instance, Shadia's conservative parents are delighted that Jeff's converting; his mother is less so. But as Shadia's family points out, her parents would not have been happy if she had converted. And Jeff's mom—who ends up attending his wedding happily—realizes she's reacting less out of religious fervor than inevitable wedding-induced stress. "Change of any type is hard," she says.

> *. . . All-American Muslim recognizes that religion is important—if it weren't, it wouldn't be religion—but not all-defining. And it's not monolithic, even within families. Free spirit Shadia has face piercings, her more conservative older sister Suehaila wears the traditional hijab, and their younger sister Samira is considering wearing it for the first time since 9/11 (when she stopped for fear of discrimination).*

In other words, *All-American Muslim* recognizes that religion is important—if it weren't, it wouldn't be religion—but not all-defining. And it's not monolithic, even within families. Free spirit Shadia has face piercings, her more conservative older sister Suehaila wears the traditional hijab, and their younger sister Samira is considering wearing it for the first time since 9/11 (when she stopped for fear of discrimination).

To tease out these differences, All-American Muslim brings the different families together between segments to discuss some of the issues that arise: the place of women in Muslim culture (a recurring theme of the show), war, intermarriage, sex, adoption. There are no pronouncements or right answers—just some well-meaning Midwesterners trying to puzzle out what God thinks about, say, going to a Red Lobster that has a bar. (This should ring true to any viewer; coming from a Jewish and Catholic family, I recall a few confused debates over the rules of Passover and Lent.) Real life is not a religious tract; it's just life, and people muddle through it, applying spiritual lessons on the fly.

The larger world's religious politics do intrude on post-9/11 Dearborn. The Tractors are taunted at away games as "terrorists," and we see deputy sheriff Mike providing security at a festival that draws a crowd of anti-Muslim protesters jeering, "Muhammad is a pedophile!" But the most intriguing incident involves something no more geopolitically charged than pancakes. Nader and Nawal go out for brunch in another suburb and wait 15 minutes before a hostess seats them. Nawal is furious, certain they're being mistreated because she is wearing the hijab. Nader disagrees, noting that they've eaten there before with no problem. Nawal considers his point: "Maybe she was just having a bad day."

Maybe it was discrimination, maybe it wasn't. The point is that they have to wonder, whereas most Americans would just assume they were getting crappy service. As we get to know Nawal, we see that she's not strident or sanctimonious; asked if she believes other Muslim women should wear the hijab, she says, "Who the hell am I to tell them?"

The most revolutionary thing *All-American Muslim* does is introduce us to a woman like Nawal, with her plainspoken *ya knows* and *kindas* and flat upper-Midwest vowels—a devout Muslim in a hijab who sounds just a touch like Michele Bachmann. TLC might have picked a more exotic immigrant community in California or Brooklyn. Instead it set the show in a town so American that Henry Ford founded his car company there and so American it then welcomed Middle Eastern immigrants to help build the machines. These characters aren't "just like us," because nobody is just like anybody. Religion is a way of distinguishing values and understanding life. But that life itself is something we all share—the pancakes and the weddings and the football games.

Speaking of which: *All-American Muslim* finished shooting before football season ended. After I watched it, I checked my hometown newspaper online for the score of the Monroe-Fordson game. Monroe won. But I was happy to read, after getting to know these characters, that Dearborn managed to qualify for the playoffs too. Go Tractors!

6

Family, Finances, and the Economy

(© Greg Federman)

Because of the economic downturn, more families are living under one roof, creating multi-generational households.

Family and the Economy

By Paul McCaffrey

The global financial panic of 2008 and 2009 and the ensuing recession have created some of the worst economic conditions since the Great Depression of the late 1920s and 1930s. Both the causes and the effects of the turmoil are many and varied, but the crisis's impact on two sectors in particular—real estate and employment—has hit American families especially hard. For example, between 2007 and 2010, according to government statistics, the average American household lost one fifth of its net value, while the Rockefeller Institute indicated that about 20 percent of US households saw their income decline by at least one quarter. The recession's toll is still coming into focus and its ramifications will be studied for decades to come, but one of the principal legacies of the recession will be how it has altered the dynamics of American families and how those changes will reshape the structure of society for the future.

The collapse of the housing sector was one of the principal causes of the 2008 and 2009 recession. The US real estate market boomed throughout much of the early 2000s. Easy credit and perennially rising property values persuaded many to enter the market under the notion that real estate investment was a sure thing. Mortgages were easy to obtain, sometimes without a credit check or proof of income. Some buyers bought their homes with exotic adjustable rate mortgages that they could not afford and did not understand. These conditions gave rise to an inflated and unsustainable housing bubble. Prices peaked in early 2006 and began a precipitous decline over the next two years. As prices fell, there was a growth in the number of underwater mortgages—those mortgages on which more was owed than the property was worth. Many homeowners started to default on their mortgages, and foreclosure rates skyrocketed. Five years into the crisis, median home prices have declined by almost 40 percent, banks have foreclosed on five million homes, and some analysts anticipate another three to five million homes will be foreclosed upon in the next few years.

The effect of the housing crisis on families, particularly on children, is especially harsh. Before the crisis is over, according to estimates, 10 percent of American children under the age of eighteen—about eight million children in total—will have suffered as a result of foreclosures. Not only do these children experience the emotional difficulty of being uprooted, but they face an increased risk of other social maladies. As Bruce Lesley, president of the children's advocacy group First Focus, commented: "Dislocation in housing is like missing a whole month of school. The chances of being held back, the chances of dropping out increase dramatically."

The employment picture is equally dismal. Thirty months into the recession, in June 2010, the Pew Research Center released a stark assessment of the jobs situation. According to the Center's survey, 32 percent of the work force had become unemployed at some point during the recession. Another 28 percent had their work hours reduced, 23 percent had taken a pay cut, 12 percent had to be put on unpaid leave, and 11 percent reported having had a full-time job reduced to part time. Unemployment peaked at a rate of 10.2 percent in October 2009, and since then the rate has not gone below 8 percent. Many of those out of work are the long-term unemployed, meaning they have been out of a job for over six months. In May 2010, 46 percent of the unemployed were long-term, while it took the median out-of-work job seeker 23.2 weeks to find a new position. The 23.2-week mark was by far the worst such rate since World War II.

For families, widespread and entrenched unemployment has had dire consequences. According to 2010 estimates by the Brookings Institution, 31 percent of the unemployed were parents of children under eighteen. In total, around 8.1 million children lived with an unemployed parent; this group constituted 11 percent, or one in nine, of all American children. "These 8.1 million children are more likely to experience homelessness, suffer from child abuse, fail to complete high school or college, and live in poverty as adults than other children," a Brookings Institution writer noted. A Pew survey further reported that nearly half of the long-term unemployed found their situations had negatively impacted their familial relationships. A joint *New York Times*/CBS poll revealed that around 40 percent of out-of-work parents believed their circumstances had led to behavioral changes in their children.

The employment situation has also helped to shift gender roles to a considerable degree. Over the past several decades, women have made vast strides in the work force. Though the recession hurt everyone, it increased the economic influence of women relative to men, as the latter suffered an overwhelming share of the job losses. This has led some analysts to refer to the recent recession as a "mancession." In 2009, women composed 47 percent of the labor force, up from 33 percent in 1960, and around 71 percent of mothers with children under 18 were working. Despite these advances, however, women tend to earn less per capita compared to men. During the recovery, men have made up some ground, but they are a long way from regaining their prerecession status. In families, the shifting fortunes of men and women in the work force are reflected in their changing responsibilities. As mothers are taking up more of the economic burden, fathers are assuming more care-giving functions.

Declining birth rates are another of the recession's principal impacts on the American family. Researchers have correlated foreclosure and unemployment rates, falling per capita income, and other figures with birth rates. As a result of the Great Depression, for example—even during a time when contraceptives were not easily obtained—the number of births per 1,000 women between the ages of fifteen and forty-four fell from an average of 102.6 in 1926 to 75.8 in 1936, a decline of more than 25 percent in the course of one decade. In 2007, 69.6 children were born per 1,000 women between the ages of fifteen and forty-four. By 2010, the rate had decreased to around 64.7, constituting about a 7 percent drop. Total US births fell during that time period from 4.32 million (the most ever recorded in the United

States) to 4.02 million. "Anyone who has wanted to have a child is concerned about whether they can afford it, but the economy has really exacerbated that," commented Linda Murray, editor in chief of BabyCenter, an online publication for parents. Indeed, a BabyCenter survey found that 43 percent of women surveyed said they would wait to have children until their financial situation was more secure, and two thirds of women surveyed said that their number of children would depend to a large extent on their economic security.

What such results mean for the future is not quite clear. Some believe the trend will leave a permanent imprint on American demographics, resulting in smaller families and, with fewer children born, an older population. Other researchers see the recent shortfall as merely a temporary lag that will be made up for in time: people have not given up on having children; they are just holding off until economic conditions improve. To support their case, they point to women between the ages of forty and forty-four whose birth rates actually increased from 2008 to 2009. The lesson, according to some, is that when age constraints make delaying childbirth problematic, economic conditions do not stand in the way of those who want to have kids.

Though the ultimate implications of the recession-inspired baby drought are as yet unclear, the trend does illustrate the economic burden of raising children. According to estimates by the US Department of Agriculture, it will cost approximately $226,920 to provide for a baby born in 2010 until the age of eighteen. Not included in those figures are the costs of college, which are considerable. Amid difficult economic circumstances, such financial burdens are too onerous for many to take up.

While the influence of the economy on birth rates is both intuitive and well established, what sort of bearing it has on marriage and divorce is not as clear cut. Marriage rates have been declining for decades, and it may seem reasonable to infer, as many have, that a tough economy—one that leaves many young adults without jobs and forces them to continue to live with their parents well into adulthood—might also keep them from marrying. But the evidence is not so conclusive. "You've probably heard the latest marriage narrative: With the recession upon us, young lovers can't afford to marry," economist Justin Wolfers declared. "As appealing as this story is, it has one problem: It's not true." Wolfers did not find any evidence to support a connection between marriage rates and economic conditions. "In fact, the marriage rate appears amazingly insensitive to the business cycle," he concluded.

Similarly, since money troubles are often a cause of marital and familial strife, some might anticipate that a dismal economy would lead to more broken marriages. Yet during tough economic periods, paradoxically, the divorce rate tends to decrease. Divorces cost money, as does maintaining two households, and in hard times people may choose to remain together for financial reasons, which is not to say that staying together necessarily offers a better home environment. "We know from the experience of the Great Depression of the 1930s that divorce rates can fall while family conflict and domestic violence rates rise," a writer for the Council on Contemporary Families observed.

Financial difficulties are also keeping families together longer. As a consequence of ongoing economic hardship, young adults are often unable to find jobs and are delaying moving out of their parents' homes. The unemployment rate for young adults between ages eighteen to twenty-nine is around 50 percent higher than for workers as whole. In May 2012, for example, 12.1 percent of young adults were unemployed, while the national rate stood at 8.2 percent. Circumstances have forced adults of all ages to move back in with their parents or to share a home with other relatives. Indeed, according to a Pew Research Center survey, during the first thirty months of the recession, 9 percent of respondents over the age of twenty-nine, and 24 percent between the ages of eighteen and twenty-nine, reported living or moving back in with their parents.

The lesson of the 2008 and 2009 recession, like other economic upheavals, is that economic instability breeds familial instability. Financial distress, whether resulting from the loss of a job, the loss of a home, or some other setback, increases the likelihood of conflict and abuse in a household, if not necessarily divorce. Whether due to financial pressure, parental conflict, or some combination of the two, children raised amid such circumstances are at greater risk of mental illness, substance abuse, and other difficulties later in life. Future families are affected by the economic unease as well. Faced with financial uncertainty, many put off having children or have fewer children, creating a lower birth rate. As young adults find it difficult to enter the job market, they are staying with their families rather than starting their own households. Though such patterns are not altogether unexpected, the severity of the recent recession will ensure that its legacy is a powerful one.

Poverty, Hardship and Families: How Many People Are Poor, and What Does Being Poor in America Really Mean?

By Philip N. Cohen
Contemporaryfamilies.org, December 5, 2011

This briefing paper describes three common misperceptions about poverty and families, and clarifies new information about recent poverty trends.

Misconception #1. Official Poverty Numbers Inflate the Problem of Poverty

In 2010, the official poverty rate in the U.S. was 15.1%, representing 46.2 million people—the largest number ever recorded and still rising despite the economy's return to growth after the recession. This is 8.9 million more poor people than in 2007, and 14.6 more than in 2000.

Critics argue that official figures greatly overestimate poverty in America because the government's traditional calculation of poverty status does not take into account non-cash benefits such as food stamps, tax benefits such as the Earned Income Tax Credit (EITC), or income contributions from non-"family" members such as cohabiting partners. So some families that are officially income-poor actually receive other support that allows them to meet their basic needs.

On the other hand, many families whose income is higher than the official poverty cut-off face expenses such as taxes and medical costs that reduce their household take-home pay below the poverty level.

To compensate for the areas where the official measure either under—or over—estimates poverty, the Census Bureau recently released a Supplemental Poverty Measure that takes into account many more sources of tax and benefit support—but also considers other burdens, including taxes, work expenses and out-of-pocket medical costs. The new measure also updates the calculation of need (which was historically indexed only to food needs) so that it now includes the price of food, clothing, shelter and utilities (adjusted for each region). The result is an indicator of poverty that better reflects Americans' actual ability to meet their needs.

Contrary to claims that the official poverty rate overstates the problem of poverty, the new poverty measure reveals a slightly *higher* overall poverty rate—16 percent in 2010, compared to 15.1 percent by the other method of calculation. However, it also leads to a significant adjustment in poverty rates by age. The new measure yields a poverty rate about 4 points *lower* for children than the official measure (18.2% versus 22.5%). But it shows a poverty rate for seniors almost 7 points *higher* than the official formula yields (15.9% versus 9%). That is mostly because many families of poor children have the benefit of the EITC and food stamps (each of which pulled about 2% of children above the poverty line), while an additional 7% of people age 65+ are below poverty because of out-of-pocket medical costs.

Rather than merely defining an arbitrary line between poor and non-poor, therefore, the new measure helps us see what most affects the ability of people living on the margin to meet their basic needs. Some policies and programs are genuinely helping poor families with children (such as the EITC, which provides an annual refund to low-income workers with children; or food stamps), and some groups are disproportionately harmed by runaway healthcare costs (especially low-income seniors).

Misconception #2. Poverty in America Is Purely a Relative Condition That Does Not Involve Serious Deprivation

According to the Heritage Foundation, U.S. living standards are so high that even the poor live well, no matter how you measure poverty. The Foundation made headlines this year by reporting that nearly all poor households have refrigerators, televisions, and microwaves. Although they may be struggling, the report's authors said, "in most cases, they are struggling to pay for air conditioning and cable TV while putting food on the table."

It is true that living standards in the U.S. today are higher than in earlier eras. Some advances in technology have reduced the cost of products that were once prohibitively expensive (such as televisions). Imports from poor countries have made some consumer goods (such as clothing) much cheaper. And poverty is far less widespread in the United States than in most Latin American, African, or Eastern European countries.

Compared with its peers, however, the U.S. does not fare well. Adjusting for taxes and government transfers, the U.S. has a higher poverty rate than all but one of the Western European, Nordic, and Anglophone countries. In fact, the U.S. poverty rate for children is more than *twice* as high as that for 8 of those countries.

Furthermore, poor people in America do experience real deprivation. As of 2010:

- More than one in five children (22%) lived in a household that was "food insecure," meaning that "[a]t times [they were] unable to acquire adequate food for active, healthy living for all household members because they had insufficient money and other resources for food."

- More than one in five adults (22%) ages 18–64 below the poverty line could not afford prescription medicines they needed at some time during the year. Even among those with incomes between 100% and 200% of poverty, nearly one in five couldn't afford necessary medicine at some point.

- More than half of children (52%) below the official poverty line experienced one of four "major hardships" during the year (very low food

security, overcrowded housing, late rent or mortgage, or forgone doctor
or hospital visit).

- During periods of cold weather, poor families and elderly individuals in
  cold areas of the country are more likely to experience food insecurity,
  as they are forced to choose between spending on heat and spending on food. These choices may become more frequent if President
  Obama's proposal to cut the Low Income Home Energy Assistance
  Program passes.

Misconception #3. Poverty Is a Static Condition

We use statistics to capture the level of poverty at a moment in time, or to track a
trend over time. But as a lived experience—especially one within families—poverty
is a dynamic condition that unfolds over a lifetime, with time spent above and below
the poverty line. The new measure of poverty reveals that there are almost twice as
many "near poor" individuals as previously thought. In addition to the 16% of the
population whose resources are insufficient to meet their needs, another 16.7%
—51 million people—have incomes less than 50% above the poverty line, allowing
them to meet only between 100% and 150% of their most basic needs without providing a cushion for emergencies.

Families with such low annual incomes are especially vulnerable to fluctuations
that result from job changes, unemployment, public assistance and variations in
family composition or needs. Here are several examples of the insecurity that pre-
vails among low-income families:

- Although the official poverty measure identified 32 million poor individuals in 2007, many more—a total of 57 million—were poor for at
  least two months at some point during that year.

- Further, millions of families move in and out of "working poor" status.
  A study from the mid-2000s found that, in a given month, 9% of families with children were officially poor even though at least one member
  was employed, as were 17% of single-mother families. But over a three-
  year period, 25% of families with children—and 43% of single-mother
  families—experienced at least one spell of below-poverty income.

Thus, to use the refrigerator example, the issue is not whether one "has" a refrigerator in the family home as much as how often—if ever—the electricity for that
refrigerator is cut off for failure to pay the utility bill.

Yes, poor and near-poor families may own microwave ovens, televisions or other
non-necessities. But a household is not a perfect economic system, in which a responsible parent can anticipate next month's medical costs in time to sell a child's
video game or forego a new pair of sneakers. The very nature of uncertainty and
insecurity is that such juggling is practically—and emotionally—difficult. And even
those poor families that do manage to maintain their food supplies, buy their prescription drugs, and heat their homes suffer the stress and anxiety associated with
living so close to falling short.

These stresses have long-term effects. The Families and Work Institute's ongoing *National Study of the Changing Workforce* shows that economic insecurity is the number one predictor of overall health problems, depression, sleep difficulties, and stress among employed workers. Children who experience crowded housing conditions or multiple residential moves are more likely to display health and developmental problems. Experiencing a parent's unemployment increases a child's chance of being held back in school by 15 percent.

> *Compared with its peers, however, the U.S. does not fare well. Adjusting for taxes and government transfers, the U.S. has a higher poverty rate than all but one of the Western European, Nordic, and Anglophone countries.*

Conclusion

Poverty in the U.S. grew substantially more common during the last decade, with hardships increasing for millions of people and their families, especially with regard to food, medical care and housing. And the Great Recession at the end of the 2000s—with high unemployment and housing foreclosures—increased the level of insecurity for millions of people who were not living below the poverty line. Although most Americans do not share the level of deprivation seen at the bottom of the income scale, the broad blanket of economic anxiety that has spread across the population should spur us to think more holistically about the impact of instability and insecurity on the social, emotional and economic well-being of the population as a whole.

References

"Income, Poverty and Health Insurance Coverage in the United States: 2010." September 13, 2011. http://www.census.gov/newsroom/releases/archives/income_wealth/cb11-157.html

The Research Supplemental Poverty Measure: 2010. By Kathleen Short. U.S. Census Bureau, November 2011. http://www.census.gov/prod/2011pubs/p60-241.pdf

"Air Conditioning, Cable TV, and an Xbox: What is Poverty in the United States Today?" By Robert Rector and Rachel Sheffield. July 19, 2011. http://www.heritage.org/research/reports/2011/07/what-is-poverty

"Child Poverty in Comparative Perspective: Assessing the Role of Family Structure and Parental Education and Employment," by Janet C. Gornick and Markus Jäntti. Luxemburg Income Study Working Paper Series, No. 570, September 2011. http://www.lisdatacenter.org/wps/liswps/570.pdf. This comparison refers to Australia, Austria, Canada, Denmark, Finland, Germany, Ireland, Luxembourg, the Netherlands, Norway, Sweden, Switzerland, and the UK. The study used the U.S. official poverty line, after taxes, as the standard of poverty.

Food Insecurity: Indicators on Children and Youth. Child Trends (2010). http://www.childtrendsdatabank.org/alphalist?q=node/363

Morbidity and Mortality Weekly Report, November 4, 2011. http://www.cdc.gov/mmwr/preview/mmwrhtml/mm6043a9.htm

"Hardship in America, Part 1: Majority of Poor Children Live in Households with Major Hardships." Center on Budget and Policy Priorities. Nov. 21, 2011. http://www.offthechartsblog.org/hardship-in-america-part-1-majority-of-poor-children-live-in-households-with-major-hardships

"Seasonal Variation in Food Insecurity Is Associated with Heating and Cooling Costs among Low-Income Elderly Americans," by Mark Nord and Linda S. Kantor. *The Journal of Nutrition*, No. 137, November 2006. http://jn.nutrition.org/content/137/11/2939.long. "Heat or Eat? Cold-Weather Shocks and Nutrition in Poor American Families," by Jayanta Bhattacharya et al.*American Journal of Public Health*, Vol. 93, No. 7, July 2003.

"Special Tabulation of Supplemental Poverty Measure Estimates," from the 2011 Current Population Survey

Annual Social and Economic Supplement. U.S. Census Bureau, Nov. 14, 2011. http://www.census.gov/newsroom/releases/pdf/CB11-TPS.51SpecTab.pdf

"Dynamics of Economic Well-Being: Poverty, 2004-2006," by Robin J. Anderson. March 2011. http://www.census.gov/prod/2011pubs/p70-123.pdf

"The Dynamics of the Working Poor: Work, Poverty, and Program Benefit Receipt Among Families with Children," by Katherine Giefer, Susan Hauan, and Bula Ghose. Presented at the National Council on Family Relations Annual Conference, November 2011.

"US Housing insecurity and the health of very young children," by D. B. Cutts et al. Am J Public Health. 2011 Aug;101(8):1508–14. Epub 2011 Jun 16. http://www.ncbi.nlm.nih.gov/pubmed/21680929 See also "The Long-Range Impact of the Recession on Families," by Valerie Adrian and Stephanie Coontz for the Council on Contemporary Families, April 2010. http://www.contemporaryfamilies.org/economic-issues/the-long-range-impact-of-the-recession-on-families.html

All Together Now: Extended Families

By Sharon Jayson
USA Today, November 23, 2011

This Thanksgiving, many families are closer—really closer—than they've been in years.

An increasing number of extended families across the USA are under the same roof, living together either permanently or temporarily. Sometimes these arrangements are multigenerational, with adult children, grandchildren or an elderly parent sharing quarters. In other cases, an extended family bunks together, with siblings, cousins, nieces or nephews sharing space.

The reasons are economic, social and demographic. The recession and its aftermath have pushed extended families to share space at a time when the average age at first marriage has climbed to 28.7 for men and 26.5 for women. And life expectancy—now 75.7 for men and 80.6 for women in the USA—continues to rise. The flow of immigrants into this country also has been a factor; immigrants are more likely than other groups to live with members of their extended family.

Taken together, the trends suggest that the rise of the extended family is going to be with us for a while, analysts say.

In Hicksville, N.Y., Gina Moscato, 26, her husband, Ian Roche Tilden, 31, and their 22-month-old son, Tyler, live with her grandmother, Christine Moscato, who will be 95 next month. The young family stays upstairs with a living area, two bedrooms and bath, while grandma is downstairs.

"We originally moved in to save money," Gina Moscato says. "We wanted to buy a house. She didn't mind because she wanted the company."

Moscato says that Thursday, they'll have a traditional Thanksgiving meal, with touches of their Italian heritage, at her father's home in the area. "We'll do, like, 7,000 courses," she jokes, listing antipasto, appetizer, lasagna, salad, turkey, dessert and dessert wines.

Living with extended family is nothing new for Valda Ford, 57, who last year moved from Omaha to High Point, N.C., to live with her son Alphonso Becote, 37, and his wife, Ronnida, 35. Ford's 80-year-old disabled cousin, T.J. Countee, also lives in the home. Alphonso Becote is his guardian.

"We always had the equivalent of an extended family, with either multiple generations in the same house or the same cul-de-sac," she says. "In Omaha, half the reason I moved there was because my oldest sister was less than a mile away with her grown daughter and her grandchildren."

So many family members live nearby that when 45 family members arrive for Thanksgiving at Becote's home, Ford says, "no one is really traveling to get there."

New 2010 Census data show that 5.1 million households in the USA (4.4%) are multigenerational, with three or more generations sharing quarters. That's a 21% increase from the 4.2 million (3.7%) such households in 2000.

"Siblings are supporting each other. Brothers-in-law are supporting their wives' sisters and brothers," says social psychologist Susan Newman of Metuchen, N.J., author of the 2010 book *Under One Roof Again: All Grown Up and (Re)learning to Live Together Happily.* "Other cultures have always lived in multigenerational families. We are slowly seeing that happening here."

Moscato and Roche Tilden moved to her grandmother's home in late 2007. "My family says it's adding years to her life," she says.

Roche Tilden, a project manager in construction, got laid off six months later and was out of work for a year. Moscato, an executive assistant, was in her last year of college. She says her husband found a job but was laid off two more times. He's employed now. She found a job in March after being home almost a year with her son.

Moscato says living with her grandmother also benefits her young family. "I see her every day. Sometimes we watch TV together. She's a big part of our lives," she says.

That's not the case for Dianah Stehle, 57, of Plymouth, Mich. This year, both her son, John Hogg, 26, and her cousin, Jim Bradford, 51, moved into her three-bedroom, one-bath home. But because of their work schedules, they barely see one another.

"I get up first and I leave the house around 5 in the morning. I think Jimmy leaves about 5:30. My son, I think he leaves around noon. I get home around 4. Jim can show up from between 5 and 9, and my son gets home around 11 or 11:30 at night," she says.

Hogg, who works two jobs, one full-time and another part-time, moved back home in June after being away three years to try to save up for a house with a garage.

Bradford, a truck mechanic who had been out of work for three years, moved there in April to be closer to his new job. A divorced father of two adult sons, he stays there during the week and spends weekends at his own home more than two hours away.

Stehle, a computer-aided designer who has been divorced 15 years, says her son and cousin each pay her $100 a month to cover utilities.

"I had some reservations because I had been in my house by myself such a long time," Stehle says.

"It was harder mentally," Hogg says. "In my book, you move out, you get a good job, you continue to progress through life. Coming back home, I felt like I was falling back a little bit. But then I just told myself this is a way to save money."

Young Adults Return Home

This is a pattern that will continue, predicts Neil Howe, 60, a historian, economist and demographer in Great Falls, Va., who has written about generational issues.

"We are clearly going to be in this era for a while," he says. "High rates of multigenerational family living had been the norm" until after World War II, when the emphasis shifted to the nuclear family enabled by construction of interstate highways, the rise of suburbs and the affluence of young adults. But by the late 1960s and '70s, "there was a generation gap and almost generational war," Howe says.

"There was a time in the 1970s when no one wanted to live together," he says. "Seniors were moving to Leisure World to get away from the culture of the kids. Couples were divorcing—it was the high tide of the divorce revolution, and Boomers wanted to strike out on their own."

> *New Census data from the Current Population Survey 2011, out earlier this month, found that between 2005 and 2011, the proportion of young adults ages 25 to 34 living in their parents' home rose from 14% to 19% for men and from 8% to 10% for women.*

But now, many young adults do return home, at least temporarily.

New Census data from the Current Population Survey 2011, out earlier this month, found that between 2005 and 2011, the proportion of young adults ages 25 to 34 living in their parents' home rose from 14% to 19% for men and from 8% to 10% for women.

Destiny Young, 26, is among them.

She earned her bachelor's degree in communications from Fayetteville (N.C.) State University in May 2010 and stayed but couldn't find work in her field. She worked part time as a receptionist at a nursing home and then moved to Raleigh for a marketing job.

Although it was full-time, Young says, it was commission-only, and she left after two months. She moved back to her parents' home in Amityville, N.Y., in April.

"They knew I was struggling," she says. "I couldn't even pay my rent. My parents were like, 'You need to come home.'"

"We gave her the option to come home one time," says her mother, Renee Young, 58. "It's not a revolving door."

Now, Destiny Young works full time as a customer-service representative; many of her employed friends aren't in their career field, either. She doesn't pay rent but does contribute to groceries. She pays for her phone and car, as well as the storage fee for her furniture, still in North Carolina. In January, she'll have to start paying on her student loans, which she had deferred. "It is difficult because I got used to being on my own," she says. "Now that I'm home, I really don't have space."

Goodbye, Empty Nest

Michele Beatty, 54, of Waynesville, Ohio, and her husband, Gordon, 56, had an empty nest for almost 2 years between the time the youngest of their three sons went to college and the return in August of their oldest, Patrick, who had been living in Dayton for about eight years. He had left his job as a graphic designer in February.

"We said, 'You can come home to your old room and continue to look for employment,' never dreaming it would go on this long," she says. "One thing we did not want was his stuff. His stuff is in storage. He came home with clothes and his cat, Sprite."

There are two closets in his room, but he lives out of suitcases, his mother says.

"It felt too permanent—like I was stuck there," says Patrick Beatty, 28. "We were all brought up with the cultural expectation that once you leave the nest, you are not supposed to return."

He's working two days a week as a freelance graphic designer and three or four days part time stocking boxes. Two of those days, he works 10 p.m. to 6:30 a.m.

"I feel part of the time like a burden," he says. "I try to contribute to the house when I can. I try to stay out of their way as much as possible. It's home, but not the home I'd be building for myself if I had my way."

According to a Pew Research Center report released earlier this month, about one in five adults ages 25–34 live in a multigenerational home. However, Pew's definition includes two or more adult generations, unlike the Census definition, which bases its data on three or more.

Caring for Family Elders

A survey of 2,226 adults, done in September by Harris Interactive for the non-profit Generations United, found that of those in a multigenerational home, 40% reported that job loss, change in job status or underemployment was a reason for the living arrangement; 20% said it was because of health care costs; and 14% said it was because of foreclosure or other housing loss. The report, *Family Matters: Multigenerational Families in a Volatile Economy*, will be released Dec. 6.

Bill Fragoso, 57, of Cleveland says his parents, both immigrants from Puerto Rico, set an example to care for family elders.

"I have to do this. That's one of the things both parents instilled in us," he says. "They took care of their parents."

Fragoso says his parents lived with his family during the last year of his father's battle with cancer. After he died in 2003, Fragoso's mother, Sarita, now 81, returned to Campbell, Ohio, about an hour away.

In 2005, she moved back in with him, his wife, Raquel, and daughter Joanna, now 17, a high school senior. Two older sons, ages 26 and 29, don't live at home.

Families don't always move to the same house to stay close. In 2008, Betty Cook, 72, and her boyfriend got an apartment at Azalea Trace, the retirement community in Pensacola, Fla., where her mother, Jean Phillippi, 98, had moved a couple of years earlier. They live in separate buildings connected by a breezeway.

On Thanksgiving, they'll gather—with Cook's son, daughter-in-law and granddaughters—in Azalea Trace's dining room.

Cook is among a growing number of seniors moving into the same retirement communities as their elderly parents. She says it allows her mother to continue living independently and is much less time-consuming and more efficient for her. In the five years before Cook moved, it was an hour's drive to Pensacola several times a week.

"When she would have a doctor appointment, it would take all day," she says.

Newman says "families have lived so far apart for so many decades" that they're now realizing that for the most part—except for some families that can't get along—their relatives are "the people they turn to when the chips are down."

"Once you work out the kinks," she says, "people realize they like the relatives."

One in Two New Graduates Are Jobless or Underemployed

By Hope Yen
The Associated Press, April 23, 2012

The college class of 2012 is in for a rude welcome to the world of work.

A weak labor market already has left half of young college graduates either jobless or underemployed in positions that don't fully use their skills and knowledge.

Young adults with bachelor's degrees are increasingly scraping by in lower-wage jobs—waiter or waitress, bartender, retail clerk or receptionist, for example—and that's confounding their hopes a degree would pay off despite higher tuition and mounting student loans.

An analysis of government data conducted for The Associated Press lays bare the highly uneven prospects for holders of bachelor's degrees.

Opportunities for college graduates vary widely.

While there's strong demand in science, education and health fields, arts and humanities flounder. Median wages for those with bachelor's degrees are down from 2000, hit by technological changes that are eliminating midlevel jobs such as bank tellers. Most future job openings are projected to be in lower-skilled positions such as home health aides, who can provide personalized attention as the U.S. population ages.

Taking underemployment into consideration, the job prospects for bachelor's degree holders fell last year to the lowest level in more than a decade.

"I don't even know what I'm looking for," says Michael Bledsoe, who described months of fruitless job searches as he served customers at a Seattle coffeehouse. The 23-year-old graduated in 2010 with a creative writing degree.

Initially hopeful that his college education would create opportunities, Bledsoe languished for three months before finally taking a job as a barista, a position he has held for the last two years. In the beginning he sent three or four resumes a day. But, Bledsoe said, employers questioned his lack of experience or the practical worth of his major. Now he sends a resume once every two weeks or so.

Bledsoe, currently making just above minimum wage, says he got financial help from his parents to help pay off student loans. He is now mulling whether to go to graduate school, seeing few other options to advance his career. "There is not much out there, it seems," he said.

His situation highlights a widening but little-discussed labor problem. Perhaps more than ever, the choices that young adults make earlier in life—level of schooling, academic field and training, where to attend college, how to pay for it—are having long-lasting financial impact.

"You can make more money on average if you go to college, but it's not true for everybody," says Harvard economist Richard Freeman, noting the growing risk of a debt bubble with total U.S. student loan debt surpassing $1 trillion. "If you're not sure what you're going to be doing, it probably bodes well to take some job, if you can get one, and get a sense first of what you want from college."

Andrew Sum, director of the Center for Labor Market Studies at Northeastern University who analyzed the numbers, said many people with a bachelor's degree face a double whammy of rising tuition and poor job outcomes. "Simply put, we're failing kids coming out of college," he said, emphasizing that when it comes to jobs, a college major can make all the difference. "We're going to need a lot better job growth and connections to the labor market, otherwise college debt will grow."

College graduates who majored in zoology, anthropology, philosophy, art history and humanities were among the least likely to find jobs appropriate to their education level; those with nursing, teaching, accounting or computer science degrees were among the most likely.

By region, the Mountain West was most likely to have young college graduates jobless or underemployed— roughly 3 in 5. It was followed by the more rural southeastern U.S., including Alabama, Kentucky, Mississippi and Tennessee. The Pacific region, including Alaska, California, Hawaii, Oregon and Washington, also was high on the list.

On the other end of the scale, the southern U.S., anchored by Texas, was most likely to have young college graduates in higher-skill jobs.

The figures are based on an analysis of 2011 Current Population Survey data by Northeastern University researchers and supplemented with material from Paul Harrington, an economist at Drexel University, and the Economic Policy Institute, a Washington think tank. They rely on Labor Department assessments of the level of education required to do the job in 900-plus U.S. occupations, which were used to calculate the shares of young adults with bachelor's degrees who were "underemployed."

About 1.5 million, or 53.6 percent, of bachelor's degree–holders under the age of 25 last year were jobless or underemployed, the highest share in at least 11 years. In 2000, the share was at a low of 41 percent, before the dot-com bust erased job gains for college graduates in the telecommunications and IT fields.

Out of the 1.5 million who languished in the job market, about half were underemployed, an increase from the previous year.

Broken down by occupation, young college graduates were heavily represented in jobs that require a high school diploma or less.

In the last year, they were more likely to be employed as waiters, waitresses, bartenders and food-service helpers than as engineers, physicists, chemists and mathematicians combined (100,000 versus 90,000). There were more working in office-related jobs such as receptionist or payroll clerk than in all computer professional jobs (163,000 versus 100,000). More also were employed as cashiers, retail clerks and customer representatives than engineers (125,000 versus 80,000).

According to government projections released last month, only three of the 30 occupations with the largest projected number of job openings by 2020 will require a bachelor's degree or higher to fill the position—teachers, college professors and accountants. Most job openings are in professions such as retail sales, fast food and truck driving, jobs which aren't easily replaced by computers.

College graduates who majored in zoology, anthropology, philosophy, art history and humanities were among the least likely to find jobs appropriate to their education level; those with nursing, teaching, accounting or computer science degrees were among the most likely.

In Nevada, where unemployment is the highest in the nation, Class of 2012 college seniors recently expressed feelings ranging from anxiety and fear to cautious optimism about what lies ahead.

With the state's economy languishing in an extended housing bust, a lot of young graduates have shown up at job placement centers in tears. Many have been squeezed out of jobs by more experienced workers, job counselors said, and are now having to explain to prospective employers the time gaps in their resumes.

"It's kind of scary," said Cameron Bawden, 22, who is graduating from the University of Nevada–Las Vegas in December with a business degree. His family has warned him for years about the job market, so he has been building his resume by working part time on the Las Vegas Strip as a food runner and doing a marketing internship with a local airline.

Bawden said his friends who have graduated are either unemployed or working along the Vegas Strip in service jobs that don't require degrees. "There are so few jobs and it's a small city," he said. "It's all about who you know."

Any job gains are going mostly to workers at the top and bottom of the wage scale, at the expense of middle-income jobs commonly held by bachelor's degree holders. By some studies, up to 95 percent of positions lost during the economic recovery occurred in middle-income occupations such as bank tellers, the type of job not expected to return in a more high-tech age.

David Neumark, an economist at the University of California–Irvine, said a bachelor's degree can have benefits that aren't fully reflected in the government's labor data. He said even for lower-skilled jobs such as waitress or cashier, employers tend to value bachelor's degree–holders more highly than high-school graduates, paying them more for the same work and offering promotions.

In addition, U.S. workers increasingly may need to consider their position in a global economy, where they must compete with educated foreign-born residents for jobs. Longer-term government projections also may fail to consider "degree inflation," a growing ubiquity of bachelor's degrees that could make them more commonplace in lower-wage jobs but inadequate for higher-wage ones.

That future may be now for Kelman Edwards Jr., 24, of Murfreesboro, Tenn., who is waiting to see the returns on his college education.

After earning a biology degree last May, the only job he could find was as a construction worker for five months before he quit to focus on finding a job in his academic field. He applied for positions in laboratories but was told they were looking for people with specialized certifications.

"I thought that me having a biology degree was a gold ticket for me getting into places, but every other job wants you to have previous history in the field," he said. Edwards, who has about $5,500 in student debt, recently met with a career counselor at Middle Tennessee State University. The counselor's main advice: Pursue further education.

"Everyone is always telling you, 'Go to college,'" Edwards said. "But when you graduate, it's kind of an empty cliff."

Associated Press *writers Manuel Valdes in Seattle; Travis Loller in Nashville, Tenn.; Cristina Silva in Las Vegas; and Sandra Chereb in Carson City, Nev., contributed to this report.*

A Long, Steep Drop for Americans' Standard of Living

By Ron Scherer
The Christian Science Monitor, October 19, 2011

Not since at least 1960 has the US standard of living fallen so fast for so long. The average American has $1,315 less in annual disposable income now than at the onset of the Great Recession.

Think life is not as good as it used to be, at least in terms of your wallet? You'd be right about that. The standard of living for Americans has fallen longer and more steeply over the past three years than at any time since the US government began recording it five decades ago.

Bottom line: The average individual now has $1,315 less in disposable income than he or she did three years ago at the onset of the Great Recession—even though the recession ended, technically speaking, in mid-2009. That means less money to spend at the spa or the movies, less for vacations, new carpeting for the house, or dinner at a restaurant.

In short, it means a less vibrant economy, with more Americans spending primarily on necessities. The diminished standard of living, moreover, is squeezing the middle class, whose restlessness and discontent are evident in grass-roots movements such as the tea party and "Occupy Wall Street" and who may take out their frustrations on incumbent politicians in next year's election.

What has led to the most dramatic drop in the US standard of living since at least 1960? One factor is stagnant incomes: Real median income is down 9.8 percent since the start of the recession through this June, according to Sentier Research in Annapolis, Md., citing census bureau data. Another is falling net worth— think about the value of your home and, if you have one, your retirement portfolio. A third is rising consumer prices, with inflation eroding people's buying power by 3.25 percent since mid-2008.

"In a dynamic economy, one would expect Americans' disposable income to be growing, but it has flattened out at a low level," says economist Bob Brusca of Fact & Opinion Economics in New York.

To be sure, the recession has hit unevenly, with lower-skilled and less-educated Americans feeling the pinch the most, says Mark Zandi, chief economist for Moody's Economy.com based in West Chester, Pa. Many found their jobs gone for good as companies moved production offshore or bought equipment that replaced manpower.

"The pace of change has been incredibly rapid and incredibly tough on the less educated," says Mr. Zandi, who calls this period the most difficult for American households since the 1930s. "If you don't have the education and you don't have the right skills, then you are getting creamed."

Per capita disposal personal income—a key indicator of the standard of living—peaked in the spring of 2008, at $33,794 (measured as after-tax income). As of the second quarter of 2011, it was $32,479—almost a 4 percent drop. If per capita disposable income had continued to grow at its normal pace, it would have been more than $34,000 a year by now.

> *Income loss is hitting the middle class hard, especially in communities where manufacturing facilities have closed. When those jobs are gone, many workers have ended up in service-sector jobs that pay less.*

The so-called misery index, another measure of economic well-being of American households, echoes the finding on the slipping standard of living. The index, a combination of the unemployment rate and inflation, is now at its highest point since 1983, when the US economy was recovering from a short recession and from the energy price spikes after the Iranian revolution.

In Royal Oak, Mich., Adam Kowal knows exactly how the squeeze feels. After losing a warehouse job in Lansing, he, his wife, and their two children have had little recourse but to move in with his mother. Now working at a school cafeteria, Mr. Kowal earns 28 percent less than at his last job.

He and his wife now eat out once a month instead of once a week, do no socializing, and eat less expensive foods, such as ground chuck instead of ground sirloin. "My mom was hoping her kids would lead a better life than her, but so far that has not happened," says Kowal.

With disposable incomes falling, perhaps it's not surprising that 64 percent of Americans worry that they won't be able to pay their families' expenses at least some of the time, according to a survey completed in mid-September by the Marist Institute for Public Opinion. Among those, one-third say their financial problems are chronic.

"What we see is that very few are escaping the crunch," says Lee Miringoff, director of the Marist Institute in Poughkeepsie, N.Y.

Income loss is hitting the middle class hard, especially in communities where manufacturing facilities have closed. When those jobs are gone, many workers have ended up in service-sector jobs that pay less.

"Maybe it's the evolution of the economy, but it appears large segments of the workforce have moved permanently into lower-paying positions," says Joel Naroff of Naroff Economic Advisors in Holland, Pa. "The economy can't grow at 4 percent per year when the middle class becomes the lower middle class."

He would get no argument from Jeff Beatty of Richmond, Ky., who worked in the IT and telecommunications businesses for most of his career—until he hit a rough patch. He and his wife are living on his unemployment insurance benefits (which will run out in months), his early Social Security payments, and her disability payments from the Social Security Administration. Their total income comes to $30,000 a year.

"Our standard of living has probably declined threefold," he says.

Mr. Beatty, who used to make a comfortable income, now anticipates applying for food stamps. He and his wife have sold much of their furniture, which they no longer need because they have moved into a one-bedroom apartment owned by his sister-in-law.

Even people with college degrees are feeling the squeeze. On a fall day, Hunter College graduate and Brooklyn resident Paul Battis came to lower Manhattan to check out the Occupy Wall Street protest. He tells one of the protesters that America's problem is the various free-trade pacts it has approved.

Mr. Battis's angst over trade is rooted in the fact that two years ago he lost his data-entry job with a Wall Street firm that decided to outsource such jobs to India.

When he had the job, he made a comfortable income. Now his income is sporadic, from the occasional construction job he lands. He used to buy clothing from Macy's or other department stores. Now he goes to Goodwill or Salvation Army stores. He has even cut back on taking the city subways, instead riding his bicycle. Separated from his wife and his 15-year-old daughter, he says, "Try making child support payments when you don't have a regular income. I'm constantly catching up."

Even recently some Americans could tap the equity in their homes or their stock market accounts to make up for any shortfalls in income. Not anymore. Since 2007, Americans' collective net worth has fallen about $5.5 trillion, or more than 8.6 percent, according to the Federal Reserve.

The bulk of that decline is in real estate, which has lost $4.7 trillion in value, or 22 percent, since 2007. In Arizona, for example, more than half of homeowners live in houses that are worth less than their purchase prices, according to some reports.

Stock investments aren't any better. Since 1999, the Standard & Poor's index, on a price basis, is off 17 percent. It's up 3.2 percent when dividends are included, but that's a small return for that length of time.

"This is really a lost decade of affluence," says Sam Stovall, chief investment strategist at Standard & Poor's in New York.

Among those who have watched their finances deteriorate are senior citizens.

"Given the stock market, they are very nervous," says Nancy LeaMond, executive vice president at AARP, the seniors' lobbying group. "They want to keep their savings."

But Ms. LeaMond also notes that about 2 in every 3 seniors are dependent not on Wall Street but on Social Security. The average annual income for those over 65 is $18,500 a year—almost all of it from Social Security, she says. "This is not a part of America that is rich," she says.

At the same time, seniors are getting pinched in their pocketbooks.

"Our members are watching all the things they have to buy, especially healthcare products, go up in price," says LeaMond.

In Pompano, Fla., some stretched seniors end up at the Blessings Food Pantry, which is associated with Christ Church United Methodist.

"We have quite a few grandparents who are raising their grandchildren on a fixed income, feeding them and buying clothes for them when they can't afford to do [that for] themselves," says Yvonne Womack, the team leader.

Others, she says, are forgoing food to pay for their medical prescriptions. "And then there is your ordinary senior whose Social Security [check] has not gone up in the last several years, but food and gasoline [prices] have skyrocketed," she says. (However, Social Security checks will go up 3.6 percent in January.) The Blessings, she notes, is now feeding 42 percent more people than last year. "We also provide food you can eat out of a can," she says. "We do have seniors who are living on the streets."

Researcher Geoff Johnson contributed to this report.

Economic Check-Up Dismal for Many U.S. Families

By Jason Kane
PBS Newshour, Septemeber 13, 2011

American families continued to take an economic pounding in 2010, with median household income declining, health insurance rates remaining dreary and the number of Americans living in poverty reaching a 52-year high, the U.S. Census Bureau reported Tuesday.

According to the yearly status update, real median income for U.S. households dipped by 2.3 percent, coming in at $49,445 in 2010.

The official poverty rate rose for the third year in a row, increasing by nearly a percentage point and topping out at 15.1 percent—the highest rate since 1993. In real terms, that means that about 2.6 million people slipped below the poverty line last year, bringing the total of those living in poverty to 46.2 million nationwide.

Christine Owens of The National Employment Law Project called the numbers "unacceptable" and urged the government to continue federal unemployment programs that have kept them from slipping even more dramatically. Unemployment insurance and Social Security, she noted, collectively kept 23.5 million Americans out of poverty in 2010.

"It's distressing but not surprising that poverty continues to increase," she said. "I think the critical thing is putting people back to work, and the plan the president proposed has a lot of important elements to move in that direction."

At the conservative American Enterprise Institute, economist Joe Antos said the release "simply confirms what we all know: 2010 was a very bad year economically and a very bad year for families." His AEI colleague, Tom Miller, blamed the stalled economy on the Obama administration's economic policies.

"Whatever changes that have happened in the past year didn't help much and didn't hurt much," he said. "We haven't solved the problem. The economy is staggering along and I don't think we'll get much progress anytime soon."

While the number of people without health insurance rose from 49 million to 49.9 million in 2010, the Census reported that the percentage without coverage remained fairly stable at 16.3 percent.

Much of the decrease in the private marketplace resulted from employers dropping their insurance coverage due to skyrocketing prices. In 2010, just a little more than half of Americans—55.3 percent—received health care through their workplace, a one percent drop from 2009 levels, and nearly 10 points lower than a decade ago.

"I think the most significant takeaway from all of this that we have an ongoing trend of people losing job-based health coverage. We now have the lowest portion of the American population covered by jobs-based health coverage since the Census Bureau has been collecting this data," said Ron Pollack, executive director of the consumer advocacy group Families USA.

> *"We now have the lowest portion of the American population covered by jobs-based health coverage since the Census Bureau has been collecting this data."*

What that means, he said, is that "more and more people needed to depend on the public safety nets, specifically Medicaid," as their lifeline for health coverage. In 2000, 28.1 million people relied on the government health care program for low-income and disabled Americans. In 2010, it's up to 48.6 million.

"This has profound implications for the current debate taking place about the budget. If Medicaid gets cut back and that lifeline is frayed, we're going to see a very significant increase in the number of uninsured," he said.

On its official blog, the Obama administration avoided all of the dreary aspects of the report and focused instead on a ray of hope: the percentage of 18–24 year olds with insurance increased by more than two percentage points in 2010—rising from 70.7 to 72.8 percent.

That translates into 500,000 more young people with insurance, Health & Human Services Secretary Kathleen Sebelius wrote in the blog post. Noting that the health care reform law allows young people to stay on their parents' plans until age 26, she pointed to the report as a sign "that the Affordable Care Act is working."

"This 2% increase in coverage for young people came as the number of Americans under 65 with insurance went down slightly," she wrote. "The Affordable Care Act will help provide coverage at a decent price for millions of uninsured Americans starting in 2014, when millions of Americans will have access to affordable insurance options."

Black Atlantans Struggle to Stay in the Middle Class

By Robert Siegel
NPR.org, December 8, 2011

There's no question that the Great Recession has meant hard times all around, but from 2007 to 2009, it sent black America into an economic tailspin.

According to the Pew Research Center, the median net worth—that's assets minus debts—of black households decreased by more than 50 percent from 2005 to 2009.

I traveled to Atlanta—a city that's virtually synonymous with the black middle class—to find out what those numbers mean in the lives of real people. I started in Fairburn, Ga., a cul-de-sac and two-car garage suburb just south of the city.

On one recent afternoon, half a dozen kids play football in the yard between two suburban houses. It's a seductive display of the American dream, and it explains how someone might buy a home with a loan they can't quite afford.

One of the kids running touchdowns on the lawn is 10-year-old Tyler Brittian. His parents, Teja and Eric, bought their Fairburn house for $155,000 six years ago. Three years later, their adjustable rate mortgage reset, and their monthly payment went up $200 to $1,400.

Then, the economy went south. Teja was a hairstylist, and business got so slow that she started losing money. Eric was an armed security guard for an IRS contractor. When his employer lost its contract, Eric lost his $40,000 a year job—now he works at Home Depot for about half that.

Like several of their neighbors, the Brittians fell behind on their mortgage and are currently facing foreclosure.

"We're not the only [ones]," Teja Brittian says. "If you actually go in the subdivision itself, there probably are a good five to eight [houses facing foreclosure]."

The Brittians got a reprieve from Bank of America after their senator, Saxby Chambliss, wrote to the bank on their behalf.

But what's at stake for them is not just a piece of property; it's the life they found for Tyler and his older sister.

"Their lives changed when we moved out here," Teja says.

Losing the Roof Over Your Head

The Center for Responsible Lending estimates that among recent borrowers, nearly 8 percent of both African-Americans and Latinos have lost their homes to foreclosure. (The rate for whites is 4.5 percent.) And losing a home is often a consequence of losing a job—as of Dec. 2, African-American unemployment is 15.5 percent, more than twice that of whites.

Nancy Flake Johnson, president of the Urban League of Greater Atlanta, says the bad economy has been devastating for *all* blacks, including college graduates.

Median Net Worth of American Households

"We've lost a third of the black middle class," she says, citing a recent Urban League study.

Moreover, Flake Johnson says she sees a stunning feature of today's long-term unemployment.

"Homelessness," she says. "People that never in a million years thought that they would be without a roof over their heads—a lot of people are without a roof over their heads."

Many of those who have lost their homes do still have a roof over their heads, but the roof is often someone else's.

For 60-year-old Foster Smith, home is a room in his best friend Mark's house. It has a big closet where Smith can fit his entire tie collection—he has more than a hundred ties, accumulated over decades of working as a salesman—and he keeps his golf bag in the corner. They are symbols of the middle-class life he had obtained by selling jewelry for more than 20 years. He says he used to make $75,000 a year, but for the past six months he has had no work at all.

When Smith, who is divorced, could no longer pay the $1,100 rent on his old house, he moved in with his friend, who lives in a middle-class Atlanta suburb. And that location is important to Smith.

"It's a reminder of where you want to stay," he says. "I grew up in Montgomery, Ala., my mother was a single parent, and we lived in housing projects."

Smith recalls taking his son to visit Montgomery a few years ago and pointing out all the guys he had gone to high school and grade school with. When his son asked him why it mattered, Smith replied, "The point I'm trying to make here is they never left this place. This is what I came from, but this isn't where I want you to go."

Falling Back on Family

At 56, Okeema Garvin is living with her mother.

In 2004, she lost her job at Bell South, where she had worked for 20 years. In 2006, she went to work at a mortgage company, but lost that job two years later when the housing market collapsed. Garvin's husband retired on medical disability years ago, after a heart attack, so when she lost her last job, they walked away from the home they had owned for 20 years and moved in with Garvin's mother.

"This is the house that I grew up in, and I'm back in the bedroom that I left many years ago. I'm right back where I started from," Garvin says. "I never imagined that I would come back, not under these circumstances. But one thing I can say: I'm glad that I have a place to stay. I'm glad that she opened her door to us. Because otherwise, I don't know where we would have gone."

> *Many of those who have lost their homes do still have a roof over their heads, but the roof is often someone else's.*

Garvin knows she isn't alone. She says that a couple of years back, the pastor at her church started asking anyone who is unemployed to stand up. At first, only one or two people stood up.

"Then as time went on, say maybe six months or a year later," Garvin says, "he would ask that question again, and you would see more people stand up. So it just became . . . a regular thing."

'They've Got a Sniffle; We've Got Pneumonia'

Atlanta is a city where civil rights leaders are the namesakes of thoroughfares the way presidents and signers of the Declaration of Independence are in most other cities. There are boulevards named not just for Martin Luther King Jr. and former Atlanta Mayor Andrew Young, but also for civil rights leaders Joseph Lowery and Ralph David Abernathy. Last year, Raymond Street was renamed SNCC Way, after the Student Nonviolent Coordinating Committee.

But no place in Atlanta embodies the progression from the civil rights movement to political empowerment to economic development quite like the Hartsfield-Jackson Atlanta International Airport. The airport is named after the city's first African-American mayor, Maynard Jackson, who negotiated a unique deal for its construction.

"That airport was constructed with a mandate of having at least 25 percent of all of the subcontracting opportunities going to minorities and women," says Thomas "Danny" Boston, a Georgia Tech economist who studies minority businesses. "First time anything like that happened in the country."

It was a kind of New Deal for blacks in Atlanta, and it grew into many other deals, including mandated set-asides for African-American and other minority contractors and subcontractors.

But the deals also made minority business disproportionately dependent on public sector work. Now, the shrinking of the public sector is having a disastrous effect on many African-American business owners, including electrical subcontractor Melvin Griffin.

Griffin's business depended heavily on public contracts for things like installing stoplights with red-light cameras. Now he gets less work and, in turn, he gives less work.

"Employees are down quite a bit," he says. "Right now, I'm only working about three people. Couple guys, I just told them don't worry about calling me because I really got no work for them."

Compare that with five years ago, when Griffin says he had enough work to keep 25 employees busy. In a time of fewer contracts, bigger contractors are competing for jobs that used to look like small potatoes, making the competition for minority contractors like Griffin much tougher.

"I look at it like this," Griffin says of his big business competition. "They've got a sniffle; we've got pneumonia."

Combine all this with the loss of public sector jobs, where many blacks found security, and you get something worse than even a Great Recession.

But Georgia Tech economist Danny Boston says, despite all this, you don't hear a lot of public discourse about how bad things are for African-Americans in Atlanta. In a nationwide survey of small-business owners he conducted, African-Americans remained exceptionally optimistic.

"And that's even magnified when you come to Atlanta, because it's always operated on this sense of optimism, whether it was well-founded or not," Boston says. "I think that that keeps the discussion about how bad things really are from coming to the surface."

The Bittersweet Side

Atlanta also has bittersweet stories, told without complaint, about the work created by the absence of work and opportunities hatched from the absence of opportunity.

Foster Smith's lifelong friend bought the house they're now living in for a song—it had been foreclosed on.

Okeema Garvin briefly had a job collecting cable boxes from customers whose service was terminated.

And Melvin Griffin had done an electrical job for a local bank, rewiring a building it had unloaded in a bank sale—vandals had stripped the copper wire from the building while it sat vacant.

There is no denying that these are still hard times.

Bibliography

Baer, Susan. "Richard Madaleno: Showing the Way on Marriage Equality." *Washingtonian*. Washington Magazine, 7 Feb. 2012. Web. 15 Jun. 2012.

Blake, John. "'Gayby Boom': Children of Gay Couples Speak Out." *CNN.com*. Cable News Network, 28 Jun. 2009. Web. 15 Jun. 2012.

Bloomberg, Michael. "NYC Mayor Michael Bloomberg Talks Marriage." *Metro Weekly*. Jansi, 26 May 2011. Web. 15 Jun. 2012.

Conners, Catherine. "Why Is Dad Blogging Important?" *Babble.com*. Babble.com, 9 Nov. 2011. Web. 15 Jun. 2012.

Cullen, Lisa. "Fatherhood 2.0." *Time* 15 Oct. 2007: 63–66. Print.

Didactic Pirate, The. "Telling My 10-Year-Old That I Am Gay." *Huffington Post*. TheHuffingtonPost.com, 13 Apr. 2012. Web. 15 Jun. 2012.

Gibbs, Nancy. "Can These Parents Be Saved?" *Time* 30 Nov. 2009: 52–57. Print.

Goldberg, Jeffrey. "A Father's Day Lesson about Children, and Life." *Bloomberg*. Bloomberg, 17 Jun. 2011. Web. 15 Jun. 2012.

Horowitz, Sara. "Welcome to Middle-Class Poverty—Does Anybody Know the Way Out?" *Atlantic*. Atlantic Monthly, 23 Sep. 2011. Web. 15 Jun. 2012.

Kaminsky, Ross. "Gay Marriage Meets Immigration." *American Spectator*. American Spectator, 26 Aug. 2011. Web. 15 Jun. 2012.

Knowles, Francine. "Tough Economy Isn't Child's Play." *Chicago Sun-Times*. Sun-Times Media, 27 Dec. 2011. Web. 15 Jun. 2012.

Landes, Luke. "Men Choosing Fatherhood over Careers." *Forbes.com*. Forbes.com, 3 May 2012. Web. 15 Jun. 2012.

Lewis, Katherine. "Why Do Dads Lie on Surveys about Fatherhood?" *Slate Magazine*. Slate Group, 17 Jun. 2010. Web. 15 Jun. 2012.

Luscombe, Belinda. "Finding Mom on Facebook." *Time* 16 Aug. 2010: 45–46. Print.

Miller, Lisa. "How to Raise a Global Kid." *Newsweek* 25 Jul. 2011: 48–53. Print.

Nance-Nash, Sheryl. "The Family Plan: Managing Life in a Multigenerational Household." *DailyFinance*. AOL, 22 Dec. 2011. Web. 15 Jun. 2012.

Nicholson, Lucy. "The Struggles of a Gay Military Family." *Reuters.com*. Thomson Reuters, 26 Sep. 2011. Web. 15 Jun. 2012.

Oduah, Chika. "Federal Grant Helps 'Concerned Black Men' Put Fatherhood First." *theGrio*. NBCUniversal, 13 Oct. 2011. Web. 15 Jun. 2012.

Onderko, Patty. "Meet the Same-Sex Parents Next Door." *Parenting.com*. Parenting, 30 Mar. 2011. Web. 15 Jun. 2012.

Paul, Pamela. "Are Fathers Necessary?" *Atlantic* Jul.–Aug. 2010: 63. Print.

Poniewozik, James. "Mideast Meets Midwest." *TIME.com*. Time, 14 Nov. 2011. Web. 15 Jun. 2012.

Rafferty, Alessandra. "Donor-Conceived and Out of the Closet." *Newsweek*. Newsweek/Daily Beast, 25 Feb. 2011. Web. 15 Jun. 2012.

Schiff, Stacy. "Dreams of His Mother." *Newsweek* 9 May 2011: 44–47. Print.

Shelly, Barb. "'Boomerang' Effect Not So Scary, Kids and Parents Say." *Midwest Voices*. KansasCity.com, May 2012. Web. 15 Jun. 2012.

Simon, Scott. "How to Say Thanksgiving in Mandarin." *Wall Street Journal*. Dow Jones, 23 Nov. 2009. Web. 15 Jun. 2012.

Tankersley, Jim. "Unemployed Autoworker One of Many Washington Forgot." *National Journal* 28 May 2011: 15. Print.

Warner, Judith. "No More Mrs. Nice Mom." *New York Times* 16 Jan. 2011, Sunday mag. ed.: MM11. Print.

Wildman, Sarah. "Children Speak for Same-Sex Marriage." *New York Times*. New York Times, 20 Jan. 2010. Web. 15 Jun. 2012.

Woolhouse, Megan. "Two Localities Are Worlds Apart." *Boston Globe*. New York Times, 18 Dec. 2011. Web. 15 Jun. 2012.

Web Sites

The Annie E. Casey Foundation
http://www.aecf.org/

A private charitable organization, the Annie E. Casey Foundation works to influence national and state policy related to children and families. The Web site offers publications on the foundation's major initiatives, as well as resources for grants, employment, and state and community activities.

Congressional Coalition on Adoption Institute
http://www.ccainstitute.org/

The Congressional Coalition on Adoption Institute is a nonprofit organization that supports advocacy for orphaned and foster youth throughout the world. The institute's Web site lists key policy issues related to adoption and children, research publications, and a broad range of opportunities to actively engage in advocacy initiatives.

Evan B. Donaldson Adoption Institute
http://www.adoptioninstitute.org/index.php

Devoted to improving adoption policy and practice, the Evan B. Donaldson Adoption Institute conducts research and offers education to citizens, professionals, and policy makers. The Web site offers publications on adoption subjects, information on community programs and events, and a list of resources for families interested in pursuing adoption.

First Focus
http://www.firstfocus.net/

A bipartisan advocacy organization, First Focus works to influence federal policy and budget decisions related to children, youth, and families. The Web site also offers a broad collection of information, news, and resources to support active advocacy for people and groups working to effect change in policy.

Parent Further
http://www.parentfurther.com/

The Parent Further Web site offers information on effective parenting and strategies to resolve a range of problem issues in family life. Through this site, the organization also offers "webinars" on a variety of parenting topics.

The Pew Research Center
http://pewresearch.org/topics/socialtrends/

The Pew Research Center is a leading resource for nonpartisan research on social trends in the United States, covering a broad range of subjects related to family and households. The Web site offers polling numbers on key social issues, data trends, and published reports going back to 2005.

United States Census Bureau
http://www.census.gov/hhes/families/

This page of the US Census Bureau Web site provides family, household, and economic data. Also, a list of related sites directs users to organizations with additional demographic data.

United States Department of Health and Human Services
http://www.hhs.gov/children/index.html

The US Department of Health and Human Services is the principal government agency providing a range of human services to Americans. Its Web site offers information on state and national policies, grant resources, health and disease, and employment and economic assistance.

The Urban Institute
http://www.urban.org/index.cfm

The Urban Institute researches and gathers data on social and economic issues important for American families. A major component of the organization is research on and analysis of public policies and programs to ensure sound and effective models and tools to achieve desired results. In addition, the Web site offers publications on issues related to families, housing, health and health care, and education.

Index

❖

About the Editor

❖

A Connecticut native, Paul McCaffrey was born in Danbury and raised in Brookfield. He graduated from the Millbrook School and Vassar College in Dutchess County, New York, and began his career with the H.W. Wilson Company in 2003 as a staff writer for *Current Biography*. He has worked on The Reference Shelf series since 2005, personally editing a number of titles, among them *The News and Its Future, Hispanic Americans, Global Climate Change,* and *The United States Election System*. As a freelance author, he has written several biographies for Chelsea House. He lives in Brooklyn, New York.